The Study of
Orchestration

The Study of
Orchestration

Samuel Adler

Eastman School of Music

W · W · Norton and Company

New York · London

Acknowledgments

Since this page cannot legibly accommodate all the copyright notices, pages 551–52 constitute an extension of the copyright page.

Belmont Music Publishers

Schoenberg, *Brahms: Piano Quartet in g minor Theme and Variations*, Op. 43a & 43b © 1944, 1949 Belmont Music Publishers; Used by permission—pp. 482–86.

Schoenberg, *Erwartung* © 1916 by Universal Ed. A.G. Vienna; Used by permission of Belmont Music Publishers, Los Angeles, California 90049—p. 296.

Belwin Mills Publishing Corp.

Gould, *Interplay* © 1960 Used by permission of Belwin Mills Publishing Corp.—p. 326

Boosey and Hawkes Inc.

Bartók *Concerto for Orchestra* © Copyright 1946 by Hawkes and Son (London) Ltd.; Renewed 1973 —pp. 23, 38, 66, 152, 170, 172, 200, 290, 323

Bartók, *Concerto for Violin* © Copyright 1946 by Hawkes and Son (London) Ltd.; Renewed 1973—pp. 100, 290

Bartók, *Divertimento* © Copyright 1940 by Hawkes and Son (London) Ltd.; Renewed 1967—p. 62

Bartók, *Mikrokosmos (Volumes 1-6)* © Copyright 1940 by Hawkes and Son (London) Ltd.; renewed 1967—p. 453

Bartók, *Music for Strings, Percussion and Celesta* © Copyright 1937 by Universal Edition; Renewed 1964; Copyright and renewal assigned to Boosey and Hawkes, Inc. for U.S.A.—p. 124

Bartók, *String Quartet Number 4* © Copyright 1929 by Universal Edition; Renewed 1948; Copyright assigned to Boosey and Hawkes, Inc. for U.S.A.—pp. 15, 37

Bartók, *String Quartet Number 5* © Copyright 1936 by Universal Edition; Renewed 1963; Copyright and renewal assigned to Boosey and Hawkes, Inc.—p. 37

Britten, *Four Sea Interludes* © Copyright 1945 by Boosey and Hawkes Ltd.; Renewed 1973—pp. 102, 281

Britten, *Serenade for Tenor, Horn and Strings* © 1944 by Hawkes and Sons, London Limited Renewed 1981—p. 242

Britten, *Young Person's Guide to the Orchestra* © Copyright 1946 by Hawkes and Son (London) Ltd.; Renewed 1973—p. 234

Copland, *Appalachian Spring* © Copyright 1945 by Aaron Copland; Renewed 1972; Reprinted by permission of Aaron Copland, Copyright owner and Boosey and Hawkes, Inc., Sole Licensees—pp. 147, 232, 390

Copland, *Billy the Kid* © Copyright 1946 by Aaron Copland; Renewed 1973; Reprinted by permission of Aaron Copland, Copyright owner and Boosey and Hawkes, Inc., Sole Publishers— p. 362

Copland, *Music for the Theatre* © Copyright 1932 by Cos Cob Press; Renewed 1960; Reprinted by permission of Aaron Copland, Copyright owner and Boosey and Hawkes, Inc., Sole Publishers—p. 153

Page makeup by Ben Gamit
Music typography by Halstan and Co., Ltd.
Photographs by Louis Ouzer
Drawings by Ralph Bentley

Copyright © 1982 by W. W. Norton & Company, Inc.

Published simultaneously in Canada by George J. McLeod Limited, Toronto.
Printed in the United States of America
All Rights Reserved
FIRST EDITION

Library of Congress Cataloging in Publication Data
Adler, Samuel, 1928–
    The study of orchestration.
    Bibliography: p.
    Includes index.
    1. Instrumentation and orchestration.   I. Title.
MT70.A3   781.6′4   81–14209
ISBN 0–393–95188–X   AACR2

W. W. Norton & Company, Inc. 500 Fifth Avenue, New York, N.Y. 10110
W. W. Norton & Company Ltd. 37 Great Russell Street, London WC1B 3NU

1 2 3 4 5 6 7 8 9 0

ISBN 0-393-95188-X

Contents

11. Scoring for Brass, and Brass Combined with Strings and Winds   300

12. The Percussion Ensemble   328

Preface

"The story of the orchestra resembles an old family chronicle, or, more exactly, the story of the rivalry among a large number of old families. Eventually, they unite for a common aim and the establishment of regular affairs of state."* This appropriate quote explains the aims of The Study of Orchestration very succinctly. Throughout the book, I have tried to describe each member of each family as carefully and thoroughly as possible and to show how each instrument "unites" with its own family, as well as other families, to achieve the best "affairs of state," namely, a good orchestral sound.

The major objectives of this book are twofold: first, to serve as a textbook for students wishing to perfect themselves in the art of orchestration, and second, as a reference book for composers, arrangers, and performers.

For the most part, the book is limited to a discussion of instruments found in the symphony orchestra literature from around 1730 to the present. Therefore, there is no chapter devoted specifically to Renaissance or Baroque instruments. However, those that have enjoyed some currency since 1730, such as the viola d'amore or the

---

* Paul Bekker, The Orchestra (New York: W. W. Norton, 1963), p. 15.

oboe d'amore, are given proper space in the book. The same is true for some instruments used exclusively in bands and specialty (ethnic) orchestras. I have quoted examples from actual orchestral works whenever possible. But some uniquely twentieth-century effects which have not, as yet, been fully utilized in orchestral writing are illustrated in excerpts drawn from the chamber or solo music repertoire; in a few cases, there are specially constructed examples to demonstrate their method of notation.

The subject of electronic instruments and amplifying devices was largely omitted, for I felt that this is a vast and as yet not fully explored subject. Rather than deal with it in a superficial way, I recommend that the interested musician consult specialty books on this important development in twentieth-century music.

The Study of Orchestration is divided into two parts:

I. *Instrumentation*

This section deals with the ranges, techniques, and timbres of each of the orchestral instruments. A chapter on each choir (string, woodwind, brass, percussion), is followed by a precise discussion of the individual instruments within that choir. Finally, there is an examination of how the instruments of one choir combine among themselves as well as with the other orchestral families.

II. *Orchestration*

The second section of the book deals with the major scoring problems, as well as the techniques of transcribing piano, chamber, and band music for orchestra. In recognition of the likelihood that the book will be used by musicians serving our public schools, special emphasis has been given to transcribing orchestral works for the odd combinations that may be found in schools or classroom situations. An important chapter on the accepted methods of setting up a score page and copying orchestral parts is also included.

There are two appendices:

I. A quick reference chart to instrumental ranges and transpositions. I have differentiated between the full ranges of instruments when performed by professionals and the more limited ranges of these instruments when played by amateurs or younger performers.

II. A substantial bibliography on orchestration and notation, as well as specialized studies of each instrument in the modern symphony orchestra.

This book is the result of twenty-five years of teaching orchestration, and I wish to acknowledge the hundreds of students who have patiently endured my classes and helped shape the approach and pedagogical presentation of the final product. I am particularly indebted to the 1980–81 classes at the Eastman School, who did not object to being used as guinea pigs in the evolution of the book. Their suggestions, criticisms, and enthusiasm made the work much easier.

I would also like to acknowledge the wonderful support of my colleagues, Warren Benson and Joseph Schwantner, who were most helpful throughout this venture. Without their active participation, especially in the early stages of the project, it would never have been completed. I was most fortunate to enjoy the close cooperation of our applied music faculty, who authenticated the information in the individual instrumental sections. In this connection, I am grateful to Abram Loft, Zvi Zeitlin, Bonita Boyd, Robert Sprenkle, Stanley Hasty, David Van Hoesen, John Beck, Louise Goldberg, and Donald Hunsberger. I am indebted to my friend, Leo Kraft, for his invaluable advice and counsel during the final stages of preparing the text. And special thanks go to my editor, Claire Brook of W. W. Norton, who has been an unfailing collaborator in bringing this book to life. Last, but not least, let me express my gratitude to Regina Graziani, who faithfully and accurately typed the long manuscript without grumbling.

Samuel Adler

II

INSTRUMENTATION

The Orchestra—
Yesterday and Today

The symphony orchestra is surely one of the noblest creations of Western art. To master its use will provide an insight into the music of the past and the present which is invaluable to composer, conductor, and performing musician, be he instrumentalist or vocalist. Its study will open up the important area of music that depends so very much on timbre and texture. The specific orchestral colors chosen by a composer add very personal touches to the music he has composed and contribute great individuality to the sound he has created. In an informative book called *The History of Orchestration*, Adam Carse concludes with this judgment:

> Orchestration has been many things to many composers. It has been a servant of the great, a support to the mediocre, and a cloak for the feeble. Its past lives enshrined in the works of the great dead, its present pants after the exertion of recent progress, and its future lies as completely hidden as it lay at the end of the sixteenth century.*

* Adam Carse, *History of Orchestration* (New York: Dover, 1964), p. 337.

As one endeavors to master the technique of orchestration, one embarks not only on a road to the acquisition of this extraordinary skill, but also toward a deeper understanding of the sensitivity with which the great masters of the past and present have handled the rich color palette we call the symphony orchestra, and how they made this remarkable instrument their servant in the search for the clearest and most vivid expression of their musical ideas.

The art of orchestration is of necessity a highly personal one. The orchestral sound of Wagner, for instance, is vastly different from that of Brahms, even though these two composers lived at the same time. In this regard, orchestration is similar to harmony, melody, or any other parameter of music. It is, therefore, imperative that one acquire the basic skills of the art in order to make it personal at a later time. The ear will be the deciding factor in the choice of instruments as well as combinations of instruments. It is for that reason that we shall immediately concentrate on developing the ear and trying to make it capable of listening and distinguishing colors.

It is the goal of this book to acquaint the reader with the distinctive, particular sound each instrument makes in solo and in combination with other instruments, as well as the techniques used to produce these sounds. Thus, when he hears a particular tone color in his inner ear (or mind), he will be able to write it down in score for realization in performance. Walter Piston put it succinctly: "You've got to hear what you put on that page." Let us call this "hearing mentally."

Compared to the development of other areas in the discipline of music, orchestration, as we know it, is a latecomer. It is very true that instruments have been used since the dawn of history, but they were employed for the most part to accompany voices or improvise during festive occasions. Furthermore, during the Middle Ages and the Renaissance, the composer rarely, if ever, specified the exact instruments which were to perform the various parts, short of designating a "soprano, alto, tenor, or bass" instrument or a color of the string, wind, brass, or keyboard families. In 1740, Leopold Mozart wrote in the preface to one of his *Serenatas* that "if the alto trombone player is inadequate, a violinist should be asked to perform the trombone part on the viola." But, by the middle of the eighteenth century, this was an anomaly rather than the norm, for in the preface to his opera *Combattimento* Monteverdi wrote: "A uniform basic mood throughout a piece postulates an unchanging combination of instruments all the way through."

From that time on, and even perhaps from as early as 1600, the orchestra as we know it began its rather slow development. We learn from such writers as Francis Bacon that in the middle of the seventeenth century in England, there were still two kinds of consorts. He refers to musica fracta, the broken or heterogeneous consort, and musica sociata, the whole or homogeneous consort. However, orchestras were springing up in many of the courts of Italy, France, and Germany. We may divide the early history into two broad periods: 1) from the beginnings of the orchestra to the death of Bach and Handel around 1750; and 2) from the Mannheim School, Haydn, and Mozart to the present.

During the first period of development, there is an emphasis on the stabilization of the entire instrument. The string choir was the first to be exploited because the construction of the four-string instruments—violin, viola, cello, and double bass—was perfected by the end of the sixteenth century. Because of the "public" concerts which were instituted at the various courts, the orchestra, with a multiple of strings especially, was slowly taking shape. The advancement of orchestral technique as well as the concern for very specific colors was also considerably aided by the media of opera and ballet. Lully, by 1686, used a string orchestra plus two flutes, two oboes, two bassoons, two horns, two trumpets, and timpani. Again, one must say that this orchestra was as yet not universally accepted. Throughout his lifetime, Bach experimented with all kinds of orchestral combinations, especially as accompaniment for his cantatas. In his case, as was so often true of composers of that period, availability of performers largely dictated the constitution of his orchestra. By the time of Haydn and Mozart, stabilization had almost been achieved, and it was accepted that an orchestra, as distinct from a large chamber group, was made up of three different choirs: the strings (first violins, second violins, viola, cellos, and double basses), the woodwinds (two flutes, two oboes, two clarinets, and two bassoons), and the brass (two horns, two trumpets, and timpani). There was no separate percussion section as yet in the standard symphony orchestra, but it did exist in the opera orchestra. Such instruments as snare drum, bass drum, triangle, and cymbals were commonly found in opera scores. Notice, however, that the timpani were classified with the brass in the Classical orchestra. The reason for this was utilitarian, since the timpani invariably played together with the trumpets. Seldom are there cases when the two are used separately. There has always been confusion as to why the trumpets are placed below the horns, even in the most modern orchestral scores, even though the trumpets usually play in a higher range than the horns. The reason is historical: horns were used in the orchestra before trumpets were introduced, and the trumpets were placed near the timpani since their music was usually coupled.

From the Classical period on, there was a rapid growth and expansion of the orchestra. First auxiliary instruments were added to increase the range of the wind choir (such as piccolo, contrabassoon, and English horn) and other instruments were brought into the symphony orchestra from the opera orchestra (trombones, harps, and the larger percussion battery). Huge orchestras were assembled by Berlioz for specific occasions in which the wind, brass, and percussion sections were more than doubled and the string choir was greatly enlarged. By the time of Mahler and Stravinsky, the large orchestra, as we know it today, was an accepted norm. The strings, instead of 6, 6, 4, 4, 2, were 18, 16, 14, 12, 10 (the numbers, of course, stand for the number of players in each of the five string sections). Nor was it uncommon to employ six flutes, five oboes, six clarinets, four bassoons, eight horns, four trumpets, four trombones, two tubas, two harps, piano, and a host of percussion instruments requiring four to five players.

Not only the size of the orchestra increased, but also the sophistication of its use. When it does not matter who plays a certain part, the composer is not really responsible for his orchestration. However, as the orchestra became a huge apparatus and every note, chord, timbre, and nuance became an integral part of the composition, it was necessary to codify the art of orchestration so it could be taught. Some of the great orchestrators of the nineteenth century felt compelled to set down their ideas and insights. Two of the outstanding orchestration texts of the last century are those by Berlioz (revised by Richard Strauss) and by Rimsky-Korsakov. Both treatises are concerned with the techniques of each instrument separately and the various combinations that have proven successful in their own works. Rimsky-Korsakov used his own works only to illustrate each point; he was, after all, a great orchestrator and a daring experimenter who provided us with insights and explanations which would not have been possible had he used works by other composers.

The art of orchestration today is a most sophisticated and intricate one. It is also highly individual, depending greatly on the taste and even the prejudice of the composer or orchestrator. Realizing this, one should master the techniques of writing for each instrument and listen carefully to the various combinations. Much can be learned from reducing a full score to its bare essentials so that it may be performed on the piano, or from "blowing up" a score from a piano part. This kind of activity has been common practice for well over one hundred years and offers invaluable lessons about clarity and coloration in the orchestra. Such fabulous orchestrators as Ravel, Debussy, and Stravinsky often composed their most advanced orchestral scores originally for piano and then orchestrated them, while Webern and Berg zealously made piano arrangements of huge orchestral scores by Schoenberg and Mahler in order to make them easier to study. In our time, the composer or orchestrator is often called upon to reorchestrate certain works for our large music-education establishment. During the course of this book, all these and other practical possibilities will be discussed. It is hoped that the organization of this text will facilitate fulfilling any task in orchestration that arises.

Throughout the book, the instruments most commonly used in the modern symphony orchestra receive the broadest exposure. On the other hand, with the advent of so many Renaissance ensembles and heterogeneous large chamber groups, it was deemed important to include instruments peculiar to such ensembles, and describe basic techniques and concepts associated with some of these instruments. In an appendix, some bibliographic references are given in case further information is desired about the instruments that are discussed less thoroughly.

Bowed String Instruments

The Violin family

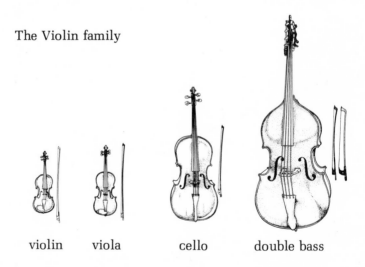

violin   viola   cello   double bass

The modern symphony orchestra is usually divided into four choirs: strings, woodwinds, brass, and percussion. The bowed string choir—violins, violas, cellos, and double basses, technically called *chordophones*—was the first to be fully exploited. This preferential treatment may be explained on two counts: the strings, of all the choirs, have the greatest number of special properties in common; and the "violin family," as it is sometimes called, reached its present state of technical perfection in construction by 1700.

Some other reasons for the chordophones' priority position as the first fully developed choir of the modern orchestra are:

1. The tone color of the string group is fairly homogeneous from top to bottom, variations in the different registers being much more subtle than in the winds or brasses.

2. The range of the group is enormous, encompassing seven octaves between the double basses and the violins.

3. The group has a wide dynamic range from an almost inaudible pianissimo to a most sonorous fortissimo.

4. As string tone is rich in overtones, all manner of close and open spacing is practical; this property produces that particular warmth and vibrancy which lends itself so well to the performance of *espressivo* passages. Further, perhaps because of this quality, one does not seem to tire of hearing string tone for extended periods of time.

5. String instruments are most versatile in producing different kinds of sound (bowed, plucked, struck, etc.) and can easily perform rapid passages, slow sustained melodies, skips, trills, double stops, and chordal configurations, as well as special (even extramusical) effects.

6. Strings are "tireless" and can play any kind of music without a rest, while a wind or brass player usually needs to stop from time to time to breathe.

The string section of a symphony orchestra consists of the following number of players:

1st Violins	16 to 18 players	8 or 9 stands
2nd Violins	14 to 16 players	7 or 8 stands
Violas	10 to 12 players	5 or 6 stands
Cellos	10 to 12 players	5 or 6 stands
Double Basses	8 to 10 players	4 or 5 stands

CONSTRUCTION

Not only is the construction of all bowed string instruments identical, but there are certain techniques common to the entire group of chordophones, which are best discussed together as a prelude to separate consideration of each instrument. Some of these techniques will have slight variations and modifications for each of the four instruments. However, discussing the group as a whole will clarify the basic principles, as well as the application of the techniques, properties, problems, peculiarities, and their execution on the four instruments.

Since we shall use some structural terms throughout this discussion, it is vital that we examine both structure and nomenclature at the very outset.

Except for the proportions, which will be given as each instrument is considered separately, it must be noted that the construction of all the instruments, as well as the names of the different parts, is identical to that of the violin diagram drawn above.

Each instrument consists of two main parts: the body and the neck. Both are made of wood. The top surface of the body, called the *belly*, the *table*, or the *soundboard*, and the bottom, called the *back*, are both curved. Together with the sidewalls, called the *ribs*, they form a hollow box which acts as a resonator and strengthens the vibrations of the strings. The overall shape of the body somewhat resembles the human form; it also appears to have a waist. Inside the body is a *soundpost*, which transmits the vibrations of the strings.

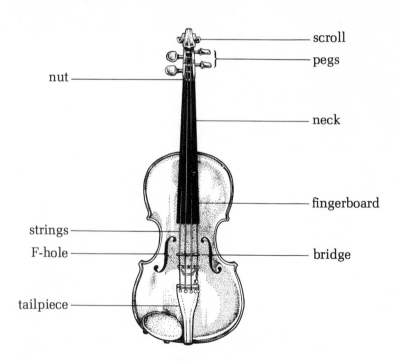

The neck consists of a long, thin, shaped piece of wood, called the *fingerboard*. At its upper end is a *pegbox*, which holds the tuning pegs, and a small curved section above the pegs, called the *scroll*. Over the fingerboard and belly are stretched four strings, or in the case of the double bass, sometimes five. The strings, each wound around a tuning peg, pass thence over a small piece of wood, called the *nut*, along the fingerboard, then over another piece of wood, called the *bridge*, and are attached to a third piece of wood or plastic, called the *tailpiece*. When a bow rubs across the string between the place where the fingerboard ends and the bridge is positioned, the string is made to vibrate, producing a sound. The bridge, which supports the strings, is also made to vibrate; its vibrations, in turn, pass to the belly and, to a lesser extent, to the back. Cutting through the belly are two sound holes, called *F-holes* because they resemble that letter in the alphabet. They permit the belly of the instrument to vibrate freely, and also provide sound-exits from the body of the instrument.

TUNING

Three of the instruments of the violin family, the violin, viola, and cello, are tuned in fifths, while the fourth, the double bass, is tuned in fourths.

Here are the pitches of the open strings of the instruments. The term *open strings* refers to the strings as they sound when they are not touched, or stopped, by any of the fingers of the left hand.

Example II–1. *Tuning of the Four Violin Strings*

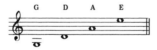

Example II–2. *Tuning of the Four Viola Strings*

Example II–3. *Tuning of the Four Cello Strings*

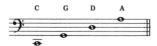

Example II–4. Tuning of the Four Double Bass Strings

A five-string double bass has a low C-string added by means of a mechanical extension. The tuning of a five-string bass is:

Example II–5.

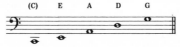

The double bass is the only transposing instrument of the violin family, for it sounds one octave lower than written.

FINGERING

In order to produce pitches higher than those of the open string, the string is firmly pressed against the fingerboard with the fingers of the left hand, thus shortening the sounding length, and consequently raising the pitch. The string itself vibrates only between the bridge and the nut. The left hand therefore moves from a position closest to the nut (*first position*) up the fingerboard toward the place where the bow is drawn across the string (between the end of the fingerboard and the bridge). As the hand moves up in order to produce higher pitches, it shifts from one position to another. It must be remembered that the index finger of the left hand and not the thumb is called the first finger. The shifting is executed in the following manner:

Example II–6.

Here is the fingering for the five basic positions of the violin and the viola:

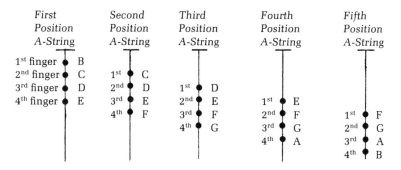

	First Position A-String	Second Position A-String	Third Position A-String	Fourth Position A-String	Fifth Position A-String
1st finger	B				
2nd finger	C	1st C			
3rd finger	D	2nd D	1st D		
4th finger	E	3rd E	2nd E	1st E	
		4th F	3rd F	2nd F	1st F
			4th G	3rd G	2nd G
				4th A	3rd A
					4th B

The principle of fingering is the same on all the bowed string instruments, but the details are quite different for the cello and the double bass and, therefore, will be discussed in greater length in the special sections devoted to each instrument.

DOUBLE-STOPS

Two notes on adjacent strings played simultaneously are called *double-stops,* of which there are two kinds:

1. those in which one of the notes is an open string;
2. those in which both pitches are stopped.

On all string instruments it is possible to play two notes on adjacent strings at the same time by fingering the two pitches and then having the bow drawn across both strings at the same time. Chords of three and four pitches, if they occur on adjacent strings, are also possible and are called *triple-* and *quadruple-stops.* With triple-stops greater bow pressure has to be exerted on the middle string of the three sounded so that all three can sound at the same time. For this reason, the simultaneous attack of three notes can only be accomplished at a greater dynamic (*f* or *mf*). When piano or pianissimo triple-stops are desired, the performer usually has to arpeggiate them slightly. When performing quadruple-stops, it must be remembered that the bow is only able to sustain properly two pitches at a time. (In the seventeenth and early eighteenth centuries, the bow was more curved than it is now and it was possible to sustain four-chord notes more readily. The curve of the wood was outward, while the modern bow is curved slightly inward.) Therefore, all quadruple-stops must be arpeggiated. The most successful triple- or quadruple-stops have one or two open notes, since these have a greater sustaining power. Here are some examples of simple double-, triple-, and quadruple-stops for each of the four instruments. A much more complete chart will be found in the chapters in which each instrument is discussed separately.

Example II–7. Violin

Example II–8. Viola

Example II–9. Cello

Example II–10. Double Bass: Only double-stops that include an open string are practical.

DIVIDED STRINGS
Divisi (*It.*), Divisés (*Fr.*), Geteilt (*Ger.*)

Since there is more than one player for each string part in a symphony orchestra, double notes (double-stops) are usually divided between the two players on the same stand. To signal this division, the part should be marked *divisi*, or its abbreviation, *div.* It is the custom for the player on the right side of the stand ("outside") to perform the upper notes, and the one on the left side (or "inside") to

* Both pitches are on the same string.

play the lower notes. When *divisi* is no longer in order and the part returns to single notes, the word *unisoni* (or more commonly the abbreviated, *unis.*), should appear on the part. Some composers wish to have each player perform double-stops. In that case, it is safer to write *non div.* so that no division between the two players will occur.

Example II–11. Debussy, *Nocturnes: Nuages*, mm. 5–15.

When triple- or quadruple-stops are to be divided, it is helpful to specify how this is to be done.

Example II–12.

If the composer wants the triple-stops to be performed by three different players, the parts should be marked *div. a3*, or in case of quadruple-stops, *div. a4*. If the division is to occur by stand, that is, first stand play the top note, second, the next lower, and so on, it is best to write out three or four different lines in the part and put the direction "Divide by stand." The Italian for "by stand" is *da leggii*; French, *par pupitres*; German, *Pultweise*.

In the following example, the composer has not only indicated the division by stand to the left of the score, but has also specified *divisi* (*geteilt*) instructions for each stand within the body of the score.

Example II–13. Strauss, *Also sprach Zarathustra,* 27

In a passage where a composer wants only half the section to play, the part should be marked "half" (in Italian, *la metà*; French, *la moitié*; German, *die Hälfte*). The "inside players" will then remain silent during such a passage. When all are to play again, the word "all" (or *tutti* [It.], *tous* [Fr.], *alle* [Ger.]) must appear on the score.

VIBRATO

When a finger is pressed down on a string and sustained for any length of time, most string performers will use *vibrato* to enhance the beauty of the tone. It is accomplished by placing the finger firmly on string at the desired pitch while performing a rocking motion in the direction of the length of the string. Besides enhancing the beauty of the tone, the use of *vibrato* increases the emotional quality and intensity of the pitch without distorting the essential frequency. A composer or orchestrator may ask for *non vibrato*, or *senza* (without) *vibrato*, if a white, pale sound is desired. Obviously an open string cannot have a fingered vibrato, but can be made to sound as if it were vibrating in either of two ways: by fingering (oscillating) the note one octave higher on the next string to set up sympathetic vibrations; or by vibrating the stopped (unison) equivalent. This latter effect can, of course, only be produced for the upper three strings.

GLISSANDO, PORTAMENTO

This is another fingered effect common to all string instruments, accomplished by sliding one finger on one string from one pitch to another. It is usually indicated by a line connecting two noteheads with or without the word *glissando* (*gliss.*) above the line. When it is done correctly, it will be executed on one long (legato) bow stroke, and all the pitches will sound, or at least be touched, between the first and last note. It is possible to glissando upward as well as downward on a string.

There is very little difference between the terms *glissando* and *portamento*. If one wishes to make a distinction, portamento is a natural, expressive way of connecting melody notes which are a great distance apart and is rarely indicated in the score. Glissando is a deliberate, notated effect. Nevertheless, one may still find composers marking *port.* instead of *gliss.* when they want a conscious slide from one pitch to another.

Example of glissandi:

Example II–14. Bartók, *String Quartet No. 4*, second movement, mm. 230–50.

If a glissando is to be performed over more than one string, it cannot be a "true" glissando, for it must be broken as soon as the open string is reached, and the player must improvise more sliding on the next string, or play a chromatic scale until the desired pitch is reached.

Example II–15. Ravel, *La Valse*, 3 measures before ⟨27⟩ to ⟨28⟩

Example II–16. Mahler, *Symphony No. 4*, third movement, mm. 72–76

There is one other kind of glissando, which may be called a "fingered glissando." It is found most often in solo literature or in string solos during an orchestral work. Sometimes called the "written-out" *glissando*, every pitch is usually notated.

Example II–17. Strauss, *Till Eulenspiegel*, mm. 205–9

THE BOW

The bow, with which most violin family instruments are played, derives its name from its initial resemblance to the bow used in archery. We find even today that Arabian and Far Eastern "fiddles" are still played with curved bows as were European string instruments until around the fifteenth century. For the next 300 years or so, various experiments brought the shape of the bow closer to what we know today. Corelli, Vivaldi, and Tartini still used bows that were slightly curved outward. Its final form—curved inward—was achieved in the Classical bows of François Tourte (1747–1833). The Classical, as well as modern bows, have the following characteristics:

1. A long tapering *bow stick* which is curved slightly inward toward the hair. It is usually made of Pernambuco wood.
2. A metal or ivory plate protecting the tip.
3. Horse-tail hair.
4. A metal ferrule (brace) at the frog which encircles the hairs and keeps them evenly spread.
5. Exact proportional measurements for balance.
6. A metal screw with which the hair is tightened or loosened.

When the hair is tightened, the elastic quality of the wood gives the entire bow a resilience that makes it possible to execute any kind of stroke desired. The tension of the hair is of the utmost importance.

Diagram of Bow

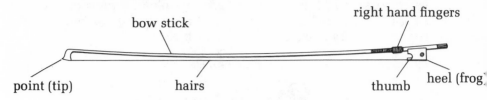

The bow is held firmly but flexibly between the four fingers and thumb in the right hand (with the exception of left-handed violinists). There are other bow hand positions, especially for the cello and the double bass, which we shall examine in specific detail when we discuss these two instruments.

BOWING

Bowing refers to the act of drawing the bow across the string. As we have said, the bow is normally drawn across the string midway between the end of the fingerboard and the bridge. In order to alter the sound of the instrument, the bow may be drawn across the string at different places.

Two symbols must be remembered: ⊓ down-bow, from the frog, drawing the bow toward* the tip; ∨ up-bow, drawing the bow from the tip toward* the frog.

A passage on any of the string instruments may be bowed effectively in a variety of ways, and even the most experienced concertmasters often disagree as to the best way to bow a given passage. Even now, bowing changes are constantly introduced in such well-established clssics as Haydn, Mozart, and Beethoven symphonies. Bowing decisions are greatly influenced by: a) the style of the music; b) its character; c) the tempo and the dynamics at which the particular work or passage is to be performed.

The composer or orchestrator should keep the following facts in mind, for these, at least, are always constant:

1. If no slurs are marked (*non legato*), each note requires a change in the direction of the bow, whether the passage is slow or fast.

---

*The word *toward* is used because the performer does not always use the whole bow, meaning all the way from the frog to the tip and vice versa.

Example II–18. Franck, *Symphony in D minor*, first movement, mm. 129–36

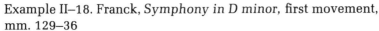

Even though changes of bow direction occur between each one of the notes above, one does not necessarily perceive these changes, since skilled performers can play the successive notes without a break or any audible difference between up- and down-bow.

2. Whenever a passage is slurred, all notes under that slur are performed on one bow, meaning all are played in one direction. This is called *legato* playing. (*Legato* means "bind together.")

Example II–19. Schubert, *Symphony No. 5*, second movement, mm. 1–8

Two observations concerning the example:

1. A performer will naturally begin an anacrusis, or upbeat, with an up-bow (V) unless the composer marks the upbeat with a down-bow sign (⊓).

2. A very common type of bowing instruction occurs on the second beat of the first measure: two up-bows are called for in order to have a down-bow on the accented first beat of the next measure. The violinist will play the quarter-note Eb, then stop his bow movement ever so briefly (the dash under the note indicates separation) before playing the eighth-note Eb while still in an up-bow motion.

Sometimes two vigorous articulations follow one another, and a double down-bow situation is called for, as in the following example. A down-bow and up-bow should be marked over the long note so that the following attack will be solid. The bow is changed almost immediately to up-bow and is then ready to give a *ff* attack on the triple-stop.

Example II–20. Beethoven, *Coriolanus Overture*, mm. 276–86

If this passage is executed well, the bow change will hardly be noticed.

It is important to remember that one is able to play louder and heavier toward the frog of the bow than toward the tip, because the pressure from the right hand holding the bow is much greater at the frog. The tendency to play a crescendo with an up-bow is quite natural due to the increasing leverage of the right hand on the bow toward the frog. Conversely, there is a tendency to perform a diminuendo with a down-bow. When bowing a passage, the composer should be aware of these tendencies and, without overmarking the parts, should indicate bow direction only where he wishes to counteract the normal habit of the players.

Never mark long phrase slurs in string parts. Such slurs only confuse the performer. The only slurs that should be used are the ones that designate the notes to be performed on one bow (legato).

There is a limit to how many notes can be played slurred on a single bow stroke. This is largely determined by the tempo and the dynamics governing a particular passage. In a fast but soft passage, a great many notes may be slurred together.

Example II–21. Mendelssohn, *Symphony No. 4*, first movement, mm. 378–83

A similar passage in the violas some measures later in the same movement shows only six notes on a bow, since the dynamic is forte.

Example II–22. Mendelssohn, *Symphony No. 4*, first movement, mm. 461–64

Even if the dynamic is soft, special caution must be taken in slow passages not to overload the bow and make the music physically impossible to perform. Remember also that the cello and bass bows are a bit shorter than those of the violin and viola.

For instance, this passage

Example II–23. Liszt, *Les Preludes*, mm. 29–35

is impossible to perform as the composer has marked while still adhering to the crescendo marks, unless it is broken up into several bows in either of the following ways:

Example II–24

Example II–25

By dividing the section and staggering the bowing among the players, one can produce a very long and effective legato line.

Besides the single bow stroke (non legato) and the slur (legato), there are various special types of bowings. Once again, all of these depend greatly on the speed and the dynamics, but are also much influenced by the style and the character of the music.

In discussing these types of bowings, we run up against an even greater diversity of views as to the meaning of each term and its execution. In addition, the terminology itself is not universally accepted, and quite often there are several names for a particular bowing in a given language. The only rational or safe way to classify the bowings is by dividing them into:

1. bowings played on the string
2. bowings played off the string ("bouncing bow")

ON-THE-STRING BOWINGS
Détaché (separate)

This is the basic stroke on all bowed string instruments. It changes direction for each note. Discussed previously as non legato bowing, this kind of bowing is sometimes referred to as "separate bows." The change of bow can be made without a break in the tone. But this détaché stroke is usually performed so that one hears the articulation of the bow changes. However, the notes are not so detached, marked, or accented that the effect could be called staccato. Ordinarily, the middle to upper third of the bow is used for best result in performing this stroke loud or medium loud at a rapid tempo.

Example II–26. Tchaikovsky, *Romeo and Juliet*, mm. 141–43

There are instances in which the composer asks that a passage be played at the tip in order to achieve a quality of extreme lightness. The marking for this effect is: at the point; *a punta d'arco* (It.); *à la pointe* (Fr.); *an der Spitze* (Ger.).

Example II–27. Bartók, *Concerto for Orchestra*, fifth movement, mm. 8–13

Conversely, composers ask for a passage to be played at the frog to take advantage of a heavy stroke which can be produced there. The marking for this effect is: at the frog; *al tallone* (It.); *au talon* (Fr.); *am Frosch* (Ger.).

Example II–28. Gluck, Overture to *Iphigenia in Aulis*, mm. 19–29

A very heavy and vigorous feeling is commonly achieved by a series of down-bows. This can be played quite fast, with the bow raised between each down-bow. It is most often performed at the frog.

Example II–29. Tchaikovsky, *Symphony No. 6*, third movement, mm. 108–12

Louré

This bowing, also called *piqué,* is a legato stroke, but a slight separation of the notes is effected while the bow is being drawn. It is a very expressive bowing used quite often in accompaniments. *Louré* is easily played both up- and down-bow. This effect is indicated by dashes under or over each of the noteheads, with slurs to designate the bow changes.

Example II–30. Handel, *Messiah,* "Comfort Ye," mm. 1–4

Staccato

Staccato comes from the Italian word "staccare," meaning to detach or separate. It is best to limit the meaning of staccato for bowed string instruments to an on-the-string effect, which may be performed by separate short strokes, or by having a series of short notes separated on one bow stroke, either up- or down-bow. Staccato is indicated by placing a dot over or under the notehead and is most effectively performed at moderate to slow tempos for reasons that will be clarified later. *Staccato* passages can be played loud or soft.

Example II–31

Because staccato bowing separates or leaves a space between the notes, this passage could sound approximately:

Example II–32

If this kind of staccato is called the *separate bow staccato*, another kind should be named the *slurred staccato*.

Example II–33

A *staccato* passage like the following is executed very much like *louré*, except that the notes are shorter (staccato) and, therefore, the space between them is longer, as in the examples above.

Example II–34. Stravinsky, *Orpheus*, Pas de deux, 109

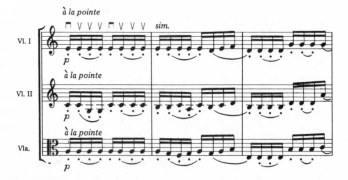

Notice that all the tempos for the staccato passages have been moderate, for a fast tempo will invariably be played off the string, with a bouncing bow. Then it should no longer be called staccato, but rather spiccato, or saltando, both terms to be discussed in the off-the-string section of this chapter.

Two other variations of the staccato on one bow, or slurred staccato, technique are very common:

1. In fast passages,   ♪·♪♪·♪   or   ♩· ♪♩· ♪

is performed  or

Notice the way it is notated; the staccato dot is placed under the short note. If both were dotted, the long note would be measurably shortened in performance.

Example II–35. Berlioz, *Symphonie fantastique*, fourth movement, mm. 140–43

2. In order to make ♩ ♪ sound crisp and light, the composer often asks to have it played with separate bow at the tip.

Example II–36. Weber, Overture to *Euryanthe*, mm. 149–52

Martelé *(Fr.);* Martellato *(It.);* or Marcato *(It.).*

The derivation of this term is from the verb to hammer. In bowing it indicates a fast, well-articulated, heavy, separate stroke, resembling a sforzando, or pressed accent. While *martelé* bowing is usually performed toward the frog of the bow, it can be done in the middle portion of the bow as well. The bow does not leave the string, even though there is a stop between the notes, and each new stroke is initiated with a heavy accent. Sometimes, instead of a simple dot, one of the following signs is placed over a note: ♪ or ♪ or ♪

Example II–37. Bruckner, *Symphony No. 9*, second movement, mm. 52–58

OFF-THE-STRING BOWINGS
Spiccato or Saltando

There are two distinct kinds of spiccato, or saltando, bowings. One may be thought of as the conscious spiccato, the other as the spontaneous spiccato. Both of these related effects depend on the speed and the dynamic of a particular passage.

1. Conscious spiccato: In a slow or a moderate tempo and at a soft dynamic, the player makes a conscious effort to make the bow "spring." The pressure of the right hand is reduced, and the wrist drops the middle of the bow on the string in a semicircular motion. The notation is similar to the staccato designation, for one places dots above or beneath the noteheads. The lightness and speed required in the passage determine whether one uses a conscious spiccato, or saltando, as it is sometimes called.

Example II–38. Beethoven, *Symphony No. 1*, second movement, mm. 154–56

2. Spontaneous spiccato: At a fast tempo with soft dynamics, the player does not have to make a conscious effort to lift the bow; rather, the short quick up–down motion controlled by the wrist alone makes the bow bounce spontaneously off the string with every stroke.

Example II–39. Rossini, Overture to *William Tell*, mm. 336–43

3. Slurred spiccato: This is very much like the grouped or slurred *staccato*, except that each of the notes is played off the string.

Example II–40. Mahler, *Symphony No. 4*, first movement, mm. 21–23

Jeté (*sometimes called ricochet*)

The upper third of the bow is "thrown" on the string so that it will bounce, producing from two to six or more rapid pitches. Usually, *jeté* is executed by a downward motion of the bow. However, it can be played up-bow as well.

One should be warned that the more notes desired on one bow stroke, the more impractical this bowing is. In an orchestral situation, it is suggested that not more than three bouncing notes at a time be used in this bowing. Solo players are perhaps more capable of including many more well-articulated notes on a single bow. Once again, remember also that the bow of the cello and double bass is slightly shorter; therefore, three, or at the most, four notes to a single *jeté* stroke are quite enough.

Example II–41. Rimsky-Korsakov, *Capriccio espagnol*, third movement, mm. 18–23

Example II–42. Rimsky-Korsakov, *Capriccio espagnol*, fifth movement, mm. 89–96

Arpeggiando

A slightly different kind of spiccato, related to jeté, is the effect called arpeggiando. This may begin with a simple slurring of an arpeggio played over three or four strings at a moderate tempo:

Example II–43

But, as the passage gets faster, the performer will spontaneously let the bow jump off the string because of the motion of his right wrist. Of course, when you begin an arpeggiated passage at a fast tempo, the bow will bounce right away, and the arpeggiando effect will naturally occur. It is most often used in solo string and chamber music literature, but is also effective as an orchestral device.

Example II–44. Mendelssohn, *Violin Concerto*, first movement, mm. 328–36

COLORISTIC EFFECTS

Trills

As in all instruments, the trill is extensively used in the strings to color tones. The motion of one finger produces a note that alternates repeatedly with a sustained tone held by another finger. The trill may be performed upward or downward, as the composer specifies. If one of the notes is an open string, the trill is not as effective because the open string quality is so different from that of stopped notes. The performance of a trill by sixteen violins or ten violas creates a most exciting and blurred rhythmic sensation, very different from the sound made by a single player on one instrument. The notation for the trill is *tr* ⌇⌇⌇over the note.

Example II–45. Hindemith, *Mathis der Maler*, third movement, 16

Tremolo

There are four kinds of tremolos:

1. bowed tremolo, unmeasured
2. bowed tremolo, measured
3. fingered tremolo (or slurred tremolo)
4. undulating tremolo (bowed or slurred)

1. Bowed unmeasured tremolo is produced by short, quick up- and down-bow strokes, repeating a single pitch as often as possible during the length of the written note.

Example II–46. Debussy, *La Mer*, first movement, mm. 5–8 after 8

2. Bowed measured tremolo is simply a convenient shorthand for writing a series of repeated *détaché* notes to give more energy or volume to a tone.

Example II–47.

Example II–48. Wagner, Overture to *The Flying Dutchman*, mm. 319–24

3. The fingered (or slurred) tremolo is the equivalent of a trill but at an interval larger than a major or minor second. One usually indicates a precise time value for the notes to make a trill-like effect feasible. It is necessary to slur the notes that are to be alternated to insure the legato movement of the bow. However, there are cases where a fingered tremolo is bowed detached rather than slurred; in those cases, of course, the slur is omitted.

Example II–49. Debussy, *La Mer*, first movement, 8 and measure following

4. The undulating tremolo is used when the two notes in the fingered tremolo are too far apart to be played on one string. The two notes are then played on adjacent strings and the bow undulates between them as quickly as possible. The undulating tremolo may be performed slurred or detached.

Example II–50. Brahms, *Symphony No. 1*, fourth movement, mm. 31–32

On the fingerboard

sul tasto *(It)*, sur la touche *(Fr.)*, am Griffbrett *(Ger.)*

In order to obtain a rather flutey, soft, and hazy tone, the composer may ask the performer to play with the bow over the end of the fingerboard. When the term *flautando* is used instead of *sul tasto*, the player should play *near* but not *on* the fingerboard. The difference is really minimal, and many composers make no distinction between the two terms.

Example II–51. Debussy, *Prélude à l'après-midi d'un faune*, mm. 96–98

On the bridge

sul ponticello *(It.)*, au chevalet *(Fr.)*, am Steg *(Ger.)*

This effect is produced by playing very near or, in fact, right on the bridge instead of in the regular space allotted for the bow stroke. Since this produces upper partials of the tone not usually heard, it gives the pitch an eerie, metallic, and somewhat glassy timbre. *Sul ponticello* is often combined with bowed or fingered tremolo.

Example II–52. Strauss, *Sinfonia domestica*,

With the wood

col legno (*It.*), avec le bois (*Fr.*), mit Holz (*Ger.*)

1. *Col legno tratto:* For this effect, the bow is turned over, and the sound is produced by the wood rather than the hair. *Tratto* means that the wood is drawn over the string. The sound is very minimal, since the friction of the wood is small compared to the hair, but it again is an eerie effect most useful for tremolo, although sometimes used in legato passages.

Example II–53. Mahler, *Symphony No. 1*, third movement, mm. 135–37

2. *Col legno battute:* This designation means striking the string with the wood of the bow. It is more commonly used than *col legno tratto*, but it, too, gives very little pitch definition. It is a percussive sound which acts like a very dry and short spiccato; do not expect to hear a definite pitch except highs or lows, depending on which of the strings are struck.

Example II–54. Berlioz, *Symphonie fantastique*, fifth movement, mm. 444–55

Every time a special effect, such as *col legno, col legno battute, sul ponticello,* or any of the others are used, one must insert the indication *naturale* or *in modo ordinario* in the score at the point where the player should resume his normal playing attitude. The English word *natural* is sometimes substituted, and is perfectly acceptable in American scores.

PIZZICATO

Now we come to another mode of producing pitches on string instruments, namely, by plucking the strings. This is called pizzicato.

The normal pizzicato procedure is as follows:

The violinist or violist usually braces his thumb on the corner of the fingerboard and plucks the strings with his index finger. The cellist or bassist simply plucks with his index finger, without anchoring his thumb. (Some violinists and violists have also adopted this non-anchored custom.) During a pizzicato passage, the bow is usually held by the other three fingers against the palm of the right hand. However, if the entire piece or a lengthy section thereof is pizzicato, preceded by rests and followed by enough time to pick up the bow, the players may elect to put their bows in their laps or, in the case of a solo performer, on a stand or even on the piano, in order to give them more freedom in executing the plucking.

Whenever pizzicato is desired, the entire word, or more often the abbreviation *pizz.*, must appear in both the score and the parts. When the player is to resume playing with the bow, the word *arco* must be printed. This effect is, of course, used very frequently. For the normal pizzicato, some short time must be allowed for the player to prepare himself to pluck and then again to resume the natural way of playing. There are instances in both solo and orchestral literature when no time is provided for either maneuver, but these are rare and should be avoided if at all possible. (This is especially true of the return from pizzicato to arco, which is a bit more awkward than going from bowing to plucking because the bow must be rearranged into playing position.) However, it is much easier to change from arco to pizzicato, if one figures out the bowing so that the players will have an up-bow stroke just before the pizzicato in order to arrive at the frog. They then have enough leverage on the bow to make the switch more quickly. If no time at all is allowed for the exchange of techniques, many players simply keep their bows in hand, extend the index finger, and pluck the string.

Example II–55. Brahms, *Symphony No. 1*, fourth movement, mm. 1–17

Left-Hand Pizzicato

This effect is much more prevalent in solo literature than in orchestral works. When a cross, +, appears above a note, it is plucked with one of the fingers of the left hand. Often, these are open strings, and the little finger is used to pluck; other times a whole series is to be plucked with the left hand. In that case, the finger producing the highest pitch plucks the next highest one in the following manner:

Example II–56

The B is played with the bow spiccato, then the fourth finger plucks the A; the third finger, the G; the second finger, the F; the first finger, finally, the open E-string.

Example II–57. Bartók, *String Quartet No. 5*, third movement,
mm. 54–56

Fingernail or Snap Pizzicato

These two modes of playing pizzicato are twentieth-century innovations often associated with Béla Bartók's works. The sign for the
snap pizzicato is ↓, and it is accomplished by snapping the string
against the fingerboard. Fingernail pizzicato is indicated by a ⌒ ,
and is achieved by pulling the string with the fingernail. Once again,
the sign must be placed above each note that is to be snapped. The
pizz. is not necessary for either the fingernail or the snap pizzicato,
since the mode of playing is implicit in the sign.

Example II–58. Bartók, *String Quartet No. 4*, fourth movement,
mm. 56–62

Arpeggiated Pizzicatos

When no preference is expressed by the composer, the performer will pluck a chord of three or four notes from the bottom up, and the arpeggiated effect can be held to a minimum by incisive, sudden finger strokes. In some cases, *non arpegg.* is specified. Otherwise, the arpeggiated pizzicato is performed:

Example II–59

Sometimes the composer wants the chord played the other way around, or in the case of a repeated chord, alternating between bottom to top, then top to bottom. In these cases, a directional sign ⇡ ⇣ should be placed in front of each chord. Occasionally, the phrase *quasi guitara* or *a la guitarre* is printed in the part and score, or arrows are placed above the chords.

Example II–60. Bartók, *Concerto for Orchestra*, fifth movement, mm. 1–9

Before leaving the subject of pizzicato, a word of caution must be added concerning endurance and speed. A long, fast pizzicato passage, played without rests, becomes very fatiguing for the performer. Some string players have perfected a technique of using the index and middle fingers alternately to facilitate a lengthy pizzicato passage. Nevertheless, occasional rests and alternation between first and second violins or violas and cellos would help alleviate any physical discomforts. Here is an example of successful lengthy pizzicato passages from the orchestral literature; notice the periodic rests in this long and very taxing pizzicato passage:

Example II–61. Tchaikovsky, *Symphony No. 4*, third movement, mm. 1–17

For additional pizzicato examples, see the pizzicato movements of Britten, *Simple Symphony,* and Foote, *Suite for Strings in E.*

Let us remember that pizzicato is similar to staccato and spiccato bowing in that the sound dies away quickly. In order to indicate that a pizzicato note is to sound as long as possible, composers sometimes write pitches with indeterminate slurs thereafter, signalling their preference for a long, "sustained" *pizz.* with the phrase "let vibrate," or *l.v.* In connection with this discussion, it is important to mention that the thickness of the string greatly affects the sustained quality of a pitch that is plucked, so that double bass strings, of course have the greatest sustaining power of all the strings of the violin family.

Example II–62. Diamond, *Symphony No. 4*, second movement, m. 1

WITH MUTES
con sordino (*It.*), avec sourdines (*Fr.*), mit Dämpfer (*Ger.*)

All string instruments may be muted. The designation most often
used when a mute is called for is *con sordino*. At that time, the
player places a small plastic, wooden, or metal object on the bridge,
thus absorbing some of the vibrations, and achieving a very soft and
smooth sound. The tone quality is radically altered, and while most
muted passages are soft, it is also effective to write forte or fortissimo
portions of a work for muted strings. The loud muted passage takes
on a special quality of restraint and a constricted, more tense sound.
The composer or orchestrator should listen carefully to both soft and
loud muted passages in order to recognize and understand this fascinating sound.

Example II–63. Weber, Overture to *Oberon*, mm. 13–21

WITHOUT MUTES
senza sordino (*It.*), sans sourdines (*Fr.*), ohne Dämpfer (*Ger.*)

A special word of caution in connection with the muting and
unmuting of strings. Enough time must be allowed to put on or take
off the mutes. Even though some players now use clips which easily
slide to the back of the bridge and clip on easily, some still use the

older version, which need to be placed on the bridge, removed from it, and put away. It is necessary to allow some time for this procedure; otherwise, chaos may result.

SCORDATURA

The open string of all string instruments can be altered for certain color effects or some practical considerations. That is, each string may be tightened or loosened to produce a pitch other than the normal tuning. This is called scordatura, an Italian term meaning mistuning. The device of scordatura tuning has been used since the seventeenth century to facilitate difficult passages in remote keys, to obtain unusual chords, and to change the tone color of the instrument. When a scordatura tuning is required the composer or orchestrator must indicate the tuning of the four strings in the score either at the beginning of the piece or at the point in the work when retuning is necessary. The same information must appear in the individual parts. Plenty of time must be allowed if the player is to return to the original tuning. This is signalized by the word *accord* or *accordatura*. Here are some examples of famous scordatura passages:

Example II–64. Saint-Saëns, *Danse macabre*, tuning and mm. 25–32

Example II–65. Mahler, *Symphony No. 4*, second movement, mm. 6–17*

*The additional flats in the signature are necessary to place the solo violin in the key of the rest of the orchestra, since all pitches must be read a major second lower than notated.

Example II–66. Stravinsky, *Le Sacre du printemps*, last 2 measures

In the Mahler example, scordatura is used coloristically to make
the violin sound like a "cheap fiddle"; the straining of all four
strings caused by raising each a whole tone removes much of the
noble sound we usually associate with the instrument. Scordatura is
used much more today for reasons like this. In years past, it facilitated playing in difficult keys; for example, a viola would be retuned
Db–Ab–Eb–Bb and its part written out in D major. This may be
observed in the solo viola part of the Mozart's *Symphonie concertante*, which is in the key of Eb; *scordatura* was thought to facilitate
the performance. Of course there is a valid musical reason for the
retuning; the increased tension on the string gives the viola much
greater brilliance.

NATURAL HARMONICS
Harmoniques *(Fr.)*, Armonici *(It.)*, Fageolettöne *(Ger.)*

To this point in our discussion, we have dealt with that series of
pitches which is produced either by the open string, or those
sounded by fingers pressing the string tightly against the fingerboard. Two other series of notes exist and can be performed easily
on all string instruments. The first series is called *natural harmonics*, which are overtones of an open string produced by touching the
string lightly at various points called *nodes*.

Every pitch produced on a sounding body, whether a string, as in
this case, or a vibrating air column, is a combination of the fundamental and overtones. These are usually heard as a single or com-
posite tone. The overtones, which give individual color or timbre to
the fundamental, can be isolated from the fundamental on a string
instrument by touching the string lightly at different nodes. Therefore, when we lightly touch the A-string of a viola halfway between
the nut and the bridge, we prevent the string from vibrating as a
whole. The vibrating lengths are now the two halves of the string,
each sounding an octave higher than the string itself (ratio 2:1). It
must be noted here that in theory it does not matter whether we draw
the bow on the nut or the bridge side of the node, since either half
of the string will give us the higher octave result.

On the violin, these natural harmonics can be translated into musical terms thus:

Example II–67

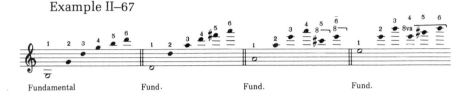

Fundamental   Fund.   Fund.   Fund.

Notice that the fundamental (marked "1") to the fifth partial are given because these are the strongest and most successfully produced harmonics, even though higher harmonics (up to the seventh or eighth partial) are quite easy to obtain on the viola, cello, and double bass, since the strings are longer and thicker.

Here is a table showing where on a given string on each string instrument the various natural harmonics can be produced:

(No. 1 is, of course, the fundamental.)

2. Lightly touching the string halfway between the nut and the bridge:

Example II–68

3. This third harmonic can be produced in two different ways:

a. Lightly touching the string of one-third of its length from the nut or one-third of its length from the bridge.

b. Lightly touching the string at two-thirds of its length from the nut or two-thirds of its length from the bridge.

Example II–69

4. The fourth partial can be obtained in two different ways:

a. Lightly touching the string at one-fourth of its length from the nut or one-fourth of its length from the bridge.

b. Lightly touching the string at three-fourths of its length from the nut or three-fourths of its length from the bridge.

Example II–70

5. The fifth overtone may be produced in four different ways, but only the circled ones are secure enough to be employed in orchestral use. The others are used, however, in solo and chamber music.

a. Lightly touching the string at one-fifth of its length from the nut (or four-fifths from the brdge).

b. Lightly touching the string at two-fifths of its length from the nut (or three-fifths from the bridge).

c. Lightly touching the string at three-fifths of its length from the nut (or two-fifths from the bridge).

d. Lightly touching the string at four-fifths of its length from the nut (or one-fifth from the bridge).

Example II–71

Notation of Natural Harmonics

1. A small circle over the note intended to sound as a harmonic; or

2. A diamond-shaped note at the pitch where the node producing the desired note may be found on the string.

Notice that in the examples given above, the string on which the various harmonics are to be reproduced is specified. That is because some pitches of the harmonic series on one string are duplicated on another. For example, on the violin, this pitch could be produced as a harmonic on the G- as well as on the D-string:

Therefore, an indication of the string on which the pitch should be obtained must be carefully marked. If it is to be on the G-string, the term *sul G* should be used. Some like to designate the strings by roman numerals. In that case, the lowest (G) string is IV. The same holds true of all the string instruments.

Nomenclature of the Strings

Violin	Viola	Cello	Double Bass
I = E	I = A	I = A	I = G
II = A	II = D	II = D	II = D
III = D	III = G	III = G	III = A
IV = G	IV = C	IV = C	IV = E

Quick Reference Table of Natural String Harmonics Practical for Orchestral Scoring*

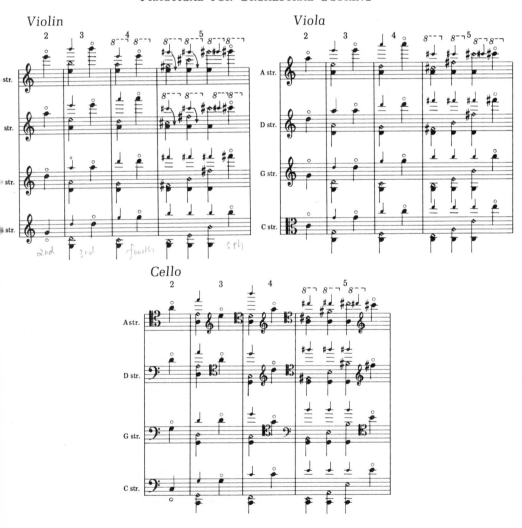

* The small notes in each case are the resultant pitches of the harmonics.

Double Bass

ARTIFICIAL HARMONICS

The second type of harmonics, *artificial harmonics*, produce the same flutey, silvery sound as the natural harmonics, but are manufactured rather than simply stopped on the open strings. On the violin and viola, the way to produce artificial harmonics is by stopping a pitch with the first finger and at the same time lightly touching a node a fourth above with the fourth finger. This produces a pitch two octaves above the stopped pitch. On the cello, this can be accomplished by using the thumb to stop the tone, while the node a fourth above is touched by the third or fourth finger. Double bass artificial harmonics are not recommended, even though some contemporary composers have called for them in solo music. The stretch of the hand makes it most impractical for clean performance. The node a fourth above the stopped pitch has been found to be most practical, and it is suggested that this manner of securing artificial harmonics be adopted for orchestral performance. Other artificial harmonic possibilities will be discussed in the separate chapters on the violin and viola, for they are used in solo and chamber works for those instruments.

Notation of Artificial Harmonics

1. A normal note with a diamond-shaped note one fourth above. One may or may not use the circle over the notes, although that makes it even clearer.

Example II–72

2. A normal note with a diamond-shaped note one fourth above, plus the actual note intended sometimes added above.

Example II–73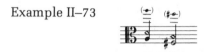

3. A small circle above the note intended to be heard as a harmonic, leaving the actual method of production to the player. This is chancy, and the orchestrator should use either of the two preceding methods instead, since the responsibility for the method of producing the harmonic should not be shifted to the performer.

Example II–74

A question often asked is how high one can or should write artificial harmonics. While theoretically there is almost no limitation, practically, the following artificial harmonics should be considered a reasonable limit, especially for orchestral use, since the higher ones are insecure and would probably squeak.

Example II–75

Two extended passages with harmonics:

Example II–76. Saint-Saëns, *Violin Concerto*, second movement, last 13 measures

Example II–77. Borodin, *String Quartet No. 1*, third movement,
Trio, mm. 1–20

CONTEMPORARY STRING TECHNIQUE EXTENSIONS

During the past thirty years, a great number of innovations and
extensions of string techniques have been added to our vocabulary.
There are so many modifications, in fact, that it has taken entire volumes to discuss these newer techniques adequately. Therefore, it is
only possible to mention some of the most important of them and to
codify those that are most commonly used in terms of notation. The
student's attention is called to such books as David H. Cope's *New
Directions in Music* (Wm. C. Brown), Gardner Read's *Contemporary
Instrumental Techniques* (Schirmer Books), and Kurt Stone's *Music
Notation in the 20th Century* (W. W. Norton) for a more complete
and detailed discussion of some of those techniques.

Here, then, are some important contemporary string technique
innovations:

a. Playing on the "wrong" (that is, the tailpiece, not the fingerboard) side of the bridge

    1.   play all four strings behind the bridge

    2.   three strings

    3.   two strings

    4.   one string only

One can also play *col legno* behind the bridge

b. Playing the tailpiece with the bow-hair or striking it with the
wood of the bow

c. Knocking, rapping, or tapping on the body of the instrument
either with one's fingers or knuckles. This is usually requested in a
footnote and further explained. Usual notation:

d. Wide vibratos, as represented in the notation:

e. Bowing on a harmonic node with great pressure in order to produce notes well below the open string of the instrument (subharmonics or undertones).

f. ⌐ = playing, in any mode specified, the highest note on a particular string (here on the G-string), or if the sign is used without designating a string, simply playing the highest note on the instrument.

g. A composer may ask for a passage to be fingered without the bow being drawn across the strings. This gives a quiet, ghostly sound, and the pitches are almost inaudible, yet make a slight sound as the fingers are slapped down hard on the strings.

h. Pizzicatos with plectrums or combs have become quite popular.

i. Half-harmonics—either touching the string lightly but not at a harmonic mode, or touching the string a little more firmly than usual at a harmonic mode. This effect is somewhat related to the sound of *sul tasto*.

Many harmonics which have been thought to be unplayable on the double bass heretofore are now being performed in solo and chamber music literature, but as yet would be dangerous to use in orchestral writing.

j. George Crumb, and others, ask for players to bow near the nut rather than the bridge "on the wrong side of the left hand," in order to produce a "viol-like" sound. The fingering, of course, would be reversed; he even asks that the beginning pitch be marked on the finger board with a chalk mark. This effect is required in Crumb's *Black Angels*, a work for amplified string quartet. It should not be casually used in orchestral works, at least right now, because few players would be able to produce it.

If any of the devices mentioned above are to be used in an orchestral score or, for that matter, anywhere in any kind of a work whether solo, chamber, or orchestral, it is strongly urged that a verbal description of the sounds the composer desires, as well as the exact technique by which the sounds may be realized, be included in the score, since the notation varies so greatly from one composer to another. In the interest of maximum communication between composer and performer, it is urged that the procedures outlined in the book by Kurt Stone mentioned above be adopted. The few notational signs given above are those most commonly used for the described effects.

3

Individual Bowed String Instruments

VIOLIN
Violino (*It.*), Violon (*Fr.*), Violine (*Ger.*)

Zvi Zeitlin, violin

Example III–1. Tuning

All music for the violin is written in the treble clef.

Example III–2. Range

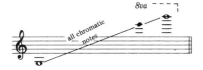

The violin is the soprano instrument of the string section. It is held on the left shoulder, supported by the left side of the chin, and held from underneath by the left arm and hand at the instrument's neck. All techniques and color effects previously discussed in the comprehensive string chapter are within the scope of this most versatile instrument. Now we will explore some particular problems, possibilities, and special properties of the violin in order to facilitate its most effective use.

The practical orchestral range of the violin extends from the low string G to the high E   but in solo or chamber music playing, the B above or even higher is possible. In the discussions of the individual string instruments, it must be kept in mind that the extremely high range is difficult to control, and only in the past 150 years has it been used extensively. During the Classical period, the limit of the violin range was   . Beyond the seventh position, in which that A is the highest note, the spaces between the fingers become progressively smaller; left-hand control is more and more tenuous as the thumb, which acts as a stabilizing lever on the neck and then the body of the instrument, loses its hold; the hand must therefore seek the higher notes without the orientation of the thumb's position. Here is a reminder of the fingering for the violin and the first five positions:

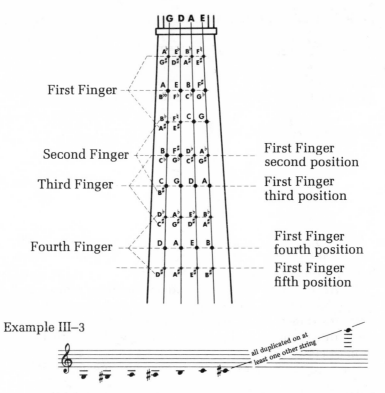

Example III–3

Notice that from the open G to the C♯ and from the high B up, the pitches are available on one string only. The D for instance, can be played on the open string or with the fourth finger on the G-string in first position. It can also be performed with the third finger on the G-string in second position, the second finger on the G-string in third position, or the first finger on the G-string in fourth position. It would be futile, then, to specify where the violinist is to play a particular pitch, which is duplicated in many places on the instrument. If the composer or orchestrator has great insight into the fingering of the instrument, the desired timbre should be the only justification for putting fingerings in the score or parts. Except under special circumstances, then, the actual fingering is best left to the performer.

Let us examine what is meant by timbral considerations. The open strings have a distinctive sound of their own. In a fast passage this may not make any difference, but in slow, expressive passages, one usually wants all the tones to be of equal and controlled texture. The open strings have a greater vibrating potential, but are not under the controlling influence provided by the finger which oscillates a stopped note. In other words, the open string on all string instruments has a characteristic sound which lends itself to great exploitation separately but stands out peculiarly in other situations. Of course, the open G-string is unavoidable, since it cannot be duplicated on the instrument; notice, for instance, how its vibrant singularity can be felt in this passage.

Example III–4. Brahms, *Symphony No. 1*, fourth movement, mm. 61–78

How different this open note sounds from all the stopped notes.

This brings us to the important but controversial subject of the particular properties and qualities of each of the four strings of the violin. It is virtually impossible to explain verbally the many shades of sound that the violin can produce. It is far more effective to illustrate the almost unlimited range of sounds that can be produced throughout the entire range of the violin with examples from the literature.

The G-string

This is the thickest and most sonorous of the four strings. As one goes into its higher positions, the sound becomes very intense and stringent because the vibrating portion of the string is constantly being shortened.

Example III–5. Tchaikovsky, *Symphony No. 5*, second movement, mm. 111–19

See also Mahler, *Symphony No. 3*, first movement, mm. 5–8.

The D-string

This is possibly the least powerful of the four. However, it has a warm and rather subdued quality, especially in contrast with the G-string. It mellows even more in its higher positions as its vibrating length is shortened.

Example III–6. Rimsky-Korsakov, *Scheherazade*, first movement, mm. 1–8

The A-string

This is quite strong in first position, but loses some of its brilliance in the upper positions. In soft, lyrical, expressive passages, the composer will often prefer the higher pitches to be performed on the A-string rather than have the player cross to the E-string, where these upper notes take on a different, more brilliant timbre.

Example III–7. Brahms, *Symphony No. 3*, third movement, mm. 13–24

The E-string

This is the most brilliant of the four strings. It has tremendous carrying power and is quite forceful, even strident, in the higher positions. At the same time, one can elicit the most ethereal sounds, which are clear and luminous when one plays softly on the E string.

Example III–8. Strauss, *Don Juan*, mm. 9–16

See also Prokofiev, *Classical Symphony*, second movement, mm. 1–4.

If one wishes to have a passage performed on one string exclusively, the passage should be marked *sul E, sul A, sul D,* or *sul G.* (The French prefer using roman numerals, as was mentioned in the previous chapter.)

Double-stops

The double-stop technique has already been discussed in general terms for all string instruments. Focusing specifically on double-, triple-, and quadruple-stopping for the violin, it is important to emphasize once again that most difficult double-stopping is reserved for solo and possibly chamber music. In orchestral writing, only the most easily accessible double-stops are usually used, particularly for *secco* chordal effects or especially sonorous passages. Since there are at least sixteen first violins and fourteen second violins in the two sections of a conventional symphony orchestra, passages that would be quite difficult for one performer are quite simple played *divisi.*

Here is a partial list of the double-, triple-, and quadruple-stop possibilities on the violin:

Example III–9. Double-stops

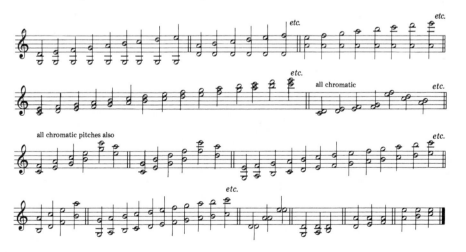

Example III–10. Chromatic Double-stops

Example III–11. Triple-stops*

Example III–12. Quadruple-stops

*Don't forget that all string triple- and quadruple-stops are of necessity played rolled.

Harmonics

Both natural and artificial harmonics have already been discussed; however, in solo and some violin chamber music, composers have required the violinist to produce harmonics in other ways than has been demonstrated

1. The most practical harmonics for orchestral writing are the "touch fourth" harmonics.

Example III–13

Actual harmonics

Fingers touching

Finger pressing

2. The "touch fifth" harmonics produce a tone which is one octave above the note that is lightly touched.

Example III–14

3. The "touch major third" harmonics produce a pitch two octaves above the lightly touched note.

Example III–15

4. The "touch minor third" harmonics produce a pitch two octaves and a major third (17th) above the lightly touched note.

Example III–16

Because Nos. 2, 3, and 4 are difficult to produce, all orchestral harmonics should be played as described in No. 1. The "touch thirds" harmonics, both major and minor, are especially weak and extremely risky.

Here are some successful orchestral passages using violin harmonics:

Example III–17. Copland, *Symphony No. 3*, fourth movement, mm. 3–8 after 128

Example III–18. Webern, *Six Pieces for Orchestra*, Op. 6, No. 5, mm. 20–26

Example III–19. Stravinsky, *Le Sacre du printemps*, 101

The Solo Violin

The violin has long been a favorite solo instrument of many composers. Almost every great master of orchestral music since the Baroque period has written violin concertos exploiting the tremendous range, versatility, and expressiveness of the instrument. Everyone should become acquainted with the masterpieces in this genre by such composers as Bach, Mozart, Beethoven, Mendelssohn, Brahms, Dvořák, Tchaikovsky, Bruch, Lalo, Schoenberg, Berg, Bartók, Prokofiev, Penderecki, and Rochberg, to name only a few. However, the special quality of the violin has also been greatly exploited as an occasional solo instrument in the orchestra. When one solo violin is called for, the concertmaster will play the part. When two soloists are required, the first stand of the first violins will be called upon. If the composer wishes some special effect, he may write one solo part for the first violin and another for the second violin. In that instance, the concertmaster and the principal second violinist will play. Some of the solo parts in the orchestral literature are quite virtuosic; therefore, today, the principal players of all sections must be of solo caliber.

Some examples of solo violin passages from orchestral works:

Example III–20. Brahms, *Symphony No. 1*, second movement, mm. 91–105

Example III–21. Strauss, *Don Juan,* mm. 73–82

Other Technical Considerations

SKIPS

Even though the violin is a most versatile and agile instrument, the problem of fast, wide skips presents real difficulties. They can sound thrilling, especially if the skips are from the extreme low register to the extreme high register. But one must realize that a soloist can execute this shift more accurately than a whole section. The difficulty is, of course, that the entire left-hand position has to be completely altered; sometimes strings have to be crossed silently yet smoothly; or a very high note must follow an extremely low one on the same string. Most skillful players can give a fairly good impression of legato playing, even when there is a string intervening in the skip, but there are difficulties in simply hitting the correct pitch.

In the following passages from orchestral violin parts, some of these difficulties are demonstrated. (Note that recordings are misleading, since in case the section does not clearly articulate the skip, the passage can be retaped until it is perfect.) These are problematical passages:

1. Wide skips on the same string:

Example III–22. Wagner, Prelude to *Die Meistersinger,* mm. 33–38

See also Shostakovich, *Symphony No. 5,* first movement, mm. 51–62.

2. Wide skips between extreme ranges:

Example III–23. Bartók, *Divertimento,* first movement, mm. 50–52

See also Copland, *Symphony No. 3,* fourth movement, mm. 2–4 after 96 .

3. Wide skips legato:

Example III–24. Berg, *Lyric Suite,* fourth movement, mm. 10–14

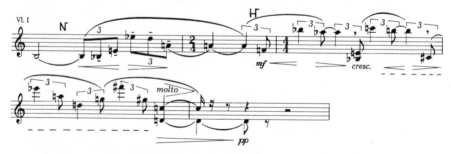

See also Stravinsky, *Agon,* Pas de deux, mm. 411–18.

CHROMATIC PASSAGES

This is a fingering problem, but should be mentioned here. All chromatic notes from the G-string to the highest register can be produced easily on the violin. Usually, the finger that is to play a pitch plays the chromatic step most closely related to it:

Example III–25

There are instances when the performer chooses not to risk the portamento that is inevitable if the chromatic scale is performed as in Example III–25. Therefore, the scale is played in "half position."

Example III–26

This is most appropriate in fast passages, for it minimizes the audible shifting of the same finger.

VIOLA

Viola (*It.*), Alto (*Fr.*), Bratsche (*Ger.*)

Francis Tursi, viola

Example III–27. Tuning

Viola music is usually notated in the alto clef, but to avoid ledger lines, the upper notes are sometimes written in treble clef.

Example III–28

Example III–29. Range

The viola is the alto voice of the string orchestra and its playing technique is similar to that of the violin. There are some problems to be kept in mind when writing for viola. The most obvious is the size of the instrument. It is quite a bit larger, sometimes as much as three to four inches, than the violin, and this means that the hand must stretch more to get the intervals in tune. The tension on the left hand is also greater, especially in the higher positions. There are variations in the size of violas, and experts do not agree on the ideal size for the most beautiful, characteristically dark-hued tone quality. Today, violists pick their instrument in proportion to the size of their left hand.

Of all the bowed strings, the viola has been the slowest to emerge. Even though trills, bowings, harmonics, arpeggios, double-, triple-, and quadruple-stops are just as successful on the viola as on the violin, this instrument has been undeservedly neglected by many great masters of the past. There are perhaps two principle reasons:

1. The eighteenth-century masters rarely wrote for four independent string voices.

2. For a long time, most violists were converted violinists and did not always enjoy the full trust of composers.

Although Bach, Stamitz, and Mozart wrote occasional solo or concertante works for the viola, it was not until Berlioz that it achieved a truly independent voice in orchestral writing.

Let us observe some differences between the viola and the violin which should help to define its function in the orchestra.

1. The viola bow is slightly heavier and thicker.

2. The strings are also heavier; therefore, they speak a bit more reluctantly and require that the player "dig in" a bit to make them sound. Hence, the lighter bowings are more difficult to produce.

3. Harmonics are easier to play because the thicker strings produce them more reliably.

Fingering

The fingering system is identical to that of the violin, and the same multiple-stop patterns are available on the viola, but a fifth lower. Similarly, all the ideas already discussed about half-positions, chromatic fingerings, pizzicato, and other color effects apply equally to this alto instrument of the violin family.

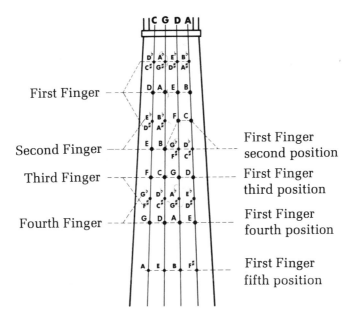

Examples of the special sound of each of the four viola strings:

The C-string

The only string not found on the violin, it is, therefore, the most characteristic of the four. It has been described by the Belgian musicologist-composer François Gevaert as "somber, austere, and sometimes even forbidding."

Example III–30. Hindemith, *Sonata*, Op. 11, No. 4, first movement, mm. 15–16

The G- and D-strings

The least characteristic, these may be called the "accompaniment strings," because it is on these that the violist performs the many accompanying figures composers have traditionally given his instrument. But they can also be exploited for their dark quality, as in the following solo:

Example III–31. Bartók, *Concerto for Orchestra*, fourth movement, mm. 42–51

The A-string

While not as brilliant as the E-string on the violin, the A-string is, nevertheless, quite piercing and nasal in quality. It combines beautifully with woodwind instruments and, in some cases, doubles well with soft trumpets and trombones. Because of its carrying power, it has been used a great deal in solo viola passages.

Example III–32. Hindemith, *Der Schwanendreher*, first movement, mm. 48–58

Double-stops

Here is a partial list of double-, triple-, and quadruple-stops which are possible on the viola. The *divisi* practice is the same as for the violin.

Example III–33. Double-stops

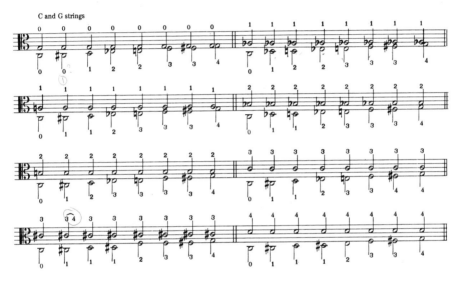

Tables of the double-stops on the G- and D-strings, as well as on the D- and A-strings, can be similarly constructed.

chord
notion

Example III–34. Triple-stops

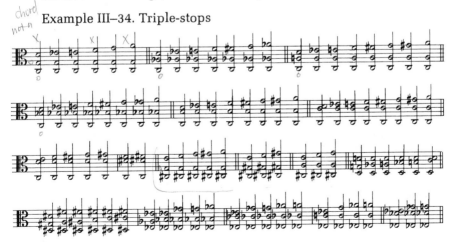

The triple-stops on the G-, D-, and A-strings should be tabulated in the same manner as those on the C-, G-, and D-strings. These triple-stops are all in the first position and are not difficult to perform, as all the awkward stops have been omitted.

Example III–35. Quadruple-stops.

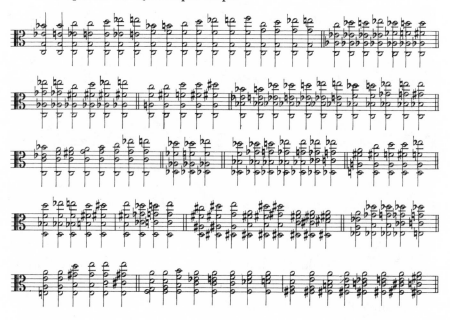

Here are some characteristic viola passages illustrating the sound of harmonics, pizzicato, double-stops, and other coloristic effects on the viola. Further, there is a passage that demonstrates the use of the viola as the bass of the string section (Example III–36), and one that is typical of the many filler or harmonic "fleshing-out" places so common in the orchestral literature (Example III–37). It would be remiss not to include one example that couples the violins and the viola in octaves (Example III–38) and one that presents the very successful coupling of violas and cellos (Example III–39).

Example III–36. Mendelssohn, Overture to *A Midsummer Night's Dream*, mm. 45–49

Example III–37. Wagner, *Lohengrin*, Act III, "In fernen Land," mm. 12–19

Example III–38. Berlioz, *Symphonie fantastique*, first movement, mm. 155–59

Example III–39. Beethoven, *Symphony No. 5*, second movement, mm. 1–10

See also:

> Stravinsky, *Le Sacre du printemps*, mm. 46–47
> Hindemith, *Der Schwanendreher*, first movement, mm. 1–11
> Tchaikovsky, *Romeo and Juliet*, mm. 114–16

The Solo Viola

The Baroque masters wrote many concertos for the viola, and some pre-Classical composers followed their lead. However, after that period, except for the *Symphonie concertante* of Mozart for violin and viola, and the solo part in Berlioz's *Harold in Italy*, there is little significant solo viola music until Wagner and Strauss in the late nineteenth century. In the twentieth century, however, the viola has finally achieved an almost equal status with its relatives in the bowed string group. We could cite as proof works like Debussy's *Sonata for Flute, Viola, and Harp*, Bartók's and Walton's viola concertos, *Der Schwanendreher* by Hindemith, and *Flos Campi* by Vaughan Williams, to name only a few. Some wonderful examples of solo or concertante viola passages from the orchestra literature:

Example III–40. Scriabin, *Poem of Ecstasy*, mm. 22–27

Example III–41. Strauss, *Don Quixote*, Variation 2, Vivace, mm. 1–13

Example III–42. Stravinsky, *Le Sacre du printemps*, 91

See also Berlioz, *Harold in Italy*, first movement, mm. 38–68.

VIOLA D'AMORE

Viole d'amour (*Fr.*), Liebesgeige (*Ger.*)

Example III–43. Usual Tuning

The principle on which the characteristic sound of this instrument is based is sympathetic vibration. Besides the seven strings which are bowed and fingered, there are seven sympathetic strings made of steel wire, which lie just above the belly of the instrument and directly below the string with which they sympathize. The sympathetic strings are generally tuned in unison with the bowed strings.

In order to allow the characteristic sound of these sympathetic strings to be heard freely in keys other than D major, alternative tunings have been used. The most common alteration is to lower the F♯ string to F♮, thus producing a D-minor tuning.

Example III–44

Hindemith used two different tunings in his works for viola d'amore:

Example III–45. *Sonata for Viola d'amore and Piano*, Op. 25, No. 4

Example III–46. *Kammermusik No. 6 for Viola d'amore and Orchestra*, Op. 46, No. 1

Vivaldi used the following tunings (six-string instruments) in his concertos:

Example III–47

Viola d'amore music is written today in the alto and treble clefs. In the past, music for the lower strings of the instrument was often notated in the bass clef, sounding an octave higher, but this is no longer done.

Example III–48. Range

In many orchestration books, instruments infrequently used in the orchestra are labeled "ancient" or "exotic" and are treated very summarily. This has proven to be rather shortsighted, since many of these instruments are today awakening from their hibernation and enjoying a renaissance. Such an instrument is the viola d'amore. It has never been a regular member of the orchestra; it has been used primarily for solo or concertante passages in such works as Bach's *St. John Passion*, several Bach cantatas, Meyerbeer's *Les Huguenots*, Massenet's *Le Jongleur de Notre Dame*, Pfitzner's *Palestrina*, and Loeffler's *La Mort de Tintagiles*. One viola d'amore accompanies the women's offstage chorus in Puccini's *Madama Butterfly*. It is doubtful that this instrument will ever enter the modern orchestra, yet every composer and orchestrator should know at least something about it.

The instrument is slightly larger than the modern violin. Some salient features of the instrument:

1. The ability to play chords and arpeggios easily, especially in keys related to the tuning used.

2. The ability to perform natural harmonics. Easily obtained are the second, third, fourth, and fifth harmonics by touching the strings lightly where one would ordinarily stop the octave, the fifth, the fourth, and the major third. Here are the resulting sounds of the harmonics in the usual D-major tuning:

Example III–49

Artificial harmonics are, of course, also possible. The most successful are the ones produced by the "touch fourth" method. All other violin techniques of fingering, bowing, and all coloristic effects may also be achieved on the viola d'amore.

Here are two passages for viola d'amore from past and present literature:

Example III–50. Meyerbeer, *Les Huguenots,* Act I, "Ah quel Spectacle," mm. 1–19

Example III–51. Hindemith, *Kleine Sonate,* second movement, mm. 14–28

See also Bach, *St. John Passion,* "Erwäge, erwäge," mm. 1–5.

VIOLONCELLO OR CELLO

Violoncello (*It.*), Violoncelle (*Fr.*), Violoncell (*Ger.*)

Robert Sylvester, cello

Example III–52. Tuning

All music for the cello is written in either the bass, tenor, or treble clef. Suggested clef changes because of ledger-line considerations:

Example III–53

A warning to score readers: in some old editions, such as the Beethoven quartets, cello parts in treble clef were meant to be transposed an octave lower when performed. This is no longer practiced. The cello always sounds where notated.

Example III–54. Range

The cello is both the tenor and the bass of the string section. The violin, viola, and viola d'amore are all held on the left shoulder and supported by the chin, but the cello's playing position is quite different. The instrument is placed between the player's knees and supported on the floor by means of an adjustable peg which slides out of the bottom just below the end of the tailpiece. The neck points over the player's left shoulder. Because of the greater length of the strings, a slightly different fingering system is used to produce all the pitches on the instrument. The second finger is only used for chromatic intervals. The normal compass in the first position between the first and the fourth fingers is a third. In the upper positions all four fingers are used more often, similar to the fingering on the viola. Because the cellist's left hand is freed from the burden of supporting the instrument to a much greater degree than that of the violinist or violist, the thumb can be used in higher positions. In the seventh position of the instrument, the left-hand thumb is forced to leave its position around the neck. It is, therefore, available to be used in actually fingering the instrument. Remember, the distance between the intervals diminishes as the hand moves to higher positions. With the additional use of the thumb, then, the cellist can stretch to octave double-stops on adjacent strings with relative ease, while anything larger than sixth double-stops is difficult in the low register. The sign for the use of the thumb is ႙.

Example III–55

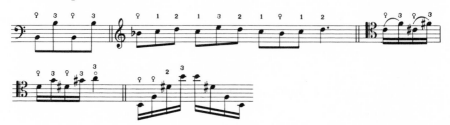

Example III–56. Double-stops

Example III–57. Triple-stops

Example III–58. Quadruple-stops

etc.

Here is a fingering chart and some combinations showing thumb positions.

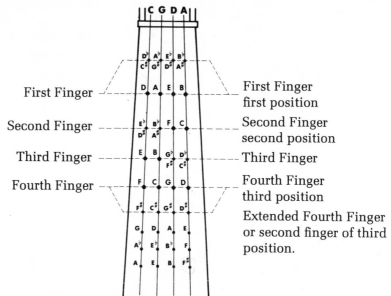

First Finger — First Finger first position

Second Finger — Second Finger second position

Third Finger — Third Finger

Fourth Finger — Fourth Finger third position

Extended Fourth Finger or second finger of third position.

It is tempting to indulge in ecstatic descriptions of the cello's tone quality. But the best evidence of the singular beauty of the instrument's sound lies in both solo passages featuring the entire section and those where the cello has a voice within the contrapuntal texture. The D is the most musically captivating string on this instrument; it has a warm and lyrical quality. The A is the most brilliant and piercing; the G, least strong, carries less well than the others. Again, because of its weight and its thickness, the lowest string, the C, is a true sonorous bass of rich quality. Berlioz once said that the cello is not "capable of extreme agility." This statement can be completely ignored today, for the cello can execute practically any technical feat possible on the viola or the violin.

Some representative passages, including accompaniment patterns:

Example III–59. Wagner, Prelude to *Tristan und Isolde*, mm. 17–32

Example III–60. Harris, *Symphony No. 3*, first movement, mm. 1–27

See also:

> Brahms, *Symphony No. 3*, third movement, mm. 1–12
> Brahms, *Symphony No. 2*, third movement, mm. 194–202
> Beethoven, *Symphony No. 3*, first movement, mm. 1–8

Harmonics

The principle of natural harmonics on the cello is identical to that for the other strings, and these harmonics are even more secure on this larger instrument because of the greater length and weight of the strings. The "touch fourth" harmonic is again the most successful for orchestral writing and produces the artificial harmonic of best quality. These artificial harmonics are played with the thumb and the third finger throughout the entire range of the instrument, with the pitch sounding two octaves above the note pressed down by the thumb.

Example III–61

Cellos are frequently used *divisi* for very rich effects, as in the following example:

Example III–62. Rossini, Overture to *William Tell*, mm. 1–10

See also:

> Mahler, *Das Lied von der Erde,* fifth movement, mm. 1–4 at 10
> R. Strauss, *Also sprach Zarathustra,* 18 measures before 10 to 1 measure before 10

The Solo Cello

The cello literature is quite rich in concertos by the major composers of all creative periods from the Baroque to the twentieth century. Some of the oustanding examples are by Boccherini, Haydn, Beethoven (triple), Schumann, Brahms (double), Dvořák, Tchaikovsky (*Rococo Variations*), Lalo, Milhaud, Hindemith, Barber, Walton, Lutosławski, and many others. Frequently, the cello is used as an occasional soloist in orchestral works. Here is a great passage from the literature:

Example III–63. Strauss, *Don Quixote,* mm. 163–76

See also:

> Brahms, *Piano Concerto No. 2*, third movement, mm. 71–86
> Bloch, *Schelomo*, mm. 1–15
> Schumann, *Symphony No. 2*, first movement, mm. 223–37

Cello in Combination

This subject will be discussed in great detail in the orchestral chapters of this book. Suffice it to point out that the cello is very compatible for coupling or doubling with a great many instruments in all the orchestral choirs. The most widely used couplings are cello and double bass, cello and bassoon, cello and clarinet or bass clarinet, cello and horn, and pizzicato cello and timpani.

Example III–64. Barber, *Essay for Orchestra No. 1*, mm. 1–8

See also:

> Beethoven, *Symphony No. 5*, third movement, mm. 162–79
> Glinka, Overture to *Russian and Ludmilla*, mm. 81–100

DOUBLE BASS
Contrabasso (*It.*), Contrebasse (*Fr.*), Kontrabass (*Ger.*)

James B. Vandermark,
double bass

Example III–65. Tuning

The double bass is notated an octave higher than it actually sounds,
thus:

Example III–66

All music for the double bass is written in bass, tenor, or treble
clef, and sounds an octave lower than written. Change of clef is suggested when there are three or more ledger lines.

Example III–67. Range

This is really the bass voice of the string choir. The practical
orchestral range is from the low E (sounding an octave lower) to the
treble B♭ (again sounding an octave lower); in solo passages and

through the use of natural harmonics, higher notes can be produced. The instrument stands on an adjustable peg and is supported by the player's body and left knee. There are two minor differences in construction between the double bass and the other members of the violin family: its shoulders are sloped rather than curved and it has cogwheel tuning pegs to cope with the thickness of its strings. Many bass players sit on a high stool while performing. Most all of the orchestral bass players use a large, full-sized instrument, while some bass solo performers have used smaller models, which are easier to play and more flexible, but these really do not have the true contra-bass quality. One very important fact must be kept in mind, and that is that despite its size, the double bass has a rather small sound by itself. Double bass solos sound thin and distant. A group or section of basses, on the other hand, can raise the roof. Further, because of the very thick and heavy strings, the instrument's "speaking," or articulation, is more sluggish than any of the other string instruments. This should be remembered when basses are doubled by cellos in fast passages, since our bass sections are much larger than those in Beethoven's time. Some of his fast passages are muddied, even by the best orchestras, and conductors have taken liberties because of this peculiar but natural acoustic phenomenon.

Example III–68. Beethoven, *Symphony No. 4*, fourth movement, mm. 319–23

Practical solution for clarification of passage above:

Example III–69

Early Uses of Double Basses

During the Baroque and Classical periods and up to Beethoven, the double bass traditionally doubled the cello for most or all of a composition. Independent bass parts appear rarely, if ever, in purely orchestral literature, although one may find some few instances in opera scores. When the composer desired a lighter bass line, he would simply write *senza basso* in the cello part, and when he wanted the double basses to resume playing, the phrase + *basso* was inserted.

Fingering

The first to fourth fingers encompass a major second in the lower position. The third finger is usually not used independently but is placed on the string, together with the fourth finger up to and including the fifth position. Therefore, first, second, and third are used, and after the seventh position, the thumb is also utilized:

Example III–70

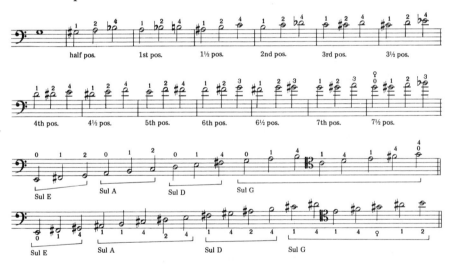

A warning must be sounded: the upper range is very effective, but great care must be given to the way it is approached. Unless one writes a piece for virtuosos, this extreme range is best approached by small-scale steps or small skips rather than large leaps. The orientation of the left hand is much more difficult because of the tremendous length of the strings.

Here is an effective orchestral double bass excerpt:

Example III–71. Wagner, Overture to *Die Meistersinger*, mm. 158–65

See also:

Verdi, *Otello*, Act IV, mm. 7–18
Beethoven, *Symphony No. 6*, fourth movement, mm. 41–47
Tchaikovsky, *Symphony No. 6*, first movement, mm. 1–6

Harmonics

As has been said before, only natural harmonics should be required of the bass player, and these are most effective. Here is a list of the simplest harmonics:

Example III–72. Natural Harmonics

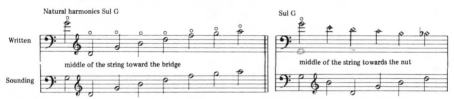

Double-stops

The use of double-, triple-, or quadruple-stops for the double bass is risky and should be avoided in orchestral writing, unless one or more of the desired pitches are open strings. In the upper positions, because of the closer proximity of the notes, double-stops are more feasible, although it is strongly urged that *divisi* instructions be given to facilitate orchestral bass parts. One can find plenty of exceptions to this rule; nevertheless, that fact does not lessen the great difficulty getting double-stops (without open strings) in tune. Further, close double-stops (seconds, thirds) on the bass in any lower register are quite thick and muddy, and unless one wishes to hear such sounds as special effects, they should be avoided.

Bowing

Bass players can use all the types of bowing already discussed. All coloristic effects are also applicable and most effective. One must remember that the bow used by double bass players is thicker, heavier, and quite a bit shorter than the violin or even the cello bow. This fact is important when one slurs long passages or asks for a lengthy *tenuto*. The way to do this is to ask the players to change bow at will.

The Five-string Bass

In most orchestras today, at least two or three members of the double bass section have instruments with a C attachment. This means that all chromatic notes from low E-string to the C below are available. If these notes are requested, and there are no players in the section with the attachment, the notes automatically will be played an octave higher. The attachment was originally installed so that all the doubled cello passages could be performed an octave lower than written without the necessity of switching octaves in the middle of the passage when the double bass ran out of notes, while the cello went down to its low C-string. There are even instances (*Pines of Rome*) of *scordatura* requests for low B.

Solo, Concertante, and Divisi Basses

The solo concerto bass literature is not very extensive, and one of the reasons is certainly because of the disappointing acoustic carrying power of the instrument as a solo performer in a large hall. After a hiatus of perhaps 200 years, great double bass solo artists have come to prominence in the twentieth century and are commissioning composers to write works for them. There are early concertos by Dragonetti, Bottesini, and Dittersdorf, and twentieth-century works by Koussevitzky, Zimmermann, and others.

Solo passages in nineteenth- and early twentieth-century orchestral literature occur rather infrequently, but concertante and *divisi* multiple independent bass parts abound.

Example III–73. Stravinsky, *Pulcinella Suite*, seventh movement, mm. 1–17

Example III–74. Milhaud, *La Création du monde*, 1 measure before 11 to 1 measure before 12

See also:

Mahler, *Symphony No. 1*, third movement, mm. 3–10
Stravinsky, *Le Sacre du printemps*, 10 to 12
Mahler, *Symphony No. 2*, second movement, 1 measure before 4 to 5 measures after 4
Persichetti, *Symphony for Strings*, first movement, mm. 16–20
R. Strauss, *Also sprach Zarathustra*, mm. 8–22 after 9

4

Plucked String Instruments

Even though only one of these instruments is a regular member of the modern symphony orchestra, the others are making their appearance more and more frequently, especially in smaller orchestral combinations. Every composer or orchestrator should know at least the number and tunings of the strings, the range compass, and the manner of performance and notation for each of the plucked string instruments currently in use. Of course, the harp, which is a standard member of the orchestra today, will be discussed in greater detail.

ZITHER
Cythare (*It.* and *Fr.*), Zither (*Ger.*)

This is an ancient instrument which is mostly used for special coloristic effects. Since it was widely played in southern Germany and Austria, composers like Johann Strauss in *Tales from the Vienna Woods* used it to evoke the locale. Not until the latter part of the nineteenth century was a practical modern version of the instrument perfected.

The zither has five melody strings upon which the upper line of the notation is performed by the left hand. These are tuned in either one of two ways:

Example IV–1. Melody Strings

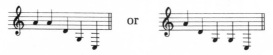

The accompaniment is played with the right hand on twenty-five accompaniment and bass strings tuned in the following manner:

Example IV–2. Accompaniment Strings

Example IV–3. Bass Strings

All these strings sound an octave lower than written.

The instrument lies on a table or stand. The left hand fingers the melody while the right-hand thumb wearing a *plectrum* plucks the strings. The accompaniment is performed by the other four fingers on the right hand plucking the accompaniment and bass strings. All the zither strings may be retuned at the composer's discretion. The tunings given above are the most usual ones.

Example IV–4. J. Strauss, *Tales from the Vienna Woods*, mm. 75–93

MANDOLIN

Mandolino *(It.)*, Mandoline *(Fr. and Ger.)*

The mandolin appeared occasionally in orchestral scores up to Grétry's and Mozart's day. It then disappeared only to resurface in late Verdi (*Othello*), Mahler (*Symphony No. 7*), Schoenberg (*Serenade*), Respighi (*Roman Festivals*), Stravinsky (*Agon*), Crumb (*Ancient Voices of Children*), and others. The instrument has eight strings tuned in pairs pitched like strings of a violin.

Example IV–5. Tuning

Example IV–6. Range

It was favored by Classical composers for the accompaniment of serenades. Single notes and double-stops are plucked with a pick or plectrum; sustained effects are achieved by playing tremolo either the same note on two like strings or two unlike notes on neighboring strings. In order to facilitate finding the notes, the fingerboard is fretted. It is a quiet instrument best used in solo or lightly accompanied by muted strings or soft winds.

Example IV–7. Mozart, *Don Giovanni*, Act II, "Deh, vieni alla finestra," mm. 1–10

Example IV–8. Crumb, *Echoes of Time and the River*, fourth movement, mm. 8–9.

BANJO

The banjo originated in West Africa and was introduced into this country by Black slaves. Thomas Jefferson wrote that the Negroes

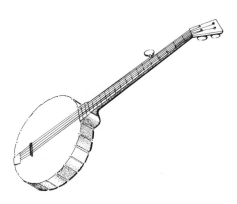

brought along an instrument they called "banger." (In Senegalese their lute is still called "banio.") Jefferson himself referred to it as the "banjar." It was a very crude instrument and not really perfected until 1847, during the career of the first banjo professional, Joe Sweeney.

At that time the banjo was very much as it is today, a body like an enclosed tambourine with a long neck. It is played either with or without a plectrum. The five-string banjo used in Blue Grass music and minstrel bands is tuned:

Example IV–9. Tuning

The high G is a short string connected to an outside peg and is called the thumb string. It is used for drones, etc. All other strings are fretted, making it easy to find the pitches. There are some banjos with only four strings, and others with five or more regular-length strings, often tuned quite differently from the five-string tuning above. As a matter of fact, the banjo has been tuned like the guitar, because in the theater orchestras and jazz bands of the '20s and early '30s, guitar players were often asked to double on the mandolin as well as the banjo. To make this more feasible, all the instruments are tuned pretty much alike. As of today, there has been no great movement to use the banjo as part of the orchestra, except in theater orchestras and imitations of Blue Grass music.

Here is a sample of what typical banjo music looks like:

Example IV–10. Gershwin, *Rhapsody in Blue,* 28 – 29

GUITAR
Chitarra (*It.*), Guitare (*Fr.*), Guitarre (*Ger.*)

The guitar has enjoyed an amazing renaissance in our time. Since folk music has become so popular, everyone seems to be playing the guitar. There are many types of guitar: Spanish, electric, Hawaiian, and classical, to name but a few. Since we are discussing orchestral instruments, we shall limit ourselves to the classical guitar, which is the one used whenever a guitar is asked for unless the composer specifies otherwise. The tuning of the guitar stems from the old lute tunings and is irregular in that it does not maintain the same intervals between each of the six strings:

Example IV–11. Tuning

Example IV–12. Range (All pitches sound an octave lower than notated.)

Single-line melodies, chords, and melodies with accompaniments are all possible on the guitar, which is fingered with four fingers of the left hand and plucked with all five fingers of the right hand. A fretted finger board makes it easier to locate pitches. Harmonics, especially natural harmonics, are very effective, but one must keep in mind that a nonamplified guitar is quite soft and harmonics are even softer than natural notes. Therefore, this too is best treated as a solo, in very small combinations of softer strings and winds, or, of course, with voice. There are guitar parts in Rossini's *Barber of Seville*, Weber's *Oberon*, Virgil Thomson's *The Plow That Broke the Plains*, Boulez's *Le Marteau sans maître*, Penderecki's *Devils of Loudon* (bass guitar), and others.

Example IV–13. Stravinsky. *Le Rossignol*, Act III, mm.136–42

HARP

Arpa (*It.*), Harpe (*Fr.*), Harfe (*Ger.*)

The harp has a very long history as a solo and accompanying instrument. It has gone through a series of alterations increasing and varying its pitches without changing its original concept. The final result is today's chromatic harp. This instrument has forty-seven strings and is basically tuned in Cb major. That is, the seven strings are tuned Cb–Db–Eb–Fb–Gb–Ab–Bb, and the range is:

Example IV–14. Range

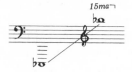

In other words, it encompasses six full octaves plus five additional notes; this means six full repetitions of the seven basic notes plus another repetition of the first five. This is important to understand because the top of each string is attached to a tuning peg and the bottom to a pedal which can raise each note one whole step. The pedal has three positions:

1. Pedals all the way up give one the original C♭ sequence;
2. Pedals one notch down raise all the notes one half step to C–D–E–F–G–A–B;
3. Pedals two notches down raise all the notes a whole step to C♯–D♯–E♯–F♯–G♯–A♯–B♯.

It must be clearly understood that, for instance, all C-strings or all G-strings are controlled by one pedal each, so that if the C♭ is depressed one notch, the entire C♭ series becomes C♮ series. One cannot play a C♭ in one octave together with a C♮ in another octave. As will be seen later, it is easy to write C♭ as B♮ and play it together with a C♮, because they would be performed on two different strings

Eileen Malone, harp

controlled by two separate pedals. This fact is too often overlooked and misunderstood, but a real comprehension of this first principle of pedaling will make the capabilities of the chromatic harp much clearer. Before we leave this brief discussion of the harp strings, it should be pointed out that the pegs around which the strings are wrapped at the top portion of the harp are turned (i.e., tuned) with a key, and like all string instruments, the pitch of the strings needs frequent adjustment. To tune a harp is a tedious task, and the harpist is usually on stage long before the rest of the orchestra preparing the instrument. The lowest eleven strings are gut wound with wire; in the remaining unwound gut strings, each C-string is red and each F-string is blue.

Arrangement of the Pedals

The pedals are arranged as follows:

D C B / E F G A

The left three are operated by the left foot while the right four are manipulated by the right foot. Obviously, the harpist cannot cross over because the harp is in the way. Therefore, it is important to know where the pedals are located in order to avoid requesting that the player change the E and G pedal at the same moment, for one foot can change only one pedal at a time.* The D and G pedals could be changed at the same time, since D would be changed by one foot and G by the other.

It is a help to the harpist to indicate how the pedals should be set at the beginning of a work. This can be done in three ways (the first two are preferred). This is the setting for the beginning of Debussy's *L'Après-midi d'un faune.*

1. This is a letter representation and a very clear one:

Db C♯ Bb / E♮ Fb G♯ Ab

2. This is a graphic representation giving the three degrees or notches, the top being the "all-flats" one.

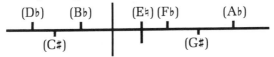

---

*It may be of help to learn a little "ditty" which was taught to me by my first orchestration teacher when I was a young boy. It has stuck with me and enabled me to remember the sequence of the harp pedals with no difficulty. I pass it on as a memorizing device:

Did Columbus Bring / Enough Food Going (to) America?

3. This is neither as clear nor as common as the other two; it gives the setting for the first, then second pedal, etc., on each side. One numbers the pedals, by the way, from the inside out, so that B is No. 1 on the left-hand side, and E No. 1 on the right.

E♮ F♭ G♯ A♭
B♭ C♯ D♭

In the famous run or glissando below, the harp really produces only four pitches, B♭, D♭, F♭, and A♭, because all the other strings are tuned enharmonically to sound: C♯ = D♭, E♮ = F♭, G♯ = A♭. This kind of enharmonic manipulation is essential, especially in highly chromatic music. The pedal setting above, for example, could also be used for a phrase such as this:

Example IV–15

On the other hand, the enharmonic spelling may be necessitated by a passage or a chord which calls for both F and F♯ for instance, in which case the F would have to be spelled E♯ or the F♯ spelled as G♭.

Example IV–16

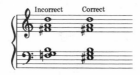

There are many such examples of strange, but practical harp spellings.

As far as pedal changes are concerned, it is usual for the harpist to change the pedal just a split second before playing the note. In this passage, for instance,

The experienced harpist usually will make the pedal change even later than it is marked. One should not worry about the changes other than to make certain the harpist does not have to change two pedals on the same side at the same time, and that the tempo will permit time for the changes. Highly chromatic music must be carefully handled, and one should study the works of composers like

Debussy, Ravel, and Stravinsky for beautiful orchestral uses of the instrument, and the solo works of the great harpists like Salzedo and Grandjany for idiomatic harp writing. Harpists are quite willing to try out new ideas as long as the composer has a well-grounded understanding of the instrument's basic problems.

The tone color of the harp is somber, dark, and sonorous in the lower two octaves, lightening progressively as one goes up the range. The middle two octaves are very rich and warm, while the top octave and a half is light and clear but does not have a great dynamic range. The upper part of the harp has neither a great sustaining power nor a great carrying potential; the *fortissimo* at the top is like a *mezzo forte* in the middle. Because the string is longest when it is in a flat position, the flat keys have more sound potential, but a good harpist can make any key sound well by the power in his hands plucking the strings.

The music for harp is notated on two staves like music for piano, using bass and treble clefs.

Example IV–17. Mozart, *Concerto for Flute and Harp,* first movement, mm. 44–54

Chords may be arpeggiated or played solidly. It is important to remember that the harpist uses only four of the fingers on each hand to play (the little finger is never used); therefore, no five-note chords should be written. Three-note chords spread wide are the most effective. The distance of an octave is much smaller than it is on the piano; for that reason tenths are quite simple to reach. Here is a passage that sounds well on the harp, and the chords are spaced in an idiomatic way:

Example IV–18

It used to be standard procedure for the harpist to arpeggiate or roll all chords, but this is no longer true. Unless a wavy line precedes a chord, the harpist will pluck the chord solidly. Just as we pointed out in string chordal pizzicato, one can indicate the direction by means of arrows ⇕ . If there are no arrows, the harpist will roll the chord from the bottom up.

An excellent chordal nonarpeggiated passage can be found at the beginning of the Bartók *Violin Concerto*, which moves from close chords to spread chords (mm. 1–18). While Brahms is not particularly known for his harp writing, there is a beautiful passage which ends the first movement of the *Requiem* (mm. 150–58).

Example IV–19. Bartók, *Violin Concerto*, first movement, mm. 1–18

Example IV–20. Brahms, *Ein deutsches Requiem*, first movement, mm. 150–58

Just to experience one more of the thousands of effective arpeggiated passages in the harp solo as well as orchestral literature, here is an excerpt from Debussy's *L'Après-midi d'un faune* with flute:

Example IV–21. Debussy, *Prélude à "L'Après-midi d'un faune,"* mm. 79–81

Harmonics

Harp harmonics are very typical, practical, and beautifully bell-like sounds. They are produced in two ways, both resulting in the octave harmonic:

1. By the left hand touching the center of the string (at the node) with the lower portion of the palm, and plucking the string with the left thumb.

2. By the right hand touching the center of the string (at the node) with the outside of the knuckle of the index finger and plucking the string with the right thumb.

Two or three or more harmonics can be played at one time by a single hand if the compass is not more than a perfect fifth.

Harmonics are usually notated with a zero over the note so that it will sound an octave higher than written. Some composers write the note at pitch and put a circle over it. This is confusing unless explained somewhere earlier in the score.

For the best results in harmonics, two factors should be kept in mind:

1. Harp harmonics are very soft and must be accompanied very lightly or played *a cappella* to be effectively heard.

2. The most practical range for harp harmonics is between C below middle C to the A above the staff. That middle register sounds best.

Above the A the strings get too short for harmonics to sound good, and below that C it is very difficult for the player to reach and stabilize a solid harmonic.

Example IV–22. Debussy, *Nocturnes: Nuages,* mm. 74–78

Example IV–23. Ravel, *Daphnis et Chloé,* symphonic fragments, *Nocturne,* mm. 49–53

The harp can be used as a melodic, as an accompanying, and as a doubling instrument with great success. There are four special color effects which should be mentioned:

1. *Près de la table,* which means plucking the string near the soundboard to give a hard, brittle, almost metallic sound.

Example IV–24. Britten, *Four Sea Interludes,* No. 4, *Storm,* mm. 109–16

2. *Sons étouffés,* which means that each note is dampened as soon as it is played. The effect is that of a *secco* pizzicato on strings. The passage must be slow enough to permit each finger on the entire hand to dampen the string or strings.

Example IV–25

3. Glissando is perhaps the best known harp sound and should not be overused for the sake of "showing off" the harp. Whenever a glis-

sando is written, one must specify how the harp is to be tuned, and give the starting pitch as well as the ending one.

Example IV–26. Glissandi

Example IV–27. Multiple Glissandi

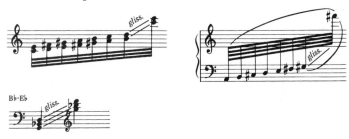

4. Trills, tremolos, and *bisbigliando* (whispering): Trills can be performed by one hand, by alternating hands plucking the same string, or by tuning two strings alike enharmonically, and having the two hands alternate on the two different strings sounding the same pitch.

The tremolo can of course be executed in a normal fashion by the two hands alternating, but a very special rustling or whispering effect called *bisbigliando* at a very soft dynamic is a unique tremolo only a harp can render.

Example IV–28. Trills

Example IV–29. *Bisbigliando*

Today, composers have devised many other harp effects for which standard notation is still being evolved (see K. Stone, *Music Nota-*

tion in the 20th Century, pp. 228–56). Some of these are: 1) knocking on the sound-board; 2) plucking the strings with the fingernails; 3) using a plectrum or pick with which to pluck the strings; 4) calling for harmonics other than the octave harmonic. All these devices are possible, and many more can be achieved. The composer should strive to make his intentions very clear in the notation, and be sure to consult a fine harpist for the feasibility of any unusual technique.

Scoring for Strings

INDIVIDUALITY WITHIN THE ENSEMBLE

The string section has been the chief lyric-harmonic element in the orchestra for much of the past 250 years. This section, which has grown into five distinct voices, has the capability to sustain major musical ideas either as a choir within the full orchestral texture or in works for strings alone. It has been said that one never tires of the varied sounds and timbres that strings can produce. This depends, of course, on how one uses this very versatile choir, and we shall try to study its potential in a variety of situations in this chapter. Even though it is not the province of this book to discuss the history and technique of string quartet and quintet writing, it is important to call the reader's attention to the great quartets of Haydn, Mozart, and Beethoven, which influenced their entire string concept. Here are some of the results of the chamber music experimentation which had far-reaching effects on the successful establishment of a five-part string choir, the forebear of the virtuosic string ensemble we find in today's orchestra:

1. the emancipation of the second violin, viola, and cello as equal partners with the first violin;
2. voice crossings for special effects;
3. the consideration of register characteristics of all the instruments for coloristic as well as structural purposes;
4. the extension of the range of all the instruments.

To illustrate some of these points, let us study twelve measures of a late Haydn string quartet, the *Emperor Quartet,* Op. 76, No. 3. This work does not, of course, include the double bass, but that instrument will enter into our discussion a bit later. We shall look at the second movement, which has the famous Austrian national anthem as its theme, and then at some of the variations.

1. The theme is presented in a simple setting with straightforward harmony. Notice the rhythmic coupling of the two violins playing the melodic material and that of the viola and cello providing the harmonic background. Also, one must call attention to the faultless voice leading so important in the exposition of a melody, so as to emphasize and feature it without complications.

Example V–1. Haydn, *String Quartet* Op. 76, No. 3, second movement, mm. 1–12

2. Now we examine a series of variations showing that Haydn regarded each of the four members of the ensemble as an equal partner. In the first variation, the second violin presents the theme while the first plays a "melodized" harmonic counterpoint against it.

Example V–2. Haydn, *String Quartet* Op. 76, No. 3, second movement, Variation I

3. The next variation gives the theme to the cello. This is an important one for us to study, for the cello rises above the second violin in mm. 10–11. One may speculate that Haydn did this because of the more intense quality of the cello in that register, whereas the second violin would be in its weakest register if it had been assigned the cello part. In this setting the second violin is only coupling the cello, which is in a much more opulent register. Notice also that the viola is simply used as a pedal instrument, emphasizing mostly the dominant and tonic notes to fill out and clarify the harmony.

Example V–3. Haydn, *String Quartet* Op. 76, No. 3, second movement, Variation II

4. In Variation III, the melody is assigned to the viola, and Haydn places it above the two violins. This results in a glorious sound brought forth by an instrument too long neglected. Here we must call attention to the fact that Haydn does not bother to place dynamics at the beginning of each variation except the first, where the direction is *sempre piano*. He relies entirely on the registers of the instruments and his scoring to achieve the correct dynamics; but more than this, he assures by his craft that the desired voice domi-

nates, while the others support. In this variation also, we find the cello taking on a supporting role, not simply providing a bass, but providing an involved contrapuntal countermelody.

Example V–4. Haydn, *String Quartet* Op. 76, No. 3, second movement, Variation III

5. The final variation is a variant of the first statement of the theme. The composer restrained himself from using the octave transposition until these last moments in the movement—and how glorious it sounds here, and how climactic! This is a wonderful lesson in orchestration, for too often the extremes in the range are wasted too early in a work, and the final buildup is, as a result, anticlimactic. The other formal factor to notice is that the entire structure is an accumulation of the elements which have slowly entered the harmonic and contrapuntal scheme in the course of the variations and have become a natural part of the statement. (Compare with first appearance of the theme.) The pedal point in the cello is another device used by Haydn to give a feeling of resolution and ending.

Example V–5. Haydn, *String Quartet* Op. 76, No. 3, second movement, Variation IV

While this is, of course, a chamber music piece for four solo play-ers, the principles it illustrates may easily be applied to the string orchestra and, by extension, to the string choir in a symphony orchestra.

A word about the double bass. As the cello took on a greater role as the tenor voice of the strings, the double bass assumed even greater significance, as we shall see in nineteenth- and twentieth-century string writing. In Haydn, Mozart, Beethoven, and Schubert, it is usual for the bass to double the cello in most passages, especially in the tutti sections. When a lighter string texture is desired, the double bass was eliminated. Independent double bass parts became increas-ingly popular as the nineteenth century progressed, as we shall see in some of the studies in this chapter. If Haydn had used a double bass in the fourth variation, he probably would have doubled the cello (an octave below) for the anacrusis plus the first three-and-a-half measures. He would then have dropped it until the tonic pedal in mm. 8–12, bringing it back once more at the cadence of mm. 15–16. Here is the way it would look:

Example V–6. Haydn, *String Quartet* Op. 76, No. 3, second
movement, Variation IV with added bass

FOREGROUND—MIDDLEGROUND—BACKGROUND

All kinds of music have been composed for the string orchestra: homophonic, contrapuntal, thematic, as well as accompaniment music. Three concepts are important to a discussion of the distribution of material in an ensemble situation:

1. *foreground:* the most important voice, which the composer wants to be heard most prominently;
2. *middleground:* includes countermelodies or important contrapuntal material;
3. *background:* accompaniment either in the form of chords or polyphonic/melodic figures.

The composer's skill can be measured by the way he orchestrates these three elements in his music. As we saw in the previous example, Haydn handled them so well that he did not even have to use dynamic markings to achieve balance among the three elements.

The composer must consider each of them, especially the foreground line, with regard to its tonal compass and the emotional intensity he wishes it to project. If this principle idea is to be scored for strings, he must consider the ranges and registers characteristic of each of its five instruments. When he has made these decisions, the resultant scoring of the main theme, idea, or gesture will then provide clues for the scoring of the middleground and certainly the background material.

An example of a successful realization of this procedure will illustrate these points better than volumes of verbiage.

Here is the opening of the slow movement of Brahms's *Symphony No. 3:*

Example V–7. Brahms, *Symphony No. 3,* third movement, mm. 1–14

Brahms chooses the cello to expose the beautiful theme (*foreground*) surrounded by the remaining strings as *background*. Let us for a moment speculate how the composer came to this decision by rescoring the excerpt in various ways.

Example V–8

1. The first violin, in this register, is very weak and without great emotional force. If it were scored an octave higher, the next statement of the theme would be anticlimactic and subsequent restatements anticipated. (See a similar consideration in the Haydn example.)

Example V–9

2. If the second violin were to play the theme on the G-string, the result would be intense, but of a much darker hue than the upper strings of the cello.

Example V–10

3. The viola sound in this register is quite nondescript and, though mellow, lacks intensity and opulence.

Example V–11

4. The double bass is an unlikely choice because, at pitch, it could only make a caricature of the melody; in a lower register it does not have enough expressive quality to carry the tune. Later in the nineteenth century, solo bass passages or section solos were used for lugubrious or humorous effects.

5. Which brings us to Brahms's choice of the cellos in their lyrical and intense register (Example V–7). The unique cello quality gives the other strings an opportunity to play a soft but exciting accompaniment (*background*) and allows the composer to build up to a higher pitch level in the violin statement. This second statement, though fuller and more heavily scored, sounds much less tense than the original. Certainly Brahms could have stated the theme in the violins as in mm. 12 ff., followed by a cello exposition, but it is the stunning and vibrant effect of the cellos that captures the listener and makes the opening so vital and engaging.

Distribution of Background Material

Before we leave this example, let us look at the distribution of the background material. Many professional orchestrators recommend staying away from the register of the melody line. In some instances, especially when foreground and background are performed by instruments of similar color, this is good advice. But in this case, we must consult our knowledge of register characteristics:

1. The foreground line is in the best register of the instrument to which it was assigned.

2. The background figures are in the palest or most nondescript registers of the instruments to which these were given, including pizzicato in the double basses.

If the violins and violas had been scored an octave higher, they would have attracted too much attention to the background; they would also have anticipated the fact that the violins would repeat the melody at the higher pitch level soon after the cellos' initial statement. In other words, Brahms saves the higher violin color for the more important foreground statement and assigns the soft swirling background to middle-register violins and violas, while the cellos dominate in their best voice.

Another important consideration is the character or the figuration of the accompaniment itself. Notice the radical rhythmic and expressive difference between the foreground and the background elements. The swirling accompaniment is repetitous and simple. It serves to add intensity to the longer notes of the melody, leaving the ♩♪ figure undisturbed. The conductor may then ask for a bit of "soloistic rubato" for the anacrusis in order to create an even freer melodic exposition of the theme. It is also important to notice how the arpeggiation is dovetailed to create extreme smoothness without any pauses in the texture.

One must not fail to mention the role of the flutes and bassoons which clarify and support the arpeggiated harmony, a purpose which will be discussed in the combination chapter of strings and winds. Here it is certainly another stabilizing and enriching element.

This passage embodies many questions the composer must answer before embarking on the orchestral scoring. There is no doubt that Brahms "heard" exactly what he put down and did not have to go through the process of elimination we employed before deciding to assign the melody to the cellos, but this decision was the result of a long and intimate relationship with the orchestra and of having heard, conducted, and yes, rescored many of his earlier works. The idea of choice is most basic not only for the compositional but also for the orchestrational process. The more a composer knows about the tonal, registral, and technical characteristics of the instruments, the more successful and colorful his score.

Other Successful Statements of Foreground Material

Sometimes a forceful unison or octave statement may be used in the antecedent of an idea, followed by a change of texture to emphasize the different emotional quality of the consequent as in the following:

Example V–12. Mozart, *Eine kleine Nachtmusik,* first movement, mm. 56–62

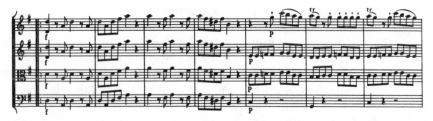

We have already used a term that needs further amplification because it will continually turn up in the discussion of orchestral processes: coupling. This term describes two instruments playing the same passage at parallel intervals, as in the second violin and viola parts, mm. 60–62 of the example above. Even though it represents only a slight change of texture and dynamic, a simple paralleling of the accompaniment in thirds registers a tremendous emotional contrast to the stark octaves in this style.

Mozart was a master at "sleight of hand." In the following short example, a sudden cessation of the Alberti-type accompaniment figure changes the mood of the predictable, settled statement to a light, ethereal texture which highlights the second phrase of the theme.

Example V–13. Mozart, *Eine kleine Nachtmusik,* second movement, mm 1–8

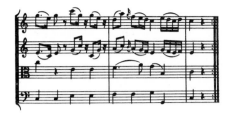

The following examples illustrate again how orchestration serves form and content, and how it can aid in clarifying a work, or even a phrase, by means of texture, accent, or color. This is true not only in the Classical era, but in all creative periods in music.

1. Building an orchestral crescendo by adding octaves to the triple *forte*.

Example V–14. Beethoven, *Leonore Overture No. 3*, mm. 514–31

2. Using string unison staccato to contrast with the piano timbre, as well as the rich harmonies and legato of the solo instrument.

Example V–15. Beethoven, *Piano Concerto No. 4*, second movement, mm. 1–30

3. The simple addition of the cellos and double basses, and a bit of "melodizing" of the harmony in the second violins sets off the first and the second statement of the theme and prepares so well for the tutti version that is to follow. Notice also that the second time the theme is stated it is an octave lower to allow the woodwinds to be heard when they enter, and to make the color more distinct.

Example V–16. Haydn, *Symphony No. 103*, first movement, mm. 40–48

4. Here is a beautiful way to open a slow movement with strings alone. Notice the violins in their rather nondescript register are doubled to give them more body. The cellos and basses are kept rather low and the violas play a contrasting rhythm *divisi* so as to not interfere in the flow of the melody.

Example V–17. Schumann, *Symphony No. 2*, third movement, mm. 1–5

5. Hindemith begins the last movement of the symphony *Mathis der Maler* with a very powerful unison. It builds great tension, and prepares well for the tutti chords to follow.

Example V–18. Hindemith, *Mathis der Maler*, third movement, mm. 1–6

6. One more effective presentation of a theme by strings alone, this one of a lighter character. The first violins present the sprightly tune, and when they reach into their lower register, they are doubled in octaves by the cellos. This addition contributes a feeling of greater resolution to the passage and prepares the listener for the woodwind scale interlude leading to the repetition of the first theme.

Example V–19. Shostakovich, *Symphony No. 6*, third movement, mm. 1–7

CONTRAPUNTAL TEXTURES

Although we have been taught that two melodies superimposed one upon the another result in a contrapuntal texture, there is a grey area of foreground, middleground, and background in orchestral music which presents serious scoring problems. The difficulty is twofold: First, one must sort out the three elements so that they communicate in the exact order of priority in which the listener is to comprehend the material. Secondly, the composer has so many choices of colors that he must limit his options, especially if a passage is to be repeated more than once.

In this example from the second movement of his *Symphony No. 7*, Beethoven has the first violins play the very simple tune, the seconds play the countertheme, and the violas, cellos, and double basses supply the background harmony:

Example V–20. Beethoven, *Symphony No. 7*, second movement, mm. 51–66

A further word about the example above: even though the voices are close together in register and homogeneous, it works successfully for two reasons:

1. Each of the three parts has its own characteristic rhythm and special articulation.

2. The foreground and middleground themes were introduced earlier without the background. As a matter of fact, the first theme was played all by itself at the very beginning of the movement.

These factors add immeasurably to the clarity of this passage and suggest ways of solving the complex foreground–middleground–background problem.

Polyphonic writing for strings has been popular since the early baroque, when the Italian masters, as well as Bach and Handel, firmly established the instrumental style. Since each of the voices of the string choir is technically capable of performing almost equally elaborate gestures, fugal, canonic, and other contrapuntal writing can be most effectively accomplished by the string section. Many times the exposition of a fugue or fugato is assigned to the strings before it is developed, colored, or doubled by other members of the orchestra. This has proven to be a most effective device.

When there are contrapuntal passages to be scored for strings alone, the two major considerations, as always, must be clarity and balance. These can best be achieved by:

1. placing the most important melody in the best possible register of an instrument;

2. thinning the counterpoint to let the main theme break through;

3. separating theme and countertheme registerally (one high, one low; or vice versa);

4. seeing to it that the countertheme is sufficiently different rhythmically from the subject (theme) so they don't interfere with one another when the two are stated together.

Of course, one can always resort to marking different dynamics such as *forte* for the foreground and *piano* for the background material, yet this is not always as effective as the other ways.

Here are some contrapuntal passages from both the string orchestra and the full orchestra literature. Study these passages.

1. Vivaldi, *Concerto Grosso*, Op. 3, No. 11

A typical fugue exposition starting with the basses and cellos, then violas, second violins, and finally the firsts—the traditional sequence of entrances. If Vivaldi had opened with the first violins, he would have been obliged to reverse the order of entrances exactly. If the second violins had begun, there would have been a choice of either first violins, then violas and basses, or violas, first violins, then basses. The first alternative discribed above (2nd Vl., Vla. C + DB) was preferred by the Baroque masters. A similar scheme would be employed if the viola were to begin the fugue. It is important to understand that although the group is homogenous, the subject comes through because of the rhythmic differences between the foreground (subject), the middleground (countersubject), and the background (continuo or harmony). In a fugal exposition the subject heard alone at the beginning carries added weight and makes the listener constantly aware of it. Further, the subject is a strong one with easily recognizable rhythmic figures. In addition, the anacrusis-type opening gives it added carrying power against a rather active counterpoint in the other voices.

Example V–21. Vivaldi, *Concerto Grosso* Op. 3, No. 11, first movement, mm. 35–54

2. Bach, *Brandenburg Concerto No. 3*

In this magnificent excerpt for six violins, three violas, three cellos, and double bass, we find very sophisticated contrapuntal writing which illustrates again how important rhythmic characteristics are in bringing forward the individual voices. During the Baroque era none of the composers extended the instrumental range too far; thus emphasizing individual parts within a basically homogenous ensemble became more of a challenge. Toward the end of the example, Bach brings the work to a rich homophonic climax which provides great contrast and fulfillment to the preceding contrapuntal section.

Example V–22. Bach, *Brandenburg Concerto No. 3*, first movement, mm. 76–92

3. Weber, Overture to *Euryanthe*

Another string fugal exposition, this time from the Romantic era. As in earlier examples, the composer is careful to separate the elements by distinct rhythmic characteristics and, like Bach, he alternates freely between contrapuntal and homophonic passages.

Example V–23. Weber, Overture to *Euryanthe*, mm. 144–59

4. Bartók, *Music for String Instruments, Percussion, and Celesta*

The exposition of this extraordinary Bartók fugue is a bit more complex and controversial than any of the previous examples. The composer sets up a formula of ever-moving eighth notes. Of course, the entrances of the subject are always noticeable, but the counterpoint balances this constant motion, giving the impression of a large arch. The freely imitative as well as canonic imitation between the voices adds to the feeling of heightening tension, which never really settles down until the entrance of the timpani in m. 34. The lack of rhythmic definition in each voice, or, to put it positively, the great similarity in the lines, creates an atmosphere of unruffled contemplation in the midst of tension.

Example V–24. Bartók, *Music for String Instruments, Percussion, and Celesta*, first movement, mm. 1–34

HOMOPHONIC WRITING FOR STRINGS

The distribution of the pitches in a predominantly harmonic or homophonic passage is an important assignment. Spacing, register, and melodic considerations should once again be the major factors in determining exactly who should play which pitches, especially in strings, where the overall color is so homogenous.

Let us first consider the scoring of some isolated chords and then study a masterful passage from the literature.

We have already referred to the importance of the overtone series in the chapter on the individual instruments. In the matter of spacing a chord and the doubling of pitches, we must invoke this musical phenomenon once again. Here is the overtone series on E:

Example V–25

A large tutti string chord could be effectively spaced:

Example V–26

Both chords can be played *piano* or *forte*. The first would be a bit darker than the second because of the lower octave of the basses and the wider spacing at the top, but the difference is not too great. All instruments are given a traditional place in the distribution. Notice that one usually leaves greater space between the lower than between the upper instruments, just as there are greater distances between the more sonorous lower partials than between the upper partials of the overtone series.

Less spread in the chords gives the composer greater choices. Considering some close chords such as these,

this progression may be scored in one of the following ways:

1. Straightforward scoring—violin I, soprano; violin II, alto; viola, tenor; cello, bass; double bass, doubling the cello an octave lower. This would result in a rather nondescript setting if the dynamic were *p* to *mf*, but would prove very bass-heavy if the dynamic were loud, since the violas, cellos, and basses are in a much better register than the violins.

2. Violas *divisi* take the upper two parts while the cellos *divisi* take the lower two. The result of this combination would be a very mellow, darkish sound.

3. Adding the bass an octave lower would greatly darken the line.

4. The first violins on the soprano with the second violins or the violas divided playing the alto and tenor part would give a slightly lighter but still subdued color to the progression.

5. All cellos with the double basses doubling the bass at pitch would, of course, be very intense.

6. The entire progression could be transposed up one octave, then two octaves, and become quite sparkling.

If there were a first-inversion chord in that passage, we would have an additional doubling problem, since we have learned that it is out of style to double the bass (the third) except when it is the first (VI⁶), second (VII⁶), fourth (II⁶), or fifth (III⁶) degree scale step. In the often-used I⁶, IV⁶, and V⁶ chords, special attention should be given to the spacing and doubling, for if there are more than four voices, the third of the chord (bass) would invariably be doubled somewhere to strengthen it. It is advisable to double it near the bottom and leave the "open" sound so characteristic of this inversion intact.

Example V–27

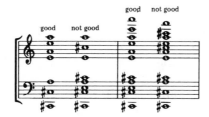

Before we discuss some homophonic passages from the string literature, let us consider the successful scoring of a string melody in an orchestral work.

What can be done to strengthen this melody?

Example V–28

1. It can be played by the first violins without accompaniment.

2. It can be played by the second violins and doubled by the first an octave higher.

3. It can be doubled at the unison by another instrument:
   a. violin I and II   c. violins and cellos
   b. violins and violas   d. violas and cellos

4. It can be played *sul G* on the violin.

5. It can be played as a viola or a cello solo, since both instruments would be more intense in that register than the violins.

6. It could be distributed over four or five octaves and played by all five strings.

7. It could be performed in unison by both violin sections, violas, and cellos.

Now let us examine the beginning of the *Serenade for Strings* by Tchaikovsky to see how he handled some of these problems.

Example V–29. Tchaikovsky, *Serenade for Strings*, first movement, mm. 1–36.

(A) The theme is presented fully and richly harmonized. All double-stops are certainly playable *non divisi*, but usually the second violins, violas, and cellos are divided, while *divisi* would weaken the first violin line. Notice that the melody notes of the first violin are always doubled but not necessarily by the same instrument at all times. In mm. 1 and 2, the second violin (lower notes) doubles, while in the mm. 4 and 5 the viola doubles. The composer emphasizes the harmony rather than the melody in mm. 3 and 6 by the phrasing and the dovetail position of the second violin, whose pitches are reinforced by doublings in violas and cellos. Notice the effective spacing of the very first chord, which is intense but quite bright, and the chords in mm. 7 and 8, which are sonorous, but a bit more mellow. The dovetailing of violas and second violins emphasizes the E, which is much stronger played by the violas than by the second violins and is, after all, the melody note.

In m. 8, a scale in octaves takes us to the second statement of the melody, this time in the bass. Great intensity is lent to this statement by the rather high double basses, and the thin texture which accompanies the tune even when played *ff* cannot interfere with it, for all violins and violas are in a nonbrilliant register. How stunning the big chord in measure fifteen sounds after this pale, subdued harmony. Be sure to notice the distribution of this chord and the ease with which it can be performed; no problem fingerings are encountered for any instrument, and since any double bass chord in the key would have to be played *divisi*, the composer chooses to assign a single well-placed tonic note to the instrument. The low C on the cello is sonorous enough to carry.

From **(C)** to **(D)** Tchaikovsky achieves a diminuendo by his scoring. From mm. 17 to 22 the close voicing, especially in the high cellos, gives a tense account of the theme and the harmony. From m. 18 to **(D)** the sound is mellow, and even though loud and intense, the homogenous sound of all the strings meshes as if it came from one instrument.

From **(D)** to the end is a marked diminuendo, in which a cadential formula is repeated three times. All instruments are in a register where a soft dynamic is easily possible, and the thinning out is emphasized by the drop-out of the bass each time it reaches the tonic note. Notice the articulation change from m. 32 to m. 33. The last time the double basses do not slur but bow the high E. Their dropping out is thus even more pronounced, and the articulation allows the E to sound a little longer, since the chords in the other strings are held.

Another most effective example of strict homophonic string writing is this excerpt from Grieg's *Peer Gynt Suite No. 1.*

Example V–30. Grieg, *Peer Gynt Suite No. 1*, "Aase's Death," mm. 17–24.

Everything is doubled at the octave, as if the piece were played on the organ with an eight-foot stop plus a four-foot stop doubling the original version an octave higher. In order that the listener may clearly hear two phrases in each of the four measures, Grieg doubles the strings differently in the antecedent and the consequent. Notice that in mm. 20 and 23–24, the second violins double the first with an added octave, instead of providing more harmony. In order to study this example more closely, it is advised that one make a simple four-part reduction for piano, and then compare it with the original orchestration. The lush romantic sound for strings is an important color to master.

Analyze the following string works for spacing, articulation, and disposition of foreground, middleground, and background material:

Dvořák, *Serenade*
Mahler, "Adagietto" from *Symphony No. 5*
Bloch, *Concerto Grosso I*
Britten, *Simple Symphony*
Honegger, *Symphony No. 2 for Strings and Trumpet*
Bartók, *Divertimento*
William Schuman, *Symphony for Strings No. 5*

A work such as the *Threnody* by Penderecki should also be studied as a prototype of a mid-twentieth-century string work. Notice that the composer specifies the exact number of instruments needed, for he often divides them so that each plays a separate pitch. Color is the important parameter here, and Penderecki takes full advantage of everything the instruments can do and invents some new tricks. Study these pages very carefully:

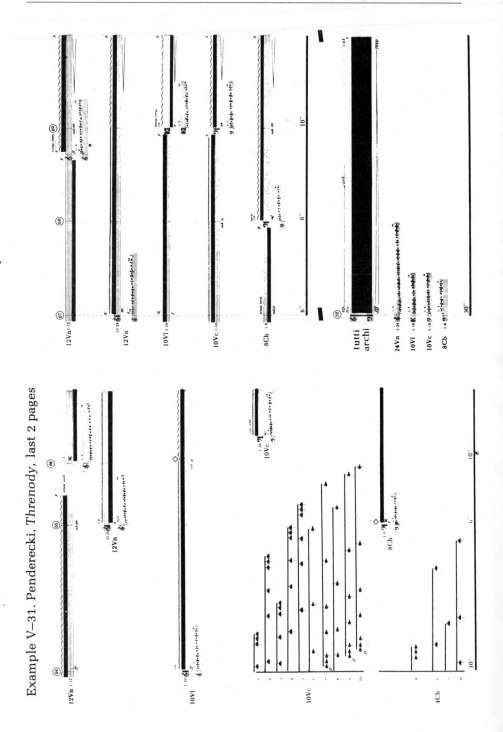

Example V-31. Penderecki, Threnody, last 2 pages

THE STRING CHOIR AS AN ACCOMPANYING GROUP

Because of the homogenous quality of the string choir and its great technical and dynamic resources, it is frequently used to accompany an instrumental or vocal soloist, a chorus, or an instrument or group of instruments in a purely orchestral work. Hundreds of different patterns have been formulated for this purpose, and we shall examine some of the more popular ones. The possibilities are almost limitless, but a quick study of these traditional formulas may give some notion of what can be done.

A. Three excerpts from Mendelssohn's *Elijah*
 1. Simple harmonic on–off beat accompaniment

Example V–32. Mendelssohn, *Elijah*, "It is enough," mm. 1–9

 2. Sustained harmony notes plus "agitated" violin figures

Example V–33. Mendelssohn, *Elijah*, "Hear ye, Israel," mm. 1–7

 3. Sustained harmony notes plus arpeggiated violin figures

Example V–34. Mendelssohn, *Elijah*, "He watching over Israel,"
mm. 1–5

B. From Mozart's *Marriage of Figaro*, a magnificent agitated string
counterpoint which highlights the frantic action in the opera at that
moment:

Example V–35. Mozart, *Le Nozze di Figaro*, Act II, No. 14, mm. 1–13

C. Two excerpts from Bizet's *Carmen*:

1. In the famous *Habanera*, the cellos provide the "ethnic" or
characteristic rhythm of the dance, while the rest of the strings
support the singer both melodically and harmonically playing
pizzicato. Notice that the singer can execute her part without
orchestral interference.

Example V–36. Bizet, *Carmen*, Act I, "L'amour est un oiseau rebelle," mm. 1–8

2. In the prelude to the opera, Bizet uses a cliché device to invest the theme with a suitably ominous quality: the cellos (doubled by trumpet, clarinet, and bassoon) render the tune with the upper strings tremolo providing the accompaniment.

Example V–37. Bizet, Prelude to *Carmen*, mm. 121–31

D. In order to produce a somber background, the lower strings only may be used to accompany the melody. Two famous examples of this practice are the first movement of the Brahms *Requiem* and Stravinsky's *Symphony of Psalms*. Another is the beautiful opening of the Fauré *Requiem*, which provides a dark-hued harmonic background for the *Requiem* text.

Example V–38. Fauré, *Requiem*, Introit and Kyrie, mm. 18–25

TRANSCRIBING FROM PIANO TO STRINGS

One is often called upon to transcribe a piano accompaniment for strings. There is a variety of ways to accomplish this task, but the most important consideration must be the realization of the composer's intent without distortion. Of course, piano figuration is not always simple to transcribe, but one must take great care to uphold the spirit of the accompaniment even though the figuration is somewhat adopted for the strings. Dovetailing becomes very important to recreate the smoothness that a single player can achieve on a single instrument. Naturally, one must not dovetail parts if an accent is required. Further, the sustaining pedal must be taken into consideration.

Let us see, first, how the effect of the sustaining pedal may be simulated:

Example V–39a. Piano Version

b. Three String Versions

Now let us take a few accompaniments and find solutions for them. Before we do, however, it is important to point out that there are many simple piano accompaniments, such as afterbeats, sustained harmonies, even certain figurations, which can simply be copied out into string parts. These we do not have to address here.

Example V–40a. Schubert, *Rückblick*, mm. 1–2: Piano Version

b. Two String Versions

Example V–41a. Brahms, *An ein Veilchen*, mm. 1–3: Piano Version (a good example for dovetailing)

b. String Version

Example V–42a. Brahms, *O liebliche Wangen*, mm. 1–3: Piano Version

b. String Version

Repeated chords in the strings have the same effect as the piano version, but are more idiomatic, especially at this fast tempo.

Example V–43a. Saint-Saëns, *L'Attente*, mm. 1–3: Piano Version

b. String Version

Similar to the previous Brahms excerpt, this accompaniment lends itself much better to repeated notes in the string version.

In this discussion of the string choir, as well as in the ensuing chapters dealing with combinations of strings, winds, then strings, winds, brass, and percussion, culminating in the full orchestra, the taste of the composer is of course the final arbiter. However, proven principles of success may help in the selection process, not only in the choice of instruments and their distribution, but also in regard to the surrounding texture. One may profit greatly by either heeding the old tried and true ways, or, armed with the knowledge of what one is rejecting, by searching for new solutions. The overriding consideration must be the realization that orchestration must serve the structure of a work. It must clarify the form and support the tonal flow by its unique contribution, the element of color.

The Woodwind Choir
(Reed Aerophones)

Whereas the string choir of the orchestra was a most homogenous group of instruments, we shall now turn to the woodwinds, the most heterogenous choir in the modern symphony orchestra.

The woodwind choir is made up of a group of instruments with the greatest variety of timbres and the most distinctive individualized tone of all the choirs of the modern symphony orchestra. Even the word "woodwinds" is simply a term of convenience rather than an accurate description of this family. While all of the major instruments in the group, except for the saxophones, were, at one time, actually made of wood, this is no longer the case. Flutes are now made of all kinds of metals, even gold, silver, and platinum; and the cheaper clarinets are made of plastic. The saxophones, being a relatively recent invention, have always been made of brass, but shall be classified under the term "woodwinds" since they are related to the group in so many ways. It is interesting to note, however, that a classic text like the Cycil Forsyth's *Orchestration* includes the saxophones in the brass instrument chapter.

Before going any further into the details of construction and categorization of these instruments, it would be wise to look very briefly at the principles on which they function.

Without too much acoustical knowledge, one can state that a body of air will vibrate when set in motion, because it possesses elasticity and inertia. The vibrating string communicates only a very small amount of sound. In order to project greater volume, that sound must be amplified by passing through a soundbox. Pipes do not require this kind of an arrangement because the vibrating air column within a conical, or a cylindrical, tube communicates the sound at a desired amplitude directly through an opening in the tube. It is, therefore, imperative for the timbre, amplitude, range, register strength, agility, articulation possibilities, and even versatility, that one know the mode of producing sound for each of the woodwinds and through what kind of tube the air column passes once it is set in motion.

The tube has to have holes, or openings, cut according to exact theoretical requirements, in order to produce all the semitones between the fundamental tone and the first partial. Until the mechanical key system invented by Theobald Boehm (1794–1881) supplanted an earlier primitive mechanism, which compensated for the inadequacy of the hand to cover the holes since they were so far apart, no real advance in the perfection of woodwind instruments was possible. The Boehm system made it relatively simple to produce all the notes on the instruments by interlocking keys which are readily worked by the fingers. This mechanical system has been continually perfected until there are hardly any skips, trills, or tremolos which cannot be performed on any woodwind instrument today.

Keeping this in mind, it is possible to classify the woodwind choir in at least five ways:

1. by families
2. by the kind of reed used
3. by the shape of the pipe
4. by the interval they "overblow"
5. by whether they transpose or not

1. Classification by Families
   a. The Flute Family*: Piccolo, Flute, Alto Flute, Bass Flute
   b. The Oboe Family: Oboe, English Horn, Oboe d'Amore, Heckelphone, Bassoon, Contrabassoon
   c. The Clarinet Family: D, Eb, Bb, and A Clarinets, Alto Clarinet, Bass Clarinets, Bassett Horn
   d. The Saxophone Family: Soprano, Alto, Tenor, Baritone, and Bass Saxophones

---

*The Recorder Consort (called the Flageolet Family)—sopranino, soprano, alto, tenor, bass—is not used in the modern symphony orchestra.

2. Classification by Reeds

In any discussion of reeds or nonreeds, of prime importance is the word *embouchure*. It refers to the method of blowing into the instrument to set the air column in motion directly (flutes) or by the reed mechanism or mouthpiece (all other woodwinds). The pitch variation—in other words, the tuning—is dependent on the embouchure, since intonation is largely controlled by the lips. The pitch can also be slightly modified by manipulating the mouthpiece joint, or, at times, the other joints, thereby changing the length of the instrument. Pulling out the mouthpiece (or *headjoint* on the flute) slightly lengthens the instrument, and therefore lowers the pitch; conversely, pushing it in raises the pitch a bit.

Oboe Reed   Bassoon Reed   Clarinet Mouthpiece and Reed

  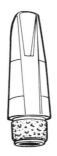 

a. Nonreed woodwinds: all flutes plus recorders
b. Single reeds: all clarinets and saxophones
c. Double reeds: oboe, English horn, bassoon, and contrabassoon

3. Classification by the Shape of the Pipe
 a. Cylindrical tube (essentially, a straight pipe): flutes and clarinets*
  1) Even though the flute is closed at both ends, the embouchure hole is so close to one end that it is called an open cylindrical pipe.
  2) The clarinet is called a closed cylindrical tube because its mouthpiece closes the tube at one end.
 b. Conical tubes (the pipe is larger at one end than at the other): oboes, English horns, bassoons, and saxophones
4. Classification by Overblowing

---

* Acousticians are still quibbling about these facts, for neither the flute nor the clarinet is a pure cylindrical shape. The flute is even being classified as a cylindro-conical pipe, but for our purposes, the simpler version suffices.

Overblowing is the woodwind equivalent of touching a node on a string at the halfway mark, producing the first harmonic. On the wind instrument, this is accomplished by blowing with more force, thereby compelling the vibrating air column to split up fractionally.

  a. All conical pipe instruments and flutes overblow the octave.

  b. All clarinets overblow the twelfth.

 5. Classification by Transposition

  a. Nontransposing woodwinds: flute, oboe, and bassoon

  b. Transposing woodwinds: piccolo, alto flute, bass flute, English horn, D, Eb, Bb, A clarinets, alto clarinet, bass clarinet, contrabass clarinet, all saxophones, contrabassoon

This category may be further broken down as follows:

  1) Those instruments that never change their interval of transposition:

Piccolo sounds an octave higher than written.

Bass flute sounds an octave lower than written.

Contrabassoon sounds an octave lower than written.

English horn in F sounds a fifth lower than written.

Alto flute in G sounds a fourth lower than written.

Alto Clarinet in Eb sounds a major sixth lower than written.

Bass clarinet in Bb sounds a major ninth lower than written (also check footnote on page 144).

Contrabass clarinet in Bb sounds two octaves and a major second lower than written.

Contrabass clarinet in Eb sounds an octave and a major sixth lower than written.

Soprano saxophone in Bb sounds a major second lower than written.

Alto saxophone in Eb sounds a major sixth lower than written.

Tenor saxophone in Bb sounds a major ninth lower than written.

Baritone saxophone in Eb sounds one octave and a major sixth lower than written

Bass saxophone in Bb sounds two octaves and a major second lower than written.

  2) Those instruments that can change their interval of transposition from work to work. (Therefore, the interval of transposition must be clearly marked in the score and in the individual parts.): all regular clarinets (excluding alto, bass, and contrabass, although in some nineteenth-century scores bass clarinets are sometimes in Eb; but in modern orchestral practice this is seldom the case).

THE PRINCIPLE OF TRANSPOSITION

A transposing instrument produces pitches that sound different from what is notated in the score. In other words, it is up to the composer or orchestrator to transpose the part so that the player may simply read it off and finger it naturally on his instrument, but produce the pitches that the music demands.

Example VI–1. Written Part

Example VI–2. Sounding Pitches

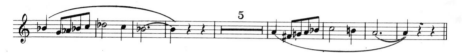

Notice: The composer writes the same notes for both Bb and A clarinet, realizing that the two phrases will sound different, since they are performed on two instruments which transpose at a different interval. Also, the composer has provided a long enough rest for the clarinetist to change his instrument. If he had wanted the clarinetist to play both phrases on the same clarinet, the music would have to read:

Example VI–3. Written Part

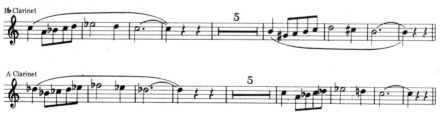

The major reason instruments at different transpositions were used was to avoid too many accidentals before the mechanical systems on these instruments were perfected. Today, switching clarinets, especially within a single work, is practically obsolete. Copland, however, uses the two clarinets alternately in *Appalachian Spring*.

The basic rule for all transposing instruments is that the written C (the fundamental) will sound the pitch by which the particular instrument is designated.

TRANSPOSING WOODWINDS

Written Pitch   Sounding Pitch

B♭ Clarinet, Soprano Sax

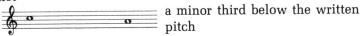 a major second below the written pitch

A Clarinet

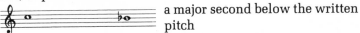 a minor third below the written pitch

E♭ Clarinet

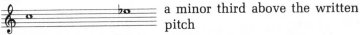 a minor third above the written pitch

D Clarinet

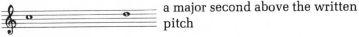 a major second above the written pitch

English Horn (always in F)

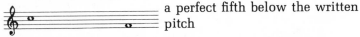 a perfect fifth below the written pitch

Alto Flute (in G)

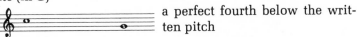 a perfect fourth below the written pitch

Alto Clarinet, Alto Sax

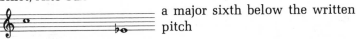 a major sixth below the written pitch

Tenor Sax, Bass Clarinet,* both in B♭

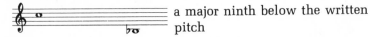 a major ninth below the written pitch

Baritone Sax

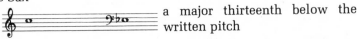 a major thirteenth below the written pitch

* If the bass clarinet is written in the bass clef it sounds only a major second below the notated pitch.

Octave transposing woodwinds: The piccolo sounds an octave higher than written; the contrabassoon sounds an octave lower than written.

In order to *sound* C major, the signature:

for an instrument in B♭ must be D major.
for an instrument in A must be E♭ major.
for an instrument in E♭ must be A major.
for an instrument in D must be B♭ major.
for an instrument in F must be G major.

Flats are cancelled by sharps, and sharps are cancelled by flats.

The decision to use a clarinet in A, B♭, D, or E♭ is usually based on the key of the work. Works in flat keys usually call for B♭ clarinets and E♭ piccolo clarinets, while those in sharp keys are best served by A clarinets and D piccolo clarinets. As has been pointed out above, today when our tonal schemes are no longer rigid or predictable, this consideration is no longer valid, and the composer is free to use either set of instruments. The larger (B♭, E♭) clarinets have a slightly more luscious sound, but the difference is hardly discernible. As a matter of fact, the irrelevance of the key relationship has existed to a greater or lesser degree since the advent of chromaticism in the latter half of the nineteenth century. With English horns, saxophones, alto and bass flutes, and, of course, piccolos and contrabassoons, the transpositions are absolute and unchanging, as we have seen.

As a matter of convenience in memorizing these transpositions, it is helpful to note that all non-octave transposing woodwinds transpose down, with the exceptions of the piccolo clarinets in D and E♭. Another useful hint is that all instruments designated tenor, baritone, or bass automatically add an octave, or two octaves in some cases, to their transposition, if notated in the treble clef.

GENERAL OBSERVATIONS

All of the general statements that follow will be discussed in greater detail in the sections dealing with each of the instruments.

Intensity and volume vary with each instrument according to the range and particular register in which the passage appears. Intonation, dynamics, and in some instances articulation, trills, and versatility are much harder to control in extreme registers than in the middle ranges of all of the instruments. This is more true of the highest than of the lowest extreme pitches. For example, the flute and piccolo are very weak in volume in the first octave of their register, while the oboe and bassoon should not be called upon to perform pianissimo in the lower fifth of their range. On the other hand, it is an outstanding, if often neglected, quality of the clarinet that it possesses a full dynamic range in all its registers from top to bottom.

All wind instruments are relatively free of problems, as long as the composer or orchestrator uses his knowledge of the possibilities and improbabilities* of the technique. Careful consideration should be given to the limitations placed on the player in certain registers of an instrument. In addition, one should not ask nonprofessional players to attempt runs or leaps that are too challenging for them. It is a fact, for instance, that breath control on the oboe is totally different from that on all other woodwinds. The player needs less breath and often has to exhale instead of inhale. Therefore, he is able to play for longer stretches than any other wind player. An analogy might be made to the camel's capacity to store water more efficiently than any other animal, slowly rationing its supply to satisfy its thirst even on long desert trips.

VIBRATO

Just as the string tone is enriched by oscillating a finger on the string to achieve a vibrato, so the wind and, for that matter, the brass instrument's tone is enhanced by its use. Vibrato is produced by engendering a pulsation of the air column more or less rapidly in one of four different ways: 1) by the lips and jaw (normal for clarinet and saxophone, seldom for oboe and bassoon); 2) by the throat muscles (sometimes for flute); 3) by the abdominal muscles (normal for oboe and bassoon); or 4) by a combination of the throat and abdominal muscles (normal for flute). The first way is dangerous, for it may upset the embouchure; therefore, the other methods are usually preferred.

One does not have to specify the use of vibrato in a score, for any good wind player will naturally color a pitch with vibrato to make it rich and round. The width of the vibrato is a matter of style and good taste and can be adjusted by a professional player. However, if a composer wishes to have no vibrato for a certain passage, he must indicate this by marking the score *senza vibrato, nonvibrato,* or as Copland does, "white tone." When the player is to return to a normal way of playing, the indication *con vibrato* or "normal" (*normale*) should appear.

---

*This word is better than "impossibilities," for today, players are able to accomplish feats on these instruments that only yesterday were thought impossible; multiphonics or rotary breathing, for example, if adopted by all players, could change the entire outlook on phrasing.

Here is a famous "white tone" passage from Copland's *Appalachian Spring:*

Example VI–4. Copland, *Appalachian Spring*, mm. 1–4

ARTICULATION, TONGUING, AND PHRASING

Articulation for woodwinds is called *tonguing.* A tone on a woodwind instrument is initiated by the sudden drawing back of the tongue as if one were saying the syllable "tu." There are instances, depending on the instrument and considerations of register and dynamic, in which the syllable "du" is used instead. The tone is stopped, either by the tongue's returning to its original position, hitting the side of the reed, or by cutting off the supply of breath. When there are no slurs marked in the music, the notes are tongued or articulated separately. When slurs are present, the player performs all the pitches under or within the slur, on one breath (like the string player on one bow; however, a wind player is able to play many more notes on one breath than a string player can play on one bow due to the limitations of bow length). This on-one-breath articulation is called legato playing.

Example VI–5. Beethoven, *Symphony No. 8*, first movement, mm. 1–4

The first few measures of Beethoven's *Eighth Symphony* would sound very different in Example VI–5 (b) than (a) because the legato playing called for in (b) gives a much smoother effect than the more spritely, mostly tongued example (a).

There are variations in straight tonguing which can be called forth by correct notation:

1. When a dot is placed over a pitch, the player will articulate a staccato note, and there will be a natural separation between the notes.

Example VI–6. Staccato

Cl. in Bb

2. In some instances, slurs are placed over repeated notes which have dots or dashes over them. This means "soft tonguing." With dots over the notes under the slur, the articulation is slightly "harder" than when dashes separate the notes. The effect is similar to slurred staccato and *louré* on strings which are played on one bow. Here they are performed on one breath.

Example VI–7. Soft-tonguing

3. In very fast passages, the player will use "double-tonguing" and, especially in fast triplet passages, "triple-tonguing." The syllables "spoken" at the time of articulation are then:

Example VI–8. Double-tonguing

Example VI–9. Triple-tonguing in Mendelssohn, *Symphony No. 4*, first movement, mm. 1–6

4. We have already mentioned the technique of tone release on a woodwind instrument, in which the tongue returns to its original position. But there is a special effect which, though not exclusive to the woodwinds, is best for these instruments. It is the *sfp, sf* $>$ *p* $<$ *f;* or vice-versa. These "envelopes" can be executed by a strong attack after which the volume is decreased and may be increased again.

Example VI–10. Beethoven, *Symphony No. 1*, first movement, mm. 1–4

Example VI–11

FLUTTERTONGUE

This is a special effect, not unlike the unmeasured tremolo for strings in notation and purpose. Of course, the sound is different; it is like a whir. It can be produced either by a rapid roll or fluttering of the tongue, or by a prolonged gutteral "r" rolled in the throat. This is relatively easy to execute on all flutes, clarinets, and saxophones, but more difficult on oboes and bassoons, even though it is seen in twentieth-century literature quite often. Fluttertonguing may be required on long notes, or an entire passage (fast or slow) may be played fluttertongue. The parts must be marked like unmeasured tremolo with three slashes through the stems or above whole notes, and the word "fluttertongue"—more commonly the German word *Flatterzunge*—must be written in the score above the passage. The abbreviation *Flt.* is certainly acceptable.

Example VI–12. Stravinsky, *Le sacre du printemps*, "Circles mysterieux des adolescentes," 1 m. before $\boxed{103}$ – 1 m. after

THE WOODWIND SECTION IN A
SYMPHONY ORCHESTRA

The instruments are listed here in the order in which they appear on the score page.

1. Classical orchestra,* up to and including early Beethoven:
   2 Flutes
   2 Oboes
   2 Clarinets (the transposition determined by the key of the work)
   2 Bassoons
2. The orchestra after Beethoven:
   Piccolo
   2 Flutes
   2 Oboes
   English Horn
   2 Clarinets
   Bass Clarinet
   2 Bassoons
   Contrabassoon
3. The large orchestra of the late nineteenth and twentieth century:

*In some early Haydn symphonies the English horn was used, but that was an anomaly; also, piccolo was used in some stage works before Beethoven. However, the norm is the orchestra as seen here.

Piccolo (sometimes 2 Piccolos or one doubling on Alto Flute)
3 Flutes
3 Oboes
English Horn
D or E♭ Clarinet
2 or 3 Clarinets in B♭ or A
Bass Clarinet (some scores ask for 2 Bass Clarinets or Bassett
Horn)
3 Bassoons
Contrabassoon

When saxophones are used, they appear in the following
sequence: soprano, alto, tenor, baritone, bass, and are placed
between the clarinets and the bassoons.

ORGANIZING THE WOODWINDS ON
THE SCORE PAGE

In order to create the most effective and legible score, the following rules should be observed:

1. The first and second parts of identical instruments (2 flutes, 2
oboes, etc.) are usually written on the same staff. The exception to
this rule occurs when the difference in rhythm and general complex-
ity in the two parts would make this practice confusing. In those
cases, a separate staff should be used for the second player. In case
there are three identical instruments, the first and second should be
on one staff, the third on a separate one. If the second and third parts
are rhythmically and melodically more akin to each other than the
first and second, the first should appear alone on one staff, while the
second and third are combined on another.

Example VI–13

2. If both first and second players are to play in unison, the part
must be marked *a2*. In case of three players in unison, it should be
marked *a3*.

Example VI–14. Bartók, *Concerto for Orchestra*, first movement, mm. 230–37

3. If the first or second player is to play alone, one can either supply the appropriate rests in the score, or mark the part 1., 1°, or 2., 2°.

Example VI–15

4. Do not use the terms *divisi* or *solo*. The first is a string term, and not applicable to the winds; the second is a nonsensical designation, for all woodwind players are soloists. In band scores, the word *solo* is used, since there is usually more than one player on each part. Some composers of orchestral music, in order to call the attention of the conductor and the player to a particular passage, have marked it *solo*. This is not necessary.

MUTING

There are no mutes for any of the woodwind instruments, yet composers have asked for muted sounds. Wind players usually accommodate by lightly stuffing a cloth or handkerchief into the opening, or by covering the open end of the bell with their hands. Obviously, this is altogether impossible for the flute.

MULTIPHONICS AND SPECIAL EFFECTS

For the past twenty years, many special techniques have been developed for woodwind instruments. The most far-reaching is the idea of multiphonics, meaning the simultaneous sounding of more than one note. This is still a subject of great controversy because not everyone can perform these, and some of the "double-stops" can be produced only on certain models of instruments. Even though some multiphonics have been called for in newer orchestral and band literature, the greater demand has been in solo and chamber music. Therefore, this technique will be discussed briefly in the sections reserved for the in-depth investigation of each instrument.

Another rather recent innovation is the use of microtones and special shadings of a pitch. This is more common for orchestral winds, but, similar to multiphonics, is a very volatile and risky subject. It is best left for personal consultation with individual players, many of whom have trick fingerings by which they produce the desired microtones or shadings. Some examples of this will appear in the individual instrumental sections.

Glissandi are most successful on the clarinet and on the saxophone, but only in an upward direction. The downward glissando is effective only between neighboring pitches. Flutes, oboes, and bassoons, as well as clarinets, can depress a pitch or raise it slightly by changing their embouchure. This sounds like the slight glissando, but should not be used between pitches greater than a second.

Example VI-16. Gershwin, *Rhapsody in Blue*, opening.

See also Crumb, *Echoes of Time and the River*, second movement, mm. 12–13.

Slap tonguing, a special effect from jazz, is most effective on clarinets and saxophones, but also possible on the flute. It produces a perky, snappy, overarticulated attack.

Example VI–17. Copland, *Music for the Theater*, 5–6

Key clicking has been used quite extensively in the last thirty years or so. It can be employed simply as a percussive, rhythmic effect; or actual pitches can be heard if the keys are slapped down hard without any air being blown through the instrument. In the flute (up close especially), one will be able to hear different pitches, much like those obtained by putting down one's fingers hard on the strings without using the bow. Once again, because of acoustical considerations, one must not expect much of this practice in orchestral music beyond a pure, soft, percussive effect.

The converse technique is also demanded at times. The composer may ask the wind players to blow through the instrument without producing a tone—in other words, simply producing the sound of blowing air through a pipe.

Example VI–18. Claire Polin, *The Death of Procris*, II, mm. 32–36

Whistletones are sometimes required of the flutist and are very effective. Instead of blowing into the mouthpiece, the flutist turns the instrument slightly away from the face and blows across the mouthpiece while fingering the pitches. This can cause a shriek, such as those required by Sydney Hodkinson in *Interplay* and Donald Erb in his *Concerto for Solo Percussionist*.

In all these cases, as with the special string effects, it is better to write out one's intentions in the score and parts, since no universally standardized notation exists as yet.*

---

* For the clearest notation of these effects, check Kurt Stone, *Music Notation in the 20th Century*.

Individual Woodwinds

FLUTE
Flauto (*It.*), Flûte (*Fr.*), Flöte (*Ger.*)

The Flute family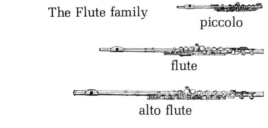
piccolo

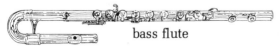
flute

alto flute

bass flute

Bonita Boyd, flute

Example VII–1. Range

The flute is the only nonreed instrument in the woodwind choir, and though all the other instruments have great agility and sensitivity, none can equal the flute in these attributes. Before looking at its range in detail and describing the almost limitless possibilities to which the flute lends itself, a general statement which should be kept in mind throughout the study of this choir of the orchestra is in order.

Each woodwind instrument has a most distinctive sound, which makes it invaluable as a presenter of melodic material. In this role, each one takes on a personality, so that not only the instrument *per se* but every segment of each instrument's range (register) is "typecast" by many composers. A great orchestrator tries to assign a part to each instrument which sounds best on it and which, psychologically as well as musically, could not be performed on any other instrument. As we examine each one of the woodwinds, we must steadfastly keep that goal in mind. Further, it is most important, in this as well as in the subsequent chapter, to concentrate on the role each instrument plays in the context of an orchestra. If a certain register is described as weak, it does not mean that one could not hear it in a solo passage or as part of a woodwind quintet. The designation of a section of its range as weak is a precautionary statement to a composer or orchestrator to be sure not to "cover" the instrument, for it is physically impossible for the player to extract more volume out of his instrument in that register. Similarly, some extreme high registers will be called shrill, and in most cases the performer can only play extremely loud. Too often these registral peculiarities are ignored by inexperienced orchestrators, who blame the players if the results do not coincide with their intentions, though they had been forewarned. In this spirit, then, let us examine the range and registers of the flute, as we shall every one of the woodwind and brass instruments.

Example VII–2. Registers

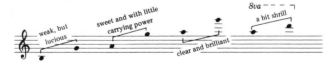

Most American flutes have a B-foot, meaning that they are able to play the low B♮. European flutists are opposed to a B-foot and feel that it takes away some brilliance from the instrument.* On the upper end, the modern flute does go beyond the high C to the C♯ and D, but one must be aware that above the A all pitches are difficult to produce, and extreme caution must be used in approaching them. The best approach is by scale. To point out the limitations, then, one must say that the highest fourth and the lowest fourth with all intervening chromatic pitches are most problematical, especially for the nonprofessional.

Here are two examples of the beautiful lowest part of the register, but notice how the composers are careful to let the flute come through by doing little with the other instruments:

Example VII–3. Dvořák, *New World Symphony,* first movement, mm. 149–56.

Example VII–4. Brahms, *Symphony No. 4,* fourth movement, mm. 97–104.

See also Debussy, *Iberia,* first movement, 4 measures before ⟨33⟩; and second movement, mm. 5–9 after ⟨46⟩.

The Brahms example affords us a wonderful opportunity to observe the profound changes of register in the flute and demonstrates that the performer does not have to struggle to be heard even in his lowest register thanks to the thin-textured accompaniment.

Next are some examples of the most nondescript part of the flute's

* Some flutists argue that a B-foot makes it easier to play the low C and strengthens that rather common note; also, the B-foot gives a slightly greater resonance or depth to the flute.

range—and yet, because of the care the composer has given the accompaniment, there are no problems for the performer, and the melody is perceived with a great deal of delicacy and vibrance.

Example VII–5. Tchaikovsky, *Piano Concerto No. 1*, second movement, mm. 5–12

Example VII–6. Debussy, *Prélude à l'après-midi d'un faune*, mm. 1–4

The upper range of the flute, which possesses such commanding brilliance, can best be illustrated by these two examples, which also show its agility. Remember that all separately notated pitches are tongued, while slurred ones are played *legato* (on one breath).

Example VII–7. Rossini, Overture to *William Tell*, mm. 209–24

Example VII–8. Bizet, *Carmen*, Prelude to Act III, mm. 1–13

See also:

Hindemith, *Symphonic Metamorphoses*, third movement, mm. 31–48

Beethoven, *Leonore Overture No. 3*, mm. 328–52

The flute is also very effective and intense in slower, long-note melodies. It is important to remember that the flute requires a great deal of breath. For best results, therefore, it is important to give the flutist time to rest after especially difficult or sustained passages.

Example VII–9. Brahms, *Symphony No. 1*, fourth movement, mm. 38–46

Example VII–10. Piston, *The Incredible Flutist*, E , mm. 1–18

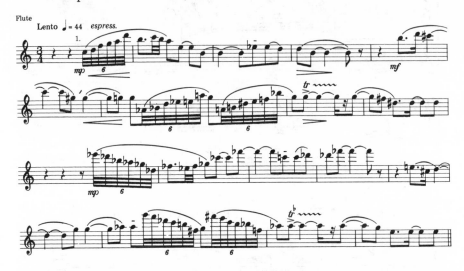

See also Shostakovich, *Symphony No. 5*, first movement, 1 measure after 39 to 41.

Double-tonguing and triple-tonguing have already been discussed in the previous chapter. The following passages may be played using either one of these techniques or simply with single-tonguing.

Example VII–11. Mendelssohn, *Symphony No. 4*, fourth movement, mm. 6–19 (triple-tonguing)

Example VII–12. Rimsky-Korsakov, *Capriccio espagnol*, mm. 6–11 (double-tonguing)

See also:

Mozart, Overture to *Le Nozze di Figaro*, mm. 276–82 (double-tonguing)

Strauss, *Don Juan*, mm. 179–83 (triple-tonguing)

Debussy, *La Mer*, 2 measures before 25 to 25 (triple-tonguing)

Trills and tremolos are also very common and successful on the flute. However, some are difficult, if not altogether impossible, and should be avoided:

Example VII–13

and the tremolo

All tremolos from and to low B♮ are weak and should not be used.

Some flutes have an added C♯ trill key to facilitate the execution of these trills. Further, all trills above high G are difficult, although possible. For the best results, do not write a tremolo which has an interval of more than a perfect fifth in the lowest octave. In the higher registers, a safe limit is a perfect fourth.

Harmonics

All the pitches above the second open C♯ on the flutes are over-blown harmonics. However, in order to get a special pale or white sound, a composer may ask the flutist to play harmonics. The notational sign is the same as for strings; a small circle above the note.

Example VII–14. Ravel, *Daphnis et Chloé*, Nocturne, mm. 5–11

Example VII–15. Ravel, *Daphnis et Chloé*, 49, mm. 1–2.

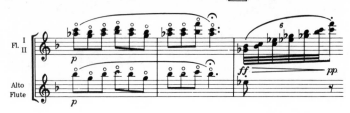

Coloristic Effects

In the previous chapter, fluttertongue, multiphonics, microtones, keyclicks, and other coloristic effects were described. The flute is able to execute all these techniques quite readily.

Example VII–16. Strauss, *Salome*, 41, mm. 1–4

Since these have proliferated in the latter half of the twentieth century, we shall indicate one example of some of the effects here and give a list of some additional places where these may be found in the literature.

Example VII–17. Claire Polin, *The Death of Procris*

See also:

A. Gilbert, *The Incredible Flute Music*
B. Jolas, *Fusain*
Berio, *Sequenza for Flute*

Multiple Flutes

During the Classical period, composers vacillated in the number of flutes they employed in each work. Haydn usually used two, but felt the need for three in his *Creation*. Mozart sometimes used only one, as did Schubert in his *Fifth Symphony*. After Beethoven two flutes in almost every orchestral work was the rule. Sometimes the second flute doubled on piccolo (in Rossini especially); other times two independent flutes plus a piccolo were used. Three flutes became the standard complement of most orchestras in the middle of the nineteenth century, and a fourth and even a fifth member of the flute section playing two piccolos or one piccolo and one alto flute have been used.

These multiple flutes either double at the octave or the unison; are scored in parallel intervals; play antiphonally one with the other; relieve one another in long, fast, or sustained passages; or have completely independent parts. Some examples of multiple flute passages:

Example VII–18. Ravel, *Daphnis et Chloé*, at ⟨165⟩

Example VII–19. Tchaikovsky, *Nutcracker Suite*, "Dance of the Toy Flutes," mm. 1–6

See also:

> Bach, *Cantata No. 106*, Sonatina (2 flutes)
> Stravinsky, *Petrushka*, m. 5 after 62 to 63 (2 flutes)
> Mendelssohn, *A Midsummer Night's Dream*, Scherzo, mm. 1–8 (2 flutes)
> Stravinsky, *Fireworks*, mm. 1–12 (2 flutes, piccolo)
> Chabrier, *España*, mm. 78–82 (2 flutes)
> Debussy, *Nocturnes: Fêtes*, mm. 48–50 (3 flutes)

The flute and its upper and lower auxiliaries are most successful doublers of other instruments, and coupling is most effective. These problems will be discussed in the chapter on woodwind scoring.

PICCOLO
Flauto Piccolo, Ottavino (*It.*), Petite Flûte (*Fr.*), Kleine Flöte (*Ger.*)

Example VII–20. Range

Each of the four fundamental woodwind instruments—flute, oboe, clarinet, and bassoon—has at least one auxiliary instrument which extends its range and, in many cases, provides intensified coloristic effects at both ends of the registeral spectrum. In the modern orchestra, these instruments are no longer considered auxiliary, but are rather full-fledged extensions of the principal woodwinds, used as a matter of course. The instrument that extends the flute range one whole octave upward is the piccolo. Because, in so doing, it extends the range of the entire orchestra, it has become especially popular in twentieth-century scores. It works on the same principle and has the same versatility and agility as the flute.

The piccolo has always been a D instrument, and there are no models that are able to play any pitches below that note. Some military bands still use the outmoded Db piccolo, but it is exceedingly rare.

Example VII–21. Registers

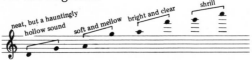

Like the flute, the piccolo can only be used effectively in its first octave if there is not much else going on in the orchestra to drown out its haunting, hollow, but very soft quality.

Above the fourth-line D, the piccolo is very commanding, as can be seen in the following examples:

Example VII–22. Mozart, *Die Zauberflöte*, Act II, "Alles fühlt der Liebe Freuden," mm. 5–9

Example VII–23. Prokofiev, *Lieutenant Kijé*, I, mm. 9–17

Example VII–24. Gluck: *Iphigénie en Tauride*, Act I, scene 3, mm. 1–9

See also:

Kodály, *Háry János Suite*, second movement, mm. 5–15
Debussy, *Iberia*, 33 , mm. 1–6
Shostakovich, *Symphony No. 15*, end of first movement
Shostakovich, *Symphony No. 6*, second movement, 51 to 53
Stravinsky, *Petrushka*, mm. 9–4 before 17
Stravinsky, *Petrushka*, mm. 11–17 after 42 (2 piccolos and 3 flutes)
Smetana, Overture to *The Bartered Bride*, mm. 427–48

The piccolo sounds very piercing in its upper notes. In these contexts that is what is desired; it is supposed to resemble a whistle. Be careful not to overuse the instrument in its extreme upper register, for the sound becomes very tiresome and it is very exhausting for the player.

ALTO FLUTE

Flauto contralto (*It.*), Flûte en sol (*Fr.*), Altflöte (*Ger.*)

Example VII–25. Range

The alto flute is the first extension of the flute family downward, and by now has become an accepted member of the symphony orchestra, although not an overwhelming number of scores ask for it. Its tube is quite a bit thicker and longer than that of the regular flute, and it is a transposing instrument. The mechanism and the fingering are the same as on the C flute, but the alto flute is in G, and therefore sounds a perfect fourth lower than written. In many orchestration texts, as well as some scores, this is called the "bass flute," but that is an erroneous designation, as will be seen in the next portion of this chapter where the real bass flute is briefly discussed.

The alto flute came into prominence in the last decade of the nineteenth century and was made popular by the scores of Stravinsky and Ravel in particular.

Example VII–26. Registers

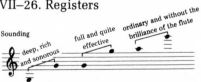

Even though all flute techniques can be realized on the alto instrument, one must remember that because of its larger size and the greater diameter of its tube, it requires more breath than the ordinary flute. Its low notes are much richer and have more carrying power, but the upper register is quite ordinary and without much brilliance. Here is a case of "personality" once again. If one elects to use an alto flute, one should certainly exploit its lower register, for the regular flute and the piccolo are capable of covering the upper part of the register most adequately.

Here are some excellent examples in which the alto flute has been used to its best advantage as a solo instrument as well as in combination with other flutes.

Example VII–27. Holst, *The Planets, Saturn,* mm. 53–66

Example VII–28. Stravinsky, *Le Sacre du printemps,* "Rondes printanieres," mm. 55–62

BASS FLUTE

Flauto basso *(It.),* Flûte bass *(Fr.),* Bassflöte *(Ger.)*

Example VII–29 Range

Ever since the middle of the nineteenth century, flutists and flute builders have acknowledged the need for a bass instrument in the family. Theobald Boehm was the first to try constructing one, but the result was too unwieldy. It was not until 1930 that a completely practical instrument was perfected, by the flute makers Rudall, Carte and Company, based on the Boehm mechanical system. The upper part of the instrument is coiled below the headjoint, and an additional bend positions the main tube across the right side of the player's body. Further, there is an adjustable light metal bracket which allows the player to balance the instrument on his right thigh when sitting down. This makes for a very comfortable playing position.

The bass flute is not any more difficult to play than the alto flute, but because it is relatively new and still very expensive, few orchestras have one and few composers score for it. It can be found, however, in solo and chamber music and in some film and band scores. Its most effective use is in the wonderfully rich low register where its unique warm "hollow" sound is unmatched.

Here is an example of a bass flute passage. It must be remembered that this is a transposing instrument and sounds an octave lower than written.

Example VII–30. Zandonai, *Francesca da Rimini*, mm. 186–90

OBOE
Hautbois (*Fr.*), Oboe or Hoboe (*Ger.*)

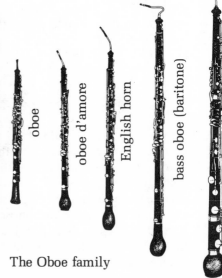

Robert Sprenkle, oboe   The Oboe family

Example VII–31. Range

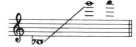

The oboe has possibly the most unique "voice" of all of the wood-winds. It is a double reed instrument and has a gently tapering conical pipe. Many people have described it as the *prima donna* of the woodwind choir. This is not because of its position in the section, but because of the many difficulties encountered in the performance of the instrument. The most volatile part of the oboe is the reed, which is inserted at the top of the pipe. Almost all oboe players make their own reeds, which must be exactly right if the player is to perform successfully. The reed must be thin enough to vibrate freely, but not too thin, or the tone quality will be poor. It must always be moist and is sensitive to all temperature changes as well as atmospheric conditions.

The professional oboist develops an extraordinary ability to hold notes for a long period of time or to play quite lengthy passages on one breath. However, it is imperative to realize that because of the sensitivity of the reed, the instrument is most taxing to play. The breath control required (holding the air in and letting it out very slowly until the next breathing point) makes frequent rest periods mandatory.

Example VII–32. Register Characteristics

Here one can strike a contrast with the flute. While the flute gets more brilliant as it goes up in its register, the oboe loses its pungency as it goes up. Conversely, while we have described the flute as weak in its lowest octave, the oboe becomes thick and tends to "honk" in the very lowest fifth of its range. Regardless of subjective description, one should never require a *pianissimo* dynamic in this register, even from the best players. The most effective range is from the F in the first space to the C above the staff; although for a thin, softly piercing effect, the oboe is sometimes most beautifully scored in the range between high C and the F above it. These notes, however, are quite hard to control, especially for nonprofessionals.

The oboe is basically a lyrical instrument, and here are some examples of the bountiful solo use in the orchestra it has enjoyed ever since the Baroque era:

Example VII–33. Bach, *Brandenburg Concerto No. 2*, second movement, mm. 9–23

Example VII–34. Schumann, *Symphony No. 2*, third movement, mm. 8–19

Example VII–35. Bartók, *Concerto for Orchestra*, fourth movement, mm. 4–12

See also:

Beethoven, *Symphony No. 3*, second movement, mm. 8–12
Beethoven, *Symphony No. 6*, third movement, mm. 91–98
Schubert, *Symphony No. 8* ("Unfinished"), second movement, mm. 207–21
Schubert, *Symphony No. 9*, second movement, mm. 8–24
Rossini, Overture to *La Scala di seta*, mm. 37–53

Bizet, *Symphony in C*, second movement, mm. 8–19
Tchaikovsky, *Symphony No. 4*, second movement, mm. 1–9

Because of the oboe reed, it is possible to single-tongue very quickly in staccato passages, but double- and triple-tonguing are seldom, if ever, used. Extremely fast repeated notes are quite unidiomatic, even though some composers have called for them. Notice that in Example VI–9 Mendelssohn writes the rapid six-eight repeated figure for all the winds except oboes. This does not imply that the oboe is not a most agile instrument. On the contrary, in the hands of the great performers of today, it can be made to play almost any run, especially if the passage is not based on extraordinarily large skips.

Example VII–36. Mozart, *Sinfonia concertante*, third movement, mm. 192–200

Example VII–37

Trills, Tremolos

It would be futile to give a list of trill and tremolo do's and don't's, for these depend very much on the model of the instrument and the proficiency of the player. On newer instruments almost all the trills and tremolos are possible except between the bottom Bb to B♮. Half-step trills from C to C♯ are not advisable. Further, all large-interval tremolos are quite difficult above the staff, and it is unwise to write tremolos of more than a perfect fifth anywhere on the instrument.

Multiple Oboes

The standard complement of oboes in a symphony orchestra is usually two, plus an English horn. Sometimes, this complement is enlarged to three oboes or more, plus an English horn. In the early

Classical orchestra, the two oboes were almost always present and most often had the task of sustaining tonic and dominant pedal notes (frequently in octaves with two French horns), in addition to playing melodic passages. Later on, they were used in many different ways.

Here are some examples in which two or more oboes are used:

Example VII–38. Berlioz, *Symphonie fantastique*, fifth movement, mm. 460–67

Example VII–39. Kodály, *Háry János*, second movement, mm. 47–51

Example VII–40. Bartók, *Concerto for Orchestra*, fifth movement, mm. 249–54

The oboe is a most poignant doubler because of its distinctive nasal quality. It can add great articulation and cutting edge to any instrument with which it is combined. Therefore, great care must be given to have it double a significant line so that an instrument that needs to be featured more prominently is not overshadowed. This problem will be discussed more fully in a later chapter.

Contemporary Extensions of Oboe Technique

In some contemporary scores, the oboe is required to execute key clicks and to blow air through the tube without producing a pitch. There are even instances when a composer asks the performer to remove the reed from the instrument and blow through it. Alternatively, if one simply wants to simulate an airflow without pitch, it is advisable to remove the reed and blow through the pipe.

Example VII–41

Bending the pitch up or down a quarter tone is also a common contemporary technique. This can be accomplished by changing the embouchure or pulling the reed out of the mouth slightly.

Example VII–42

Multiphonics are quite successful on the oboe, but often sound ugly. At this writing, even though quite a few composers have demanded multiphonics, not all oboists are able to produce them. It is strongly suggested, therefore, that a composer consult with a performer as to the best available multiphonic and its fingering before writing it into a score. The fingering should always accompany the multiphonic.

ENGLISH HORN

Corno Inglese *(It.)*, Cor anglais *(Fr.)*, Englisch Horn *(Ger.)*
Oboe da caccia *(Hunting Oboe)*

Example VII–43. Range

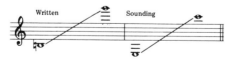

The English horn is a transposing instrument, sounding a perfect fifth lower than written. There are no standard instruments in the oboe family that extend the range upward, but there are at least three that add notes below the oboe range. The English horn, the alto instrument of the family, is the most popular downward extension and works on the same principle as the oboe. It is a conical tube instrument, double reed, with both the tube and the reed slightly longer than those of the oboe. Added to the flared part of the oboe tube is a bulb-shaped bell (d'Amore bell), which gives the English horn a more sonorous, more melancholy sound, rather like a quail.

There is a great deal of conjecture concerning the name English horn. It is neither English nor does it resemble the horns in the brass family. The most plausible—though partial—explanation is that it was called "cor anglé" because of the bent shape of some of the older instruments. The French word *anglé* was then mistranslated as *anglais*, or English. Even though the modern instrument is perfectly straight, the false translation has prevailed, and it is universally known by the name English horn.

The direct antecedent of the English horn was the *oboe da caccia* (hunting oboe), which was widely used through the Baroque period. It too was a transposing instrument, sounding a perfect fifth lower than written. Bach often notated this instrument at pitch in the alto clef, while the more antiquated French notation was in the mezzo-soprano clef. Today, if one wishes to use this practically obsolete instrument (at one's own risk), it should be notated like the English horn. It has the same range and registral characteristics as that instrument. With Medieval and Renaissance bands becoming popular these days, the *oboe da caccia*, as well as the shawm (which came in at least seven sizes in the sixteenth century), may enjoy a renaissance in our own time.

It is strange that although the English horn (or, more exactly, the *oboe da caccia*) was often used in the Baroque era, it was rather neglected from Haydn's time to Wagner's, especially in Germany. There are notable exceptions, of course, in the works of Berlioz and Meyerbeer. However, from the middle of the nineteenth century on, the English horn enjoyed a lofty position in the orchestral repertoire.

Example VII–44. Register Characteristics of the English Horn

The registral properties of the English horn are like its sister instrument, the oboe: it gets thinner as it gets higher. In its upper register, the English horn sounds so much like an oboe that it loses its personality. However, its lowest fifth or sixth is richly beautiful, with tremendous expressive carrying power.

There are countless examples in the orchestral repertoire of English horn solos, both *a cappella* and accompanied. Here are some outstanding ones:

Example VII–45. Berlioz, *Roman Carnival Overture*, mm. 21–36

Example VII–46. Wagner, *Tristan und Isolde*, Act III, scene 1, mm. 5–11

Example VII–47. Sibelius, *The Swan of Tuonela*, mm. 18–32

See also:

Rossini, Overture to *William Tell*, mm. 176–80
Franck, *Symphony in D minor*, second movement, mm. 16–32
Dvořák, *Symphony No. 9* ("From the New World"), second movement, mm. 7–18

Tchaikovsky, Romeo and Juliet, mm. 183–89
Debussy, Nocturnes: Nuages, mm. 5–8
Copland, Quiet City, mm. 22–27
Stravinsky, Le Sacre du printemps, mm. 14–20

Trills and Tremolos

The same trill and tremolo problems that plague the oboe exist for the English horn, and tremolos should be carefully written and confined to small intervals, especially when they occur above the staff.

Other Considerations

The English horn is as agile as the oboe and can easily execute all active figures with the rest of the woodwinds.

As far as contemporary extensions of the technique are concerned, the great virtuoso Heinz Holliger has written and commissioned a great many works which make use of multiphonics and other microtonal sounds. These occur mostly in solo literature thus far, but they can be produced on this instrument as readily as on the oboe.

OBOE D'AMORE
Hautbois d'amour (Fr.)

Example VII–48. Range

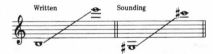

The oboe d'amore is the mezzo-soprano instrument of this family. It is a transposing instrument, which sounds a minor third lower than written. Occasionally, Bach and other Baroque composers notated the actual sounding pitches of the instrument (for instance, in Bach's Christmas Oratorio); it is strongly recommended that this not be done today.

This instrument was very popular in the Baroque period, but as a larger sound was needed for the larger orchestras and halls, it fell out of favor and was supplanted by both the oboe and English horn. Nevertheless, after close to two hundred years' neglect, it is making an appearance once again.

The sound of the oboe d'amore is much gentler than that of the oboe, but since it has a bulblike bell like the English horn, its lower notes are quite full, dark, and beautiful. The upper register is quite thin and almost useless, although Strauss in his *Sinfonia domestica* calls for an F above high C. Gunther Schuller writes consistently above the staff for it, but he doubles it with other instruments in his *Concerto for Orchestra No. 2.*

Here are some examples of the oboe d'amore as a solo instrument, as well as within an orchestral frame:

Example VII–49. Bach, *Christmas Oratorio*, Sinfonia, mm. 9–11

Example VII–50. Strauss, *Sinfonia domestica*

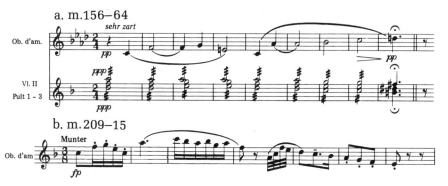

The oboe d'amore may also found in the following works:

Bach, *Cantata No. 37: Gottes Zeit*, "Der Glaube schlafft der Seele Flügel," mm. 1–6
Debussy, *Gigues*, 10 to 11 .
Ravel, *Bolero*, mm. 77–84
Schuller, *Concerto for Orchestra No. 2*, second movement, mm. 76–77

OTHER MEMBERS OF THE OBOE FAMILY

Two other members of the oboe family deserve mention. Although they are not used very frequently, the composer or orchestrator should have some superficial knowledge of their sound and notation.

The *heckelphone* is named after its inventor, Wilhelm Heckel, an instrument maker in Biebrich, Germany, who perfected this pseudo-bass oboe around 1904. It sounds an octave lower than the regular oboe and adds a semitone, the low A.

The *baritone oboe*, sometimes called the *bass oboe*, has the same range and a very similar sound as the heckelphone; the difference is in appearance. The heckelphone was made by a bassoon maker; hence, the instrument resembles a bassoon, while the baritone oboe was manufactured by an oboe maker and looks very much like a big English horn, since it also has a d' amore bell.

Example VII–51. Range

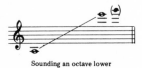

Sounding an octave lower

These provide an excellent bass for the oboe family, but as in the case of the bass flute, there are very few instruments extant, and very few orchestras would be able to supply one if it were called for in a score. Richard Strauss, in his operas *Elektra* and *Salome*, and Frederick Delius are two of the very few composers who have used the heckelphone. All parts may be performed equally well on the bass oboe.

Example VII–52. Strauss, *Salome*, 326 , mm. 1–5

Example VII–53. Delius, *Dance Rhapsody,* mm. 1–10

CLARINET

Clarinetto (*It.*), Clarinette (*Fr.*), Klarinette (*Ger.*)

All clarinets have the same written range.

Example VII–54. Range

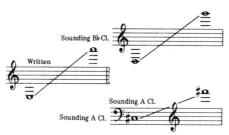

The Clarinet family

Stanley Hasty, clarinet

The lowest written note on all clarinets (with the exception of specially constructed bass clarinets) is this E: The sound produced when that pitch is played depends, of course, on the particular instrument being used.* It is important to introduce a term which is most commonly used to distinguish between the written pitch and the sounding pitch on a transposing instrument. The note one sees on a page is usually referred to as the *written pitch*. The resulting pitch emanating from the instrument is called *concert pitch*. A similar differentiation is made for key signatures: the key in which the entire orchestra is playing is called *concert key*.

Example VII–55. Written Pitch, Concert Pitch

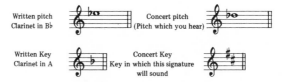

It is important to emphasize that all clarinets have the same fingering system, and all clarinetists are able to play all clarinets in the entire family. The performer will read any part as though it were written for a clarinet in C, and the instrument itself transposes according to its size. The actual clarinet in C is now obsolete; therefore, the notes written for a clarinet can always be expected to be

* It would be wise to review the entire transposition portion of Chapter VI.

different from the concert pitches one will hear. If a part is correctly transposed, therefore, there will be no problems with the written parts of any of the clarinets.

The instrument itself is constructed of a cylindrical tube with an added bell which flares slightly more than that of the oboe. A mouthpiece with a single reed is inserted as the uppermost joint of five sections making up the instrument. The mouthpiece is sometimes referred to as the *beak*.

Before we discuss the quality of the different registers, it is important that one fingering phenomenon on clarinets be mentioned. "The break" on the instrument occurs between B♭ and B♮. This simply means that whereas the note B♭ is played with no keys depressed or holes covered—in other words, with the entire tube open—the B♮ requires the entire tube closed (all holes covered), with the exception of the vent hole, which is opened by the left thumb depressing the register key in back of the instrument. Since this finger transition presents problems to all but the most expert player, it is advisable that the composer or orchestrator be aware of it. The same phenomenon occurs in the other winds, but with less devastating effects, because all the other winds overblow the octave, while the clarinet overblows the twelfth. The problem of coordinating the break completely disappears as the performer becomes more experienced, so that in the end, it presents no difficulties whatsoever.

Example VII–56. Register Characteristics

The clarinet has the most homogeneous range of any of the woodwinds, no matter what part of its register it plays in. Furthermore, a good clarinettist can play the entire dynamic spectrum, from the faintest *pianissimo* to the most forceful *fortissimo*, beginning with the lowest and extending to the highest range of the instrument.

Some of the registers of the clarinet are designated with names which recall the ancestry of the family. The lowest register is called the *chalumeau* register, after the Medieval instrument, a single-reed cylindrical pipe construction antedating the modern clarinet. The third and largest register is called the *clarino* register: The word clarinet is a diminutive form of the old Italian word for trumpet which played the high parts. *Clarinetta* (little trumpet) became the name of our modern instrument because in the eighteenth century, when it first entered the symphony orchestra, the parts assigned to it could be described as "little trumpet" parts. It is strange that the designation stuck, for the instrument began to develop a very different personality in the nineteenth century. In fact, nineteenth-century composers thought of it as the nightingale of the orchestra.

Both B♭ and A clarinets are used in our modern symphony orchestras, and as has been said before, the determination of which one to use most often depends on the key of the work. For predominantly flat keys, one uses the B♭ clarinet, while the A clarinet serves best in mostly sharp keys. Nevertheless, if one were to make a statistical survey of twentieth-century scores, one would find a greater preponderance of B♭ clarinets, regardless of keys, especially since the tonal element has been so obscured in modern times.

As can be seen in the following examples, the clarinet is a most agile and versatile instrument, equally effective in lyrical as well as active running passages in all registers. The staccato, while very dry and sharp, is less pointed than the oboe, but perhaps a bit more articulate than the flute. While single-tonguing is mostly used, some clarinetists are able to perform double- and triple-tonguing.

One effect that can be accomplished on the clarinet better than on any other woodwind instrument is the *niente* attack, in which the tone starts from almost complete silence without articulation.

Example VII–57. *Niente* Attack

In contemporary scores, this extreme dynamic is called for in passages to be played in subtones.

Example VII–58. Subtones

Here are some representative solo clarinet passages from the orchestral literature:

Example VII–59. Tchaikovsky, *Symphony No. 5*, first movement, mm. 1–10

Example VII–60. Wagner, Overture to *Tannhäuser*, mm. 295–98

Example VII–61. Rimsky-Korsakov, *Le Coq d'or*, 4, mm. 33–36

Example VII–62. Stravinsky, *L'Histoire du soldat*, "The Soldier's March," mm. 47–52

See also:

Thomas, Overture to *Mignon*, mm. 1–11
Tchaikovsky, *Symphony No. 6*, first movement, mm. 325–35
Beethoven, *Symphony No. 6*, second movement, mm. 72–77
Mendelssohn, *Symphony No. 3*, second movement, mm. 8–16
Mussorgsky, *Night on Bare Mountain*, mm. 432–40
Copland, *El Salon México*, mm. 294–308
Kodály, *Dances of Galanta*, mm. 43–57
Weber, Overture to *Oberon*, mm. 64–72
Prokofiev, *Symphony No. 5*, second movement, mm. 82–88

As in the case of the other three fundamental woodwinds, the clarinets come in pairs. Again, one has to mention that in the enlarged orchestra since Wagner, there can be as many as three or more, in addition to the "piccolo" clarinets and downward extension instruments, such as bass clarinets, alto clarinets, basset horns, and even contrabass clarinets.

The clarinets in multiples may play in unison, alternate parts, or, in many cases, two or more completely independent parts.

Example VII–63. Mozart, *Symphony No. 39*, third movement, Trio, mm. 1–8

Example VII–64. Mendelssohn, *Hebrides Overture*, mm. 202–14

Example VII–65. Mahler, *Symphony No. 7*, fifth movement, ☐252☐, mm. 6–9

See also:

Stravinsky, *Petrushka*, second tableau, ☐49☐, mm. 1–4
Mozart, *Cosí fan tutte*, Act I, No. 14, mm. 15–19; and Act II, scene 3, mm. 1–12
Wagner, *Siegfried*, Act III, scene 3, mm. 93–100

Trills and Tremolos

There are no trills or tremolos that cannot be negotiated on the clarinet. The larger-interval tremolos are more difficult above the staff, but are certainly possible.

Example VII–66. Kodály, *Psalmus hungaricus*, [20], mm. 2–7

N.B. Double-tonguing is almost never used by clarinetists.

Contemporary Extensions of Clarinet Technique

As has already been demonstrated, the clarinet can execute glissandi between notes. Here the "break" becomes important, for it is easier to perform glissandi above the break than below, and they can only be done upward. "Bending" the tone downward is certainly possible, but that is accomplished by the embouchure alone and should only be used if microtones are desired.

Example VII–67. Bending the Tone

The subtones, which are phenomenally quiet and ethereal, are favorites of many contemporary composers.

Example VII–68. Subtones

Keyclicks, blowing air through the tube, and playing pitches through the mouthpiece separated from the rest of the instrument are common contemporary devices, as are multiphonics for the clarinet. It is hoped that eventually most performers will be able to execute all of these techniques and that some standard notation will evolve. Until then, especially in orchestral scores, the composer must not expect every clarinetist to play all these new techniques successfully, and he should describe in words, besides symbols, exactly what his intentions are in a nonstandard passage.

"PICCOLO" CLARINET, CLARINET IN D OR E♭

Example VII–69. Range

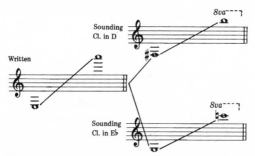

The two small clarinets that extend the range upward stand in the same pitch relationship as the B♭ and A instruments and were created for similar key considerations. They both have the same mechanical and fingering systems; however, the clarinet in D is very seldom, if ever, used today. All parts for the clarinet in D are performed on the E♭ clarinet with the player transposing the part by reading all the pitches a half step lower than written. All piccolo clarinet parts should be written for E♭ clarinet from now on.

A few special considerations must be given to these instruments, for one must keep in mind that they are smaller than the fundamental clarinets:

1. When a B♭ or A player has to switch to E♭, be sure he has enough time to change instruments, and allow for a moment of adjustment.

2. Even though the piccolo clarinet is constructed to emphasize its upper register, it is more difficult to play than its "sister" clarinets. Since it requires greater effort, frequent rest periods are recommended.

3. Its lower range is quite thin but certainly useful, and its upper register is quite shrill. The safest upper note is written G, although A above that is certainly possible.

4. The E♭ clarinet is used a great deal as a high solo instrument,

but its personality and agility mix well with the other clarinets as a contrapuntal or harmonic partner. Further, as will be explained later, it is an excellent doubler to reinforce the flute, the violin, and even a high trumpet.

5. It has a most penetrating tone at the upper end of its register, an incisive staccato, an effective legato, and is able to perform any trills, tremolos, and contemporary devices desired of the other clarinets. The E♭ clarinet also is capable of a full range of dynamics anywhere in its range, except possibly in the last major third of its extreme high register.

Examples from the literature include:

Example VII–70. Berlioz, *Symphonie fantastique,* fifth movement, mm. 40–45

Example VII–71. Strauss, *Till Eulenspiegel,* mm. 43–35 before the end

Example VII–72. Mahler, *Symphony No. 3,* first movement, 12, mm. 1–3

See also:

Strauss, *Ein Heldenleben,* mm. 124–29
Ravel, *Daphnis et Chloé,* 5 measures before 202 to 202

BASS CLARINET

Clarinetto basso (*It.*); Clarinette basse (*Fr.*); Bassklarinette (*Ger.*)

Example VII–73. Range

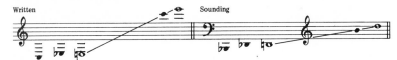

The bass clarinet is most commonly in B♭. Although composers in the past have asked for a bass clarinet in A, this is no longer in use. In their desire to add depth and a lower range to this instrument rather than resorting to the more cumbersome contrabass clarinet, some composers have simply demanded an extension of the lower range of the orchestral bass clarinet. The low E was the accepted low note for all bass clarinets for a long time, and then an E♭ was added. In the 1930s and 1940s, Russian composers in particular called for an instrument which had a range to low C, meaning B♭ concert pitch. Nowadays, one can reasonably expect every bass clarinet to have a low E♭, but writing all the way to C is still risky, for not all symphony orchestras have instruments with such extensions.

There is a further complication in the method of notating a bass clarinet part. The problem was alluded to in the footnote on page 144. In German scores, the instrument is usually notated in the bass clef, in which case one transposes each pitch one whole step down from where it is written. The French notate the B♭ bass clarinet part in the treble clef, to be transposed down a major ninth from where it is written. The French way is most commonly used in all scores today, and it is recommended that composers and orchestrators use it rather than the German method.

Register

The bass clarinet has the same register designations as the fundamental B♭ clarinet. Here are some special considerations one should remember when writing for the bass clarinet:

1. It is a bass instrument and the bass member of the clarinet family. Therefore, the *chalumeau* register, which in this case is the first octave and a third, has the most distinctive, the warmest, and the most effective sound, followed by the *clarino* register, which would

go to the G above the staff in the treble clef. The *chalumeau* register is mysterious and shadowy and can be quite sinister, but as it goes up, it loses some of this quality.

2. The upper notes from the G above the staff to the C or even E are thin and very difficult to produce. It is true that they are often demanded, but that does not really make them any more accessible.

3. The bass clarinet can play lyrical legato as well as all kinds of staccato passages, but it speaks a bit less incisively than its smaller relatives because of its size.

Here are some examples from the literature which will demonstrate the different registers, as well as the bass clarinet in combination with other clarinets:

Example VII–74. Wagner, *Die Götterdämmerung*, Act I, scene 3, mm. 1–13

Example VII–75. Wagner, *Tristan und Isolde*, Prelude to Act II, mm. 13–20

Example VII–76. Stravinsky, *Le Sacre du printemps*, mm. 28–31

Example VII–77. Strauss, *Salome*, 320 , mm. 1–8

See also:

Tchaikovsky, *The Nutcracker*, "Dance of the Sugar-Plum Fairy," mm. 5–14

Strauss, *Don Quixote*, Variation I, mm. 2–4

ALTO CLARINET IN E♭

Clarinetto alto *(It.)*; Clarinette alto *(Fr.)*, Altklarinette *(Ger.)*

Example VII–78. Range

The alto clarinet in E♭ is seldom, if ever, used in the orchestra, but it has become a more or less regular member of the standard band and wind ensemble literature of this century. Though it has the same fingering and mechanical system as the fundamental B♭ or A clarinets, it does not have their assertive powers and is most effective in the first two octaves of its range. It is most useful for filling in the harmony and for rather soft solo passages. Good performers on the instrument can play *legato* as well as staccato passages, and long, lyrical melodies are as easy for them as fast, agile runs. Since so few orchestral scores have made use of this instrument, here is a passage from the band and wind ensemble literature:

Example VII–79. Ingolf Dahl, *Sinfonietta*, second movement, mm. 1–5

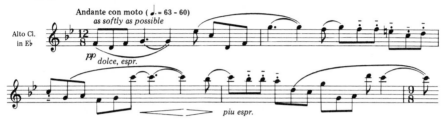

BASSET HORN

Corno de bassetto (*It.*); Cor de basset (*Fr.*); Bassethorn (*Ger.*

Example VII–80. Range

The basset horn is sometimes described as the real orchestral tenor clarinet. Curiously enough, like the English horn, it always transposes a perfect fifth down. Like that double-reed instrument, it is certainly not a horn but is so called probably for its sickle-shaped appearance. The confusing term *basset* may be interpretted as a diminutive form of *bass*. Invented c. 1770 by the Mayrhofers, this instrument has gone out of style in the twentieth century.

The bore of the basset horn is somewhat narrower than that of either the alto or bass clarinet, and it has quite a distinctive timbre described once as "unctuous seriousness." Here are some examples of the use of the basset horn in the orchestral literature:

Example VII–81. Strauss, *Capriccio*, 208 , mm. 1–4

Example VII–82. Strauss, *Capriccio*, scene 2, mm. 22–26

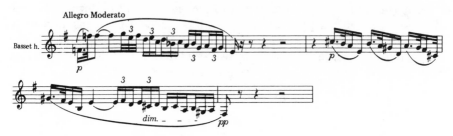

See also:

> Mozart, *Die Zauberflöte*, Act II, "O Isis und Osiris"
> Mozart, *Requiem*, "Dona eis requiem" (Agnus Dei), mm. 14–17
> Strauss, *Der Rosenkavalier*, mm. 18–22

CONTRABASS CLARINET

This is a clarinet in Bb (or Eb) which has a range an octave lower than the bass clarinet. It is made of metal, while most clarinets are made of wood (except for the bass clarinet or alto clarinet bells), and looks like a diminutive contrabassoon, for it is folded in upon itself.

Example VII–83. Range

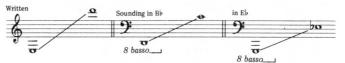

The instrument has a very rich sound, especially in its lowest register, but does not have the agility of the bass clarinet. As yet, the contrabass clarinet, which, of course, is of rather recent vintage, does not appear in many orchestral scores, but is used frequently in works for band and wind ensemble. Here is a passage using the Bb contrabass clarinet:

Example VII–84. Schuller, *Concerto for Orchestra No. 2*, second movement, mm. 113–20

SAXOPHONE
Saxophono *(It.),* Saxophon *(Ger.)*

Raymon Ricker, saxophone

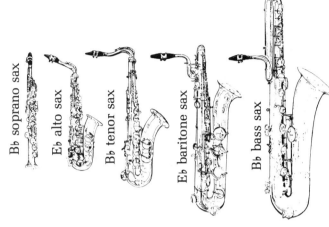

The Saxophone family

Though made of brass and having a conical pipe, the saxophones need to be discussed in proximity to the clarinets for several important reasons: First and foremost, their tone is closer to the clarinet family than to any other. Secondly, they are played with a mouthpiece and a single reed very much like that of the clarinet. Thirdly, most clarinetists "double" on saxophones because they can master the fingering (which is very similar to that on the clarinet) and all other saxophone techniques without much retraining. The instrument is used primarily as a member of the woodwind rather than the brass choir.

The saxophone was invented by Adolphe Sax in Paris around 1840. There are a great variety of saxophones in use today, and we shall discuss them as a family of instruments, since their use is somewhat limited in the standard orchestral repertoire, but very extensive and in multiple numbers in the band and jazz band literature. The entire saxophone family is most homogeneous, but for one reason or another, they have never been fully accepted into the symphony orchestra, though a great many composers of the nineteenth and twentieth centuries have used them to great advantage, especially in solo passages. The sound of all "saxes" is quite distinctive, and one may speculate that the major reason for their rejection from the symphony orchestra may be the fact that they do not blend well with the other instruments but tend to dominate whenever used. A second reason may be that the manner of playing the instrument and the sound it produced in its early days was too primitive to be acceptable. This situation has changed drastically since the 1920s, and the great virtuosos of today, with their fantastic control of every register in each instrument of the family, continue to convince composers, as we shall see in the works we examine.

Example VII–85. Range and Transpositions of All Saxophones

As far as the range properties are concerned, it is important to say that most players have great difficulty playing very softly at both extremes of the registral spectrum, but most especially at the very bottom of it. The register after the first perfect fifth of each instrument for almost two octaves up can be controlled beautifully. There is a difference between the jazz sound of the instrument and what is called the classical sound. The jazz sound is either quite sweet, sentimental, and full of vibrato, or very raucous, while the symphonic or classical sound tends to contain less vibrato and to be more dynamically controlled. Many of the composers of this century have used the saxophone to suggest jazz or popular music, but as great saxophone players develop their techniques, this is becoming less and less the case.

Symphonic composers have made most use of the alto saxophone (in Eb), but soprano, tenor, and baritone are also in evidence. In the symphonic band, the saxophone family is usually represented in one of the following complements:

1. two altos	2. one soprano
one tenor	one or two altos
one baritone	one tenor
(one bass)	one baritone
	one bass

The sopranino saxophone in F is very seldom used, but should be mentioned especially because Ravel gave it prominence in his *Bolero;* there is also chamber music in which this instrument appears.

Here are some examples from orchestral music since 1840. We shall encounter others in the chapter on band and wind ensembles later in this book:

Example VII–86. Ravel, *Bolero,* mm. 2–18 after 7 (Sopranino in F [usually played on the soprano] and Soprano in Bb)

Example VII–87. Bizet, L'Arlésienne Suite No. 2, second movement, mm. 17–20 (alto)

Example VII–88. Strauss, Sinfonia domestica, mm. 950–51; mm. 964–84

See also:

> Copland, Piano Concerto, mm. 254–56 (soprano)
> Gershwin, An American in Paris, 63 , mm. 1–9 with upbeat
> Vaughan Williams, Symphony No. 6, first movement, mm. 5–10
> Mussorgsky-Ravel, Pictures at an Exhibition, "The Old Castle," mm. 7–14
> Prokofiev, Lieutenant Kijé, second movement, 18 , mm. 1–4 (tenor)
> Rachmaninoff, Symphonic Dances, first movement, mm. 105–20 (alto)

BASSOON

Fagotto (It.); Basson (Fr.); Fagott (Ger.)

Example VII–89. Range

K. David Van Hoesen, bassoon

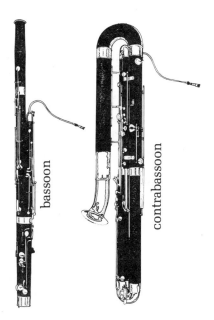

The Bassoon family

The bassoon is notated in the bass clef, but when the ledger lines begin to accumulate, the tenor clef is used (from about the G above middle C upward).

The bassoon, a double-reed instrument with a conical bore, is the bass voice of the wind section. The reed is fitted onto a curved metal mouthpipe called the *crook* or *boçal*. The pitch can be adjusted by pulling this mouthpipe out slightly, thus lengthening it, or pushing it in a bit to shorten it. Although the bassoon, by virtue of its double reed as well as its conical shape, is related to the oboe, its tone is much less nasal. On the other hand, it rivals the oboe in the incisive way it can produce attacks and staccato passages, and like the oboe, the bassoon performs lyric melodies beautifully.

Example VII–90. Register Characteristics

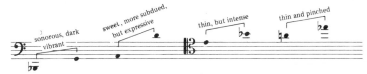

A few warnings on scoring for the bassoon: as a solo instrument, it is superb in all its registers, but when accompanied, it has a tendency to get swallowed up for it blends incredibly well with other instruments, especially in its higher registers. The low register is a very strong and noble bass for the wind choir, but at the same time, it has been a favorite register in which to double with cellos and basses. In this combination, the cello tone predominates, but the doubling bassoon or bassoons give added body to the sound even as they are absorbed in the whole.

The bassoon is as versatile and agile as any woodwind instrument today, and it has been a favorite solo instrument for composers in orchestral compositions since the early Baroque period. Composers have exploited its dark, foreboding lower range as well as its pinched extreme high notes. The latter, of course, recalls the famous beginning solo in *Le Sacre du printemps* by Stravinsky, which people at the first performance mistook for a saxophone. Other composers in the past one hundred years have treated the bassoon as the "clown of the orchestra" and have assigned certain staccato passages to it that truly sound humorous.

Single-tonguing is the norm for the bassoon, and this can be executed with remarkable speed. There are performers who are able to perform double- and triple-tonguing, although this is seldom called for. Slurs upward can be played with great rapidity, and large skips are quite easy to perform even between the extreme registers. However, some downward skips, because of the acoustics of the instrument, are very difficult.

Caution must be exercised in the use of dynamics for the bassoon. It is extremely difficult to play the notes of the lowest perfect fifth *pianissimo*. On these notes, one must expect a firmer attack, for it takes that to make them secure. Conversely, the extreme upper perfect fifth does not project as well as most of the lower register. If a bassoon solo is accompanied in that register, care must be taken to mark the dynamics of the accompanying instruments so that they do not overshadow the soloist.

Trills are most effective on the bassoon, but there are some to be avoided:

Example VII–91.

Tremolos are not very idiomatic; if needed, they should never exceed a compass of a perfect fourth. Avoid all trills from 𝄢 up, except 𝄢 and 𝄢 . Here are some examples of significant bassoon passages from the orchestral literature:

* Some instruments have a special trill key for this trill.

Example VII–92. Mozart, Overture to *Le Nozze di Figaro*, mm. 1–7

Example VII–93. Bizet, *Carmen*, Entr'acte before Act II, mm. 1–20

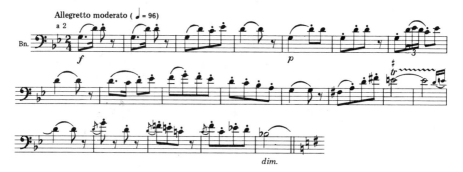

Example VII–94. Tchaikovsky, *Symphony No. 6*, first movement, mm. 1–12

Example VII–95. Stravinsky, *Le Sacre du printemps*, mm. 1–15

See also:

Tchaikovsky, *Symphony No. 5*, third movement, mm. 197–205
Beethoven, *Symphony No. 4*, fourth movement, mm. 184–87.
Rimsky-Korsakov, *Scheherazade*, second movement, $\boxed{I}$, mm. 2–7
Mozart, *Symphony No. 38*, first movement, mm. 111–115
Haydn, *Symphony No. 104* ("London"), second movement, mm. 17–25
Haydn, *Symphony No. 103* ("Drumroll"), second movement, mm. 74–84
Mahler, *Symphony No. 9*, second movement, mm. 8–15
Prokofiev, *Peter and the Wolf*, $\boxed{15}$, mm. 1–6
Ravel, *Bolero*, mm. 41–48

As it was with the flutes, oboes, and clarinets, the basic orchestral complement of bassoons is two. As the symphony orchestra expanded, bassoons in threes and even fours, with the last one usually but not necessarily doubling on the contrabassoon, were employed. The bassoons in multiples have been used in many ways, from unisons and parallel interval passages to complex contrapuntal phrases. Here are some passages for two or three bassoons without the contrabassoon:

Example VII–96. Dukas, *The Sorcerer's Apprentice*, mm. 72–99

Example VII–97. Bartók, *Concerto for Orchestra*, second movement, mm. 164–70

See also:

> Strauss, *Don Juan*, mm. 1–3
> Wagner, *Tristan und Isolde*, Act III, "Mild und leise," mm. 9–12
> Tchaikovsky, *Symphony No. 6*, fourth movement, mm. 21–36
> Bizet, *L'Arlésienne Suite No. 2*, fourth movement, mm. 10–16
> Mozart, *Symphony No. 40*, second movement, mm. 68–71
> Debussy, *Nocturnes: Fêtes*, mm. 33–35
> Berlioz, *Symphonie fantastique*, fifth movement, mm. 255–77

CONTRABASSOON

Contrafagotto (*It.*), Contrebasson (*Fr.*), Kontrafagott (*Ger.*)

Example VII–98. Range

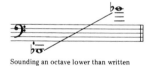

Sounding an octave lower than written

Both fundamental double reed instruments, the oboe and the bassoon, have no auxiliaries which extend their ranges upward, but both have downward extension instruments. The bassoon's downward-extension auxiliary instrument is the contrabassoon, which sounds an octave lower than notated and widens the bassoon's range by an octave.

All that was said about bassoon technique applies also to the contrabassoon, only this larger instrument, especially in its lowest register, is a little bit more stubborn and resistant as far as articulation is concerned. In other words, it is a little less agile and speaks a bit more slowly at the bottom of its range than does the bassoon. This impression of clumsiness in the low register is often exploited as an asset by composers. As a matter of fact, the lowest octave is its most effective range. When sustained tones are held, the contrabassoon acts like a 32-foot organ pipe; even though the tones have a "buzz" because of the slow vibrations, it provides a solid foundation for a chord or passage, especially when it doubles cellos, basses, and bassoons at the octave. A word of caution is in order in regard to the lower range: the amount of breath it takes to produce these notes is considerable. Therefore, it is advisable to provide quite a few periodic rests so that the player can replenish his breath more easily.

Even though many composers have asked for the contrabassoon to play in its higher and even its highest register, this is not advisable, for it takes the instrument out of its most characteristic register, the lowest twelfth, and makes it just another bassoon, a little weaker and paler than its relatives.

Both legato and staccato passages are effective; but the staccato on this lowest of the woodwinds is difficult to produce quickly. Therefore, fast, repeated staccato notes are very treacherous and risky, since the air column is too large and responds too sluggishly, especially at the lower end of the register.

There are not too many contrabassoon solo passages (and even fewer concertos, although Gunther Schuller has recently written one). However, here are a few representative passages from the orchestral literature featuring the contrabassoon:

Example VII–99. Strauss, *Salome*, Act I, scene 3, 151 , mm. 6–27

Example VII–100. Ravel, *Mother Goose Suite*, "Beauty and the Beast," mm. 114–23

Example VII–101. Ravel, *La Valse*, [37]–[38]

Example VII–102. Brahms, *Variations on a Theme by Haydn,* mm. 1–10

See also:

Beethoven, *Symphony No. 9,* fourth movement, Alla marcia, mm. 1–28.

Brahms, *Symphony No. 1,* fourth movement, mm. 47–51

Mahler, *Symphony No. 9,* second movement, mm. 35–28 before the end

Strauss, *Till Eulenspiegel,* mm. 551–58

Strauss, *Elektra,* [186], mm. 1–18

Bloch, *Schelomo,* last five measures

Scoring for Woodwinds and Woodwind-String Combinations

"To orchestrate is to create, and this cannot be taught." This statement by Rimsky-Korsakov would seem to come a bit late in this text. Why here? And why quote such a negative statement in an orchestration book? The answers to these questions will, it is hoped, dispel a great deal of misunderstanding concerning the handling of the woodwind section. It will also shed light on the manipulation of the brasses and percussion as a part of the symphony orchestra, which are dealt with later in the book.

While the string choir is more or less homogenous in sound, and plays more or less continuously throughout most orchestral compositions, the woodwind choir, which is not at all homogenous, is reserved for specific functions. The most common of these have been:

1. a harmonic background to a string foreground;
2. solo passages—either entire melodies, melodic fragments, or smaller melodic gestures;

204

3. as contrasting color repeating or echoing a passage previously played by the strings; or dividing a passage between strings and winds;

4. to double other instruments of the orchestra.

Though a great deal of wind chamber music has been written, there are very few compositions for winds which rival the string orchestra literature of the past 300 years. Exceptions, such as the *Divertimenti* of Mozart, the *Serenades* of Dvořák and R. Strauss, and the *Symphonies* of Gounod and Milhaud, are sometimes programmed as "relief" pieces on symphony programs. It is noteworthy to observe that in most of the aforementioned works two or more horns are included as part of the woodwind section. We shall continue to notice the inclusion of horns as we study the use of winds in the symphony orchestra, because from the Classical orchestra onward, horns were considered part woodwind, part brass, and their function was also divided. Often they are assigned pedal dominant or tonic notes similar to those given to the oboes in the early Classical symphonies. Other times they double the winds to strengthen them. Traditionally, the horn is a member of the woodwind quintet as well as the brass quintet.

WINDS IN THE SYMPHONY ORCHESTRA

As we examine the use of the winds in the symphony orchestra, preference, taste, choice, and even prejudice enter more and more into our considerations. It was certainly simpler to figure out why Brahms used the cello to introduce the slow movement theme in his *Third Symphony* than it is to determine by logical means why a certain woodwind instrument or combination states a given theme, except possibly for reasons of range.

1. Why did Schubert use a combination of unison oboe and clarinet for the first theme in the *Unfinished Symphony*?

2. Why did Debussy have a combination of unison flute and oboe play the long theme in the final movement of *La Mer*?

3. Why did Berlioz choose the English horn to introduce the *idée fixe* in the *Symphonie fantastique*?

4. Why did Stravinsky open *Le Sacre du printemps* with the bassoon?

Since we are dealing with the heterogeneous members of an instrumental choir, questions of taste and color preference become all-important. We have already discussed the sound and registral characteristics of each woodwind instrument; now we must learn how to use them in combination. Experimentation with the next few examples from the great symphonic literature will greatly aid the student orchestrator, who should be thoroughly familiar with the exact sound of the different combinations. We will begin with Schubert's *Symphony No. 8 in B minor* ("Unfinished").

1. The first major theme after the opening is introduced by the first oboe and first clarinet in unison. Both instruments are in a good register, and both can play *pianissimo*. In every orchestration book, the student is told not to use this doubling in a melody for three reasons:

    a. The oboe with its nasal quality will overshadow the clarinet.

    b. The conductor will have to balance the two by having the oboe play softer.

    c. Clarinet and oboe will have great difficulty staying in tune with each other.

Example VIII–1. Schubert, *Symphony No. 8*, first movement, mm. 12–35

How fortunate that Schubert did not read any of these books and took a chance on this passage, which has a mysterious color because of the doubling. Every live performance will be slightly different;

the instruments, the players, and the acoustics of the hall are variables which will influence the results.

2. Let us combine flute and oboe in the same passage. The oboe, being in a more advantageous register, will certainly stand out, but the flute will somewhat neutralize the nasal quality of the oboe and give the passage a rounder, richer sound.

Example VIII–2

3. The combination of flute and clarinet would eliminate the bite of the oboe sound. In this pairing, the clarinet would be the most poignant factor, while the flute would contribute little more than a thickening of the resulting tone.

Example VIII–3

4. The bassoon does not have the range to play this tone in unison with any other wind instrument, but could be coupled at the octave. All of these combinations would be most sonorous. Here is a version for oboe and bassoon in octaves, and another in Mozart's favorite color combination, flute, clarinet, and bassoon in a three-octave spread.

Example VIII–4

Example VIII–5

Examples VIII–4 and 5 are both unacceptable, because they antic- ipate the expansion of the registers to which Schubert is heading (see the "comment interlude" of the bassoons and horns, mm. 20– 21, and the climactic cadence, mm. 28–29). Notice that in the score the flute enters almost undetected in m. 26, doubling the oboe for the crescendo, but is not really heard until it plays the highest notes of the cadential chords in mm. 28–29. All these considerations prob- ably have something to do with Schubert's original choice of the oboe-clarinet combination.

Before leaving this work, it is important to note that the woodwind role in the introduction to the second main theme is reversed: first the clarinets combine with the violas, then with the bassoons to

Example VIII–6. Schubert, *Symphony No. 8*, first movement, mm. 36–79

assume the duties of accompanists. By orchestrating each major thematic element differently, Schubert enhances the clarity of the form and the ease with which each idea is communicated.

We will be looking at other excerpts that illustrate the melodic function of the woodwinds. However, the winds (and horns) served another important purpose, especially in forte tutti passages of the Classical and Romantic repertoire: They were used to strengthen the harmony, providing pedals which gave a strong, continuous, and solid quality to the music. Here is the opening statement of the theme from Mozart's *Symphony No. 29*, K. 201, which is scored for the typical early Classical orchestra:

Example VIII–7. Mozart, *Symphony No. 29*, first movement, mm. 1–5

Now here is the first tutti of the first movement, with the traditional use of the pedal A in both the oboes and horns:

Example VIII–8. Mozart, *Symphony No. 29*, first movement, mm. 13–23

Just for the sake of comparison, let us consider this passage without the tonic pedal. Notice the lack of stability and grandeur without those sustained tones in the first six measures. Notice, too, how much the pedal added to the power of the cadence (especially the skip of an octave by the second horn which so dramatically emphasizes the dissonance.)

Example VIII–9

We encounter a more sophisticated kind of sustained woodwind writing over an active string theme in the overture to Mozart's *Marriage of Figaro*. The flute and oboe play a sustained harmonic background, while the bassoon doubles the cello part. The bassoon doubling is certainly audible even when performed softly, since it is the only nonstring playing the part. It adds a wonderful new color, but in Mozart's time was probably used for more pragmatic reasons. Since the cello and bass sections in the theater orchestras of that day were very small, the bassoons were frequently used to bolster the bass. Today the beautiful coloristic effect remains. Notice the wide distance between the strings and the flute and oboe. This adds great prominence to the sustained counterpoint without detracting from the major thematic idea.

It is very beneficial to study this overture for the different ways in which the sustained pedal or other sustained harmonic gestures are employed. Two more will be pointed out in this discussion, after which the student is urged to analyze the score to find other instances where this device is used, since it is the trademark of much orchestral music of the late eighteenth and early to late nineteenth centuries.

1. Chords built by flutes, oboes, and clarinets sustain and clarify the harmony, aid in the *fp* effect of mm. 35, 37, and 39, and lend weight to the tutti effect of the cadence at m. 45.

Example VIII–10. Mozart, Overture to *Le Nozze di Figaro*, mm. 19– 42

2. Immediately thereafter, the winds, brass, violas, cellos, and double basses play a melodic or thematic fragment, while the violins perform what we may call an agitated pedal or an ornamented pedal on A. This kind of pedal was more popular in strings than in woodwinds, especially during Mozart's time.

Example VIII–11. Mozart, Overture to *Le Nozze di Figaro*, mm. 43– 58

In a subsequent chapter the idea of pedal orchestration will come up again, for the brass section was often called into play also; therefore, one more example here should suffice for the moment. This example from the overture to *Die Fledermaus*, by Johann Strauss, Jr., should illustrate that the pedal harmonic effect does not lessen the light character of this passage, but simply ties it together harmonically, while pointing up the spiccato nature of the tune and accompaniment by contrast. Strauss uses a valuable trick after the first statement of the melody in m. 83. He suspends the pedal for a moment so that the anacrusis to the second statement in the first violins is clearly heard; thus, this repetition is separated from the initial exposition. This device also provides a natural breathing space. Its omission later on contributes to the tension after m. 99.

Example VIII–12. J. Strauss, Overture to *Die Fledermaus*, mm. 76–101 (upbeat to m. 76 omitted)

When called upon to orchestrate or transcribe a work by masters who worked in this style between 1750 and 1880, one should employ this pedal or sustained harmony effect to great advantage whenever possible.

TRANSCRIBING FROM PIANO TO WINDS AND STRINGS

Here are two rather simple and straightforward examples of transcriptions in which the material seems to call for pedal effects. The first is the beginning of the final movement of Mozart's *Piano Sonata* in *A major*. It is marked *alla Turca,* and therefore the use of double-reed instruments suggests itself as a suitable color for the sustained tonic and dominant pitches.

Example VIII–13a. Mozart, *Piano Sonata* K. 331, third movement, mm. 1–8: Piano Version

b. Orchestral Version

The second example is a short piano piece by Robert Schumann (first eight measures). The setting is for winds in pairs, and the harmony, which is only outlined in the piano version, has been slightly enriched and octaves added to give a more orchestral sound. Schumann's own orchestration is usually quite heavy in octave doublings; therefore, these octaves are consistent with his style. The sustained quality of the sostenuto pedal is easily provided first by the clarinet and then the bassoon. Before one sets out to transcribe or orchestrate anything by any master of the past, it is important to study his orchestration technique carefully and learn all about his idiosyncrasies and preferences in order to retain that composer's style. This is especially true on the use of wind instruments. Which were his favorites? And for what kinds of gestures did he use winds? What kinds of doublings are found in his most characteristic orchestral works? The answers to these questions can give great insight into the individual sound of a particular composer.

Example VIII–14a. Schumann, *Melody*, mm. 1–8: Piano Version

b. Orchestral Version

MELODIC TREATMENT

We have already discussed the assignment of a melody to a wood-wind instrument when we introduced each instrument separately in the previous chapter. Let us suppose we have chosen an instrument for a certain passage, and it is perfect in all ways, but we question whether it will be strong enough to carry the tune alone. When do you double an instrument with a like instrument? In other words, do two flutes sound louder than one? Is the sound of two clarinets playing the same gesture more intense than one playing alone?

These are very controversial issues, and experts disagree. The question is best rephrased by asking what is the difference between the sound of one oboe or bassoon on a part, and two oboes or bassoons on a part. The answer may recall the discussion concerning muted strings and brass. The mute may soften the instrument, but it also changes its basic color. This is also true of doubled solo passages by the same two instruments. Since they can never be absolutely in tune with one another, the overtone balance is upset, the sound thickened, and in certain registers, muddied. The essential timbre of the solo instrument is altered. Further, a unison solo of two like winds limits and impedes the expressive quality and prohibits any slight rubato which a single player would add to the interpretation. We are speaking now of ordinary solo passages, not tutti sections where simple volume is required and the characteristic timbre not crucial.

To illustrate the sound difference, let us take the following tune by Rossini from his *Semeramide* overture, consider it on each of the four basic instruments, and then "a 2."

Example VIII–15

Doubling wind passages in octaves has already been established as an accepted norm, and a student may want to turn to pipe organ registration for hints of fine orchestration in this regard. When an organist wishes to add color and volume to a tone, he usually couples the fundamental (eight-foot stop) with an octave (four-foot) and a double octave (two-foot). This gives a transparent but forceful sound, while simply adding more fundamentals (eight-foot stops) would take away a great deal of the clarity. Octave doubling is a good idea for winds a 2.

Example VIII–16

Since we have just abused Rossini for our didactic purposes, let us give him his due and show how he actually handled the passage using the eight-foot–four-foot principle beautifully.

Example VIII–17. Rossini, Overture to *Semiramide*, mm. 177–92

VARIETY OF ORCHESTRAL TREATMENTS

Keeping these discussions in mind, let us now briefly analyze some passages from the orchestral literature in which the wind section is used idiomatically:

1. as relief color or contrast to string passages;
2. in purely homophonic wind choir writing and chord spacings;
3. to clarify a gesture or a whole passage by the choices of colors;
4. in novel articulations;
5. with doublings of strings;
6. in contrapuntal examples for winds.

1. Contrast or Relief Color

In the third movement of Brahms's *Second Symphony*, there is a very beautiful use of alternation or, in this case, of "melting" one section (winds) into another (strings). This familiar technique is an important tool for the orchestrator. Five measures before the end, the woodwind chord dissolves into a string chord; then, at the very end, the final chord is colored by a wind chord with slightly different voicing, but in a similar juxtaposition to the strings, as before.

Example VIII–18. Brahms, *Symphony No. 2,* third movement, last 8 measures

Another lovely example of this effective alternation of voices is the beginning of the first Trio in Schumann's *Symphony No. 1.* Here, a short gesture, initiated by the strings, alternates with winds, including first horns then trumpets, and serves as a unifying element

in the movement. Note that whenever the choirs are first used separately and then together, a most satisfying sense of completion or resolution results.

Example VIII–19. Schumann, *Symphony No. 1*, third movement, mm. 49–73

Another short but famous example of "throwing the ball around" is very much in order. Beethoven was very fond of assigning little thematic gestures to different members of the winds and strings and then summing them up with a cadential tutti phrase. After the opening exposition of the main idea, and a bombastic tutti in the first movement of the *Third Symphony*, Beethoven provided instant contrast with a three-note gesture that is played at different pitch levels by oboe, clarinet, flute, and first violin twice, in that order. The third time, the oboe, followed by the clarinet and bassoon in octaves, introduces the summation gesture played by all the winds and strings, with the horns and trumpets providing the pedal dominant–tonic progression.

It may be important at this point to make an observation that any student of orchestration should keep in mind. Although there are exceptions, most of the great masters try to alter something, no matter how slightly, the *third* time they use the same orchestration. This is often true of any sequential material. It may be exactly the same voice, but, the third time it must be a bit different, in order to renew interest in the phrase. A principle like this, while not foolproof or absolute, is a good one to remember.

Example VIII–20. Beethoven, *Symphony No. 3*, first movement, mm. 38–57

2. Homophonic Wind Choir Writing in Orchestral Music

The wind choir with or without horns was not widely used homophonically until the nineteenth century. From then on, we find many excellent examples of purely homophonic writing lasting as little as four measures, or encompassing very long passages.

For study purposes it is suggested that the student reduce each of the following examples for piano (VIII–32, 33, 34, and 35) and analyze the doubling and spacing of each melodic line, each harmony, and the spacing of the chords, keeping in mind the registral characteristics of each wind instrument. The most important thing to remember is that the melody must come through (if it is important, that is) and not be obscured by the harmony. However, if the chord progression is the focal point of interest, then it must be orchestrated with the following in mind: shade (light or dark), dynamic (loud or soft), inversion (root position or inversion). These factors should influence the choice of instruments, as well as the spacing and doubling of the chordal passage.

Let us isolate a few chords before we look at the examples. Too many orchestration books give pat formulas for this task. Of course there are some obvious ways of spacing and doubling which are more effective than others. However, homophonic wind writing, doubling–spacing, and instrument selection have all been used by various composers in ways characteristic of their personal orchestration style. Here are some norms one can build upon:

Chords for winds in pairs may be voiced in four ways:

a. juxtaposed or superimposed one pair on the other;
b. interlocked;
c. enclosed;
d. overlapped.

Example VIII–21.

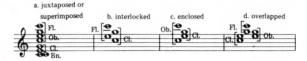

a. Juxtaposition is probably the most frequently used voicing, but one must be sure that the most prominent melody note is in a good register for the instrument to which it has been assigned.

b. Interlocking is a more imaginative voicing because it mixes the wind colors, but it has some greater registral dangers.

Example VIII–22

c. Enclosing another instrument may present similar problems, namely the prominence of some registers on some instruments and the lack of carrying power in other registers.

Example VIII–23

Also, the third example encloses the oboe within two different timbres, which not only gives better balance since the clarinet is stronger on the fourth-line D than the second flute, but provides added color interest.

d. Overlapping was in much greater use in the past than it is today, for doubling instruments at the unison (discussed earlier) robs the timbral characteristics from both and usually only results in a stronger pitch. In full-orchestra tutti this practice is still common.

Why have we not mentioned a chord where each note has a different timbre? Because such chords are difficult to balance, and unless the work is for small orchestra with single winds, this kind of writing is avoided. There are tuning difficulties to boot; however, a chord that is spaced wider is easier to handle with four different colors than a close chord, since each instrument can be placed in its most advantageous register.

Example VIII–24

One should notice that the greater gaps exist between the bass and the next highest voice. This spacing is preferred, and it is usual to voice the upper woodwinds or the upper notes of the chord in close position. Special consideration should also be given to the spacing of a first inversion in which the third (bass) should be doubled toward the bottom rather than the top. The "open" quality of the first inversion is thus preserved.

Example VIII–25

When multiples of three and four instruments are used in a wind section, the same principles of juxtaposition, interlocking, enclosing, and overlapping are also operational. Even greater care must be given to assign pitches that are registrally and technically practical so as not to upset the balance of the chord or the flow of the melody.

As we mentioned, spacing is often a very personal matter. Here are a few examples of this:

Example VIII–26. Typical Spacing in a Beethoven Work

Example VIII–27. Romantic Spacing

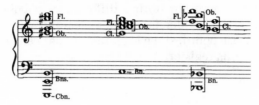

Example VIII–28. Two Typical Stravinsky Spacings

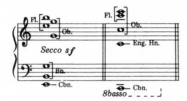

The bright or dark hues result from the choice of instruments and the position of the chord. Here are a few examples:

Example VIII–29

FOR CLASS DISCUSSION

Study these four homophonic excerpts from the orchestral literature:

a. A fast passage from the end of the Minuet from the "Will o' the Wisp" section of Berlioz's *Damnation of Faust*. The two piccolos and flute doubled by the oboe play continually, while the two clarinets and bass clarinet provide a marchlike rhythmic-harmonic background. (See Example VIII–30.)

b. More characteristic of wind homophonic writing are these eight measures from the *Second Symphony* of Robert Schumann (Example VIII–31). The doubling of the oboe line at the octave by the violas and the doubling of the bass line by the cello make a smooth transition to the introduction of the entire string section. This color will be retained for several measures after the G octave is reached.

Example VIII–30. Berlioz, *The Damnation of Faust,* Minuet of the Will-o'-the-Wisps, mm. 125–40

Example VIII–31. Schumann, *Symphony No. 2,* fourth movement, mm. 272–91

c. The opening of William Schuman's *New England Triptych* is an excellent example of a simple hymn setting in which the winds simulate the organ a bit. The doublings and voicings are most important. The flute robs the oboe of some of its nasal quality to make the sound even more organlike. At m. 13, the bass clarinet enters, providing a welcome, if not radical, change from the mass wind color so well established. If he had introduced a cello or a bass, it would have spoiled the beginning of the new section and the novelty of hearing a string sound.

Example VIII–32. W. Schuman, New England Triptych, third
movement (Chester), mm. 1–19

3. The Choice of One Color to Characterize or Clarify a Melodic Gesture or a Whole Melodic Passage

This technique is frequently used to represent a person or an object by an instrument in a tone poem. In more abstract cases, it may be the representation of an *idée fixe* or *Leitmotif* by a single instrument or a small group of instruments. Hundreds of examples exist, from Berlioz's use of the English horn in the *Symphonie fantastique* to the Strauss's horn in *Till Eulenspiegel* and the incredible bassoon opening in Stravinsky's *Sacre*. The clarinet, for instance, was thought to represent a nightingale by some nineteenth-century composers. The technique of assigning a motive or melody to a particular instrument or group of instruments remains valid today and can be an important device in bringing greater clarity to the form of a piece.

To illustrate the technique, we look at *Nuages*, the first movement of Debussy's *Nocturnes*. The first element of the work is a series of parallel chords introduced by clarinets and bassoons; the only contrasting gesture that appears in the entire piece is the following little figure, always played by the English horn.

Example VIII–33. Debussy, *Nocturnes: Nuages*, mm. 21–28

If one considers the entire movement as an *A–B–A* form, this gesture helps clarify the form: it appears only in the *A* group of events, and neatly reintroduces these when the fragment returns after a long absence at the change of key (the return to the original key 23 measures before the end).

In the second *Nocturne*, *Fêtes*, there are similar techniques used. Debussy reserves certain colors for specific groups of instruments each time they appear. Especially noteworthy is the biting combination of instruments that expose the staccato figure at 2:

Example VIII–34. Debussy, *Nocturnes: Fêtes*, mm. 25–29

This same combination is used again four measures later and then, significantly repeated when the recapitulation of the first part appears at mm. 208–10. While this movement is full of extremely colorful combinations, Debussy chose to reiterate a certain melodic fragment with the same instrument throughout the piece. This gives great clarity and unity not only to the orchestration but to the entire form of a work.

4. Some Novel Ideas concerning Articulation

As we have discussed in the previous chapters on winds, there are basically two articulations possible—slurred or tongued. The tonguing may be single, double, or even triple. There is such a thing as hard and soft tonguing to give different kinds of articulations when one or the other is appropriate. Some twentieth-century composers have devised a number of novel articulation formulas which are most useful and worthy of study. We shall look at two excerpts from the literature which provide interesting ideas to ponder.

a. A long solo passage for flute and oboe in a "strange unison" taken from the final movement of Debussy's *La Mer*. Here the oboe "pulsates" quite a few of the sustained pitches of the tune to make it

Example VIII–35. Debussy, *La Mer*, third movement, mm. 157–72

seem quite a bit more animated than it would be if the oboe simply doubled the flute. Further, it draws attention to the difference between the quality of the flute and the oboe. As the two reach their lower register, the "pulsating" oboe gains prominence over the more placid flute. After the long passage is completed, Debussy echoes it with English horn and piccolo in octaves and gives it an extra sheen by adding the Glockenspiel yet another octave higher. Notice that in the "echo" only the English horn and the Glockenspiel articulate the first and third beats, while the English horn pulsates on afterbeats a little like a second violin or viola part. It certainly makes for an exciting and unusual presentation of this wonderful tune.

b. In this short excerpt from the first movement of Stravinsky's *Symphony of Psalms*, the winds are divided so that one slurs a gesture while, at the same time, another tongues the same pitches. The only gesture that is entirely slurred is the sung melody doubled by the first and third oboe, and the little arpeggio figure in the English horn. The overall effect of this marvelous accompaniment is similar to that of violins being divided, with the firsts playing arco while the seconds play the same pitches pizzicato.

Example VIII–36. Stravinsky, *Symphony of Psalms*, first movement, mm. 26–36

5. Winds as Doublers of Strings

The woodwind choir is often called upon to double the string choir, especially in tutti sections. In the eighteenth and nineteenth centuries, doublings of winds with strings "at pitch" in unison were very popular. Today, however, we feel that octave doublings are more successful. Even though a passage may look as if the doubling is ineffective, the timbre would be changed without it. To experiment, let us take a doubling that seems unlikely and wasted and consider it first with the flute doubling the first violin and then without the doubling. The performance without doubling has neither the warmth nor richness of the alternative, especially as the line goes up.

Example VIII–37. Berlioz, *Symphonie fantastique*, third movement, mm. 19–36

Another unusually beautiful doubling is found at the beginning of the second movement of Brahm's *First Symphony*. We have already experienced the terrific effect of the two bassoons doubling the bass line in the opening theme of Mozart's overture to *The Marriage of Figaro*. Here we have a single bassoon doubling the opening theme in octaves with the first violins. This lends added warmth to the already rich harmony, and brings out the melody even more clearly despite the rather thick harmonic background.

Example VIII–38. Brahms, *Symphony No. 1* second movement, mm. 1–6

Now for a few examples of "normal" doubling of winds and strings:

a. A most effective beginning with the first violins doubled by the flutes and piccolo, the oboes, and clarinets filling out the upper-octave harmony by doubling the violas an octave higher, and the bassoons doubling the cellos at pitch plus an octave higher.

Example VIII–39. Dvořák, *Carnival Overture*, mm. 25–31

Example VIII–40. Tchaikovsky, *Symphony No. 6*, first movement, mm. 237–44

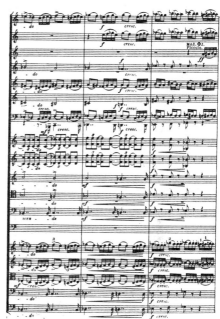

b. This excerpt starts with a very dark coloring, and only as it goes up does it get more and more brilliant. Of course, the trick is to keep the volume of the brass down enough to let the strings and winds through. This passage would sound much more exuberant if the piccolo were used an octave higher and doubled at the beginning, but then the subdued feeling would not be as pervasive, and that is obviously what the composer intended.

c. Here is quiet doubling at its best. A completely restful summation of two previous phrases, one for strings alone, the other for winds alone. At this point they come together for a third statement preceeding the final coda. Notice the voicing with the violas above the second violins for the first four measures. The second violins therefore need the heavy doubling of the second clarinet and the muted horn. Also, mark the way Copland orchestrates a diminuendo by cutting out the first oboe in the fifth measure, for it honks too much in that extreme low register, and substitutes for it the quiet, rich sound of the second flute to complete first violin doubling. It is interesting

Example VIII–41. Copland, *Appalachian Spring,* 70 – 71

that the horn, which doubles the second violin for seven measures, switches at the end to emphasize the third of the chord, E. Without a dominant note (G) in the chord, it is a relative of the famous final chord of the *Symphony of Psalms,* only very quiet, dark, and subdued compared to the bright spacing in the Stravinsky work.

6. Contrapuntal Writing for Winds

Since the winds in the orchestra were not a prime factor in either the Baroque or the Classical periods, there are not many examples of fugal or imitative composition written specifically for the wind section in the orchestral repertory. Of course there are hundreds of instances where individual winds play imitatively with strings or other wind instruments. However, since each of the woodwinds has such a unique color, contrapuntal writing, especially rhythmical, is very effective. Here are four very different kinds of contrapuntal examples for winds from the orchestral literature.

a. This passage needs little explanation. Its marvelous woodwind imitation adds to the happy nature of the phrase.

Example VIII–42. Mozart, *Symphony No. 38,* third movement, mm. 120–38

b. Here is one of the few full-fledged fugue expositions exclusively for woodwinds, making full use of the registral differences of the choir and giving a good opportunity to study the sound of two like instruments playing in unison. A most effective and beloved piece which should tell us that it is quite possible to write such contrapuntal passages for winds today.

Example VIII–43. Britten, *The Young Person's Guide to the Orchestra,* Fugue, mm. 1–55

c. Probably four of the most ingenious pages in all of the orchestral repertoire, this is counterpoint in the most sophisticated manner. Here, almost each instrument has an entirely separate part at all times except for a few homophonic measures. The effect evokes the sensation of listening to the sound of nature on a spring night. Nothing seems symmetrical, yet everything is perfectly notated in 2/4 and 3/4 time. The extreme rhythmic variation in the parts gives that magnificent freedom. Even though there are so many diverse parts, the excerpt is very clear, because Stravinsky has orchestrated each gesture in the best register of each instrument. There are no "gimmicks." The fluttertongue sounds just right, as does the mixing of rhythms three against two, four against six, etc. Notice also a typical Stravinsky device, the division of grace notes: in m. 40 the first clarinet plays the grace note on the first beat, the second on the third, the first on the fifth, etc. This makes the grace notes fresher, for the same person is not worn out by repeating the same figure constantly; also, each player articulates just a bit differently, so each grace note is enhanced. Stravinsky uses this division of grace notes on many similar occasions, notably in *Petrushka*.

Study the excerpt below very carefully and listen to it often, since it contains some of the most thoughtful and colorful wind writing ever written and is perhaps the apex of contrapuntal writing in the twentieth century. The beautiful divided bass harmonics in m. 58 add a mysterious texture to the whole.

Example VIII–44. Stravinsky, *Le Sacre du printemps*, mm. 41–61

NEW TECHNIQUES

Every chapter in a book like this must be open-ended, since composers are constantly experimenting with new sounds and fresh approaches to all instruments, woodwinds in particular. The hundreds of new uses have not yet found their way into the new orchestral repertoire for the most part. That certainly does not mean that one should not try them. However, consultation with an experienced professional orchestral musician on the feasibility and practicability of a desired effect is the best assurance of its success in performance. One of the most experienced orchestral composers of our time, Gunther Schuller, in one of his best works, experiments with the oboe in combination with harp and viola, and in an ingenious little trio gives an example of what can be done to enlarge techniques today. Here is a bit of this passage from Schuller's *Seven Studies on Themes of Paul Klee*.

Notice that specific instructions for the instruments are clearly given. This is an important addition to any score that requires unorthodox methods of production. The object here is to simulate the sound of an ethnic Arabic dance.

Example VIII–45. Schuller, *Seven Studies on Themes of Paul Klee*, "Arab Village," mm. 60–73

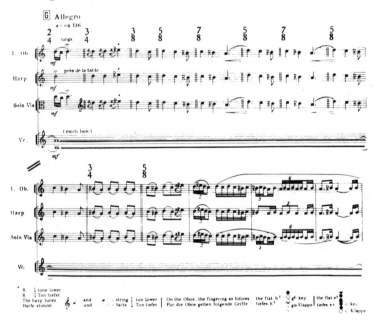

Most problems that arise in contemporary scores stem from notation that is foreign to the performer and is not explicitly explained at the beginning of each work. Here are two excerpts from contemporary Polish scores that require some brand-new effects:

1. Penderecki, *Dies irae*

Winds first play the highest pitch they are able to produce. Then they trill on the specified notes until the end of the dark line with arrow.

Example VIII–46. Penderecki, *Dies irae*, "Apocalypsis," mm. 2–4

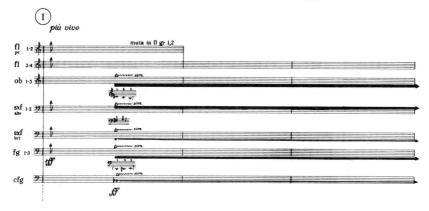

2. Stachowski, *Irisation for Orchestra*

The composer asks the winds to remove their mouthpieces from their instruments and "play" through them.

Example VIII–47. Stachowski, *Irisation for Orchestra*, third movement, mm. 79–83

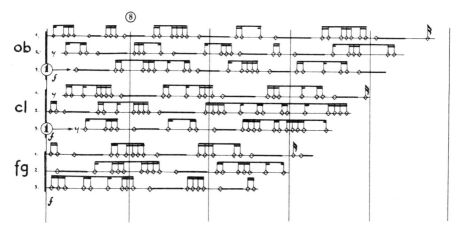

The solo and chamber music for woodwinds is more technically advanced than orchestral writing for these instruments. One important reason is acoustical, since many contemporary woodwind effects are very soft and therefore much more effective in smaller halls and in smaller, more intimate groups. Two additional reasons are important to bear in mind when one wishes to use contemporary techniques that are as yet not universal: 1) only a few players are able (or in many cases willing) to perform them; 2) Some techniques are more successfully performed on certain makes of instruments. Instances of that are the multiphonics mentioned in some European texts, which are impossible or at least extremely difficult to produce on American instruments. Nevertheless, if a composer hears a certain sound in his inner ear and consults with an experienced professional, all things are possible.

Can orchestration be taught? Of course, if the ear is sharpened by familiarity of the orchestral repertoire and careful analysis of each interesting sound one hears for future use. The facts learned in this chapter should be kept in mind as we go on with the brasses and percussion and their combinations, culminating in the full orchestra in subsequent chapters.

Introduction to
Brass Instruments

Even though most instruments in the brass section of our modern symphony orchestras have been in use for hundreds of years, the standardization of these instruments is a rather recent development and, in some cases, is still in flux. For example, Walter Piston in his orchestration book, published in 1952, makes the statement that trumpets in D "appear rarely" in the orchestra today. Since then, however, many trumpeters have taken up this instrument, and it is manufactured and played frequently once again.

With renewed interest in the performance of older music, especially from before 1650, we face great problems concerning the kinds of brass instruments that were used in those days. If we wish to be authentic, we must be aware that the strange sound and pitch inaccuracy of the trumpets and horns, attributable to their rather primitive construction, were accepted phenomena of the times. Further, the character and the gestures of the music were dictated by these limitations until around the middle of the nineteenth century.

It is therefore imperative to pay close attention to the evolution and development of this choir. Today, brass instruments suffer few of the limitations which formerly frustrated them and are rapidly taking their places among the most agile and versatile members of the modern orchestra.

COMPOSITION OF THE BRASS SECTION

The brass section of the modern symphony orchestra is usually made up of four horns, three trumpets, three trombones, and a tuba. Larger numbers of these instruments may be employed, and some composers augment these basic instruments with cornets, euphoniums, and Wagner tubas. In some early nineteenth-century scores, we often find the outmoded ophicleide, whose parts are mostly performed on the tuba today.

While the brass choir is more homogeneous than the woodwind group, it would be altogether simplistic to make this an unqualified statement. Practically, there are two major divisions:

1. the horns
2. the trumpets, trombones, and tubas

This most important division of the instruments is a consequence of the way in which they are constructed with respect to the shape of the tube and the bore, as well as the small but radical differences in the shape and size of the mouthpiece.

A minor division is possible between the brass instruments when we consider the question of transposition:

1. transposing: horns and trumpets (cornets)
2. nontransposing: trombones and all tubas (euphoniums)

TONE PRODUCTION, ARTICULATION, TONGUING

Just as the reed performs the function of a sound generator for the clarinet, oboe, and bassoon, so the lips of a player held against a mouthpiece at the small end of the main tube of the instrument perform this function for all brass instruments. When the player forces a stream of air through the tube, the air column within the tube is set in motion.

One is able to generalize about the embouchure on brass instruments in the following manner: the lips are loose for low notes and tighten as the player goes up into the higher registers. The timbre of the individual instrument depends on the size and shape of the mouthpiece. Forsyth says "the shallower the cup, the more brilliant the tone";* this is an excellent generalization to remember. Therefore, we can see in the illustration below that the trumpets have a cuplike, shallow mouthpiece which makes their tone much more

* Cecil Forsyth, *Orchestration* (New York: Macmillan, 1949), p. 90

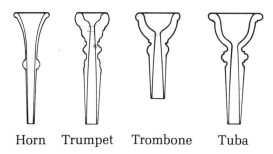

Horn   Trumpet   Trombone   Tuba

brilliant than the mellow horns, which are fitted with a funnel-shaped mouthpiece.

The problems of tonguing for brass instruments are similar to those of the woodwinds. While the woodwind tongue stroke was *tu*, the attack for brass is *ta*. All variants of tonguing are available, and double- and triple-tonguing is feasible for all. A great variety of attacks are possible on all brass instruments, although as one considers the problems of each of these instruments closely, one will find that, for instance, because of the loose embouchure of some extremely low notes, certain attacks and articulations may be problematic. Conversely, the soft attacks and controlled articulations for the very high extreme register on most of the brass instruments are fiendishly difficult, because of the firmness of the lips and the velocity of the breath required to produce these notes. All this will be discussed in the systematic examination of the instruments of the brass choir.

OVERBLOWING AND THE PRINCIPLE OF THE HARMONIC SERIES

Early in the nineteenth century, trumpets and horns were not equipped with valves or pistons to produce the various pitches, but simply worked on the principle of overblowing the harmonic series. To restate the operative acoustical principle: The longer the tube, the lower the pitch of the fundamental, and vice versa. Let us take an eight-foot-long tube, which is theoretically capable of sounding the low C, and therefore produces the following harmonic series:

Example IX–1. Harmonic Series on C

The brass player isolates these pitches or partials of the harmonic series with his embouchure. The skill of the individual brass player is determined by his ability to find any notated pitch (or partial) by a combination of embouchure and breath control. In other words, he has to have a mental image of what the pitch sounds like and then what the pitch feels like while he is performing it. One should keep in mind some general problems faced when playing natural instruments, that is, brass instruments which have no valves or pistons to change the pitches. They are entirely dependent on the length of the tube for their harmonic series and the skill of the performer to find each prescribed pitch:

1. Only the notes of the particular harmonic series can be sounded on an instrument with a tube of a given length. For example, on the instrument which produces the harmonic series and therefore the partials of the above example, the performer could not, under any circumstance, play the following notes or any of their chromatic alterings:*

Example IX–2

2. While theoretically all pitches are producible in the harmonic series, most players cannot produce pitches above the sixteenth partial.

3. There are certain partials which are out of tune compared with our present tempered scale when performed on natural instruments. This is especially true of the seventh, eleventh, thirteenth, and fourteenth partials, but upon close examination, we shall also find that the two major seconds between eight, nine, and ten are intervals of unequal length. In our day, some composers want this out-of-tune sound as a special effect. Notice in this example from Benjamin Britten's *Serenade* that the pitches with crosses over them are out of tune because Britten specifies that this passage be played on an "open" horn utilizing, if necessary, the modern horn by playing the series on F without manipulating the notes by means of the valves.

Example IX–3. Britten, *Serenade*, mm. 1–14

* As we shall find out later, there were ways in which skilled performers overcame this problem, but many times sacrificing good intonation.

4. For beginners, the fundamental is usually difficult to produce, and the Classical composers seldom ask for notes higher than the twelfth partial. Here are three typical passages from the Classical literature, one of which does demand the higher partials:

Example IX–4. Mozart, *Symphony No. 40*, third movement, mm. 74–78

Example IX–5. Beethoven, *Piano Concerto No. 5*, first movement, mm. 43–47

Example IX–6. Beethoven, *Symphony No. 3*, third movement, mm. 174–81

5. Bach, Handel, Vivaldi, Telemann, and their Baroque contemporaries were very daring and demanding when it came to brass writing, and the virtuosos of their day made the upper range a particular specialty. When the player found certain notes out of tune or "missing" from the particular harmonic series, he "found" the miss-

* ᵛ means pitch to be adjusted by the player.

ing note or corrected the bad notes by varying the existing pitches by means of his embouchure. In the case of the horn, the right hand was placed into the bell of the instrument, in effect shortening the tube and raising the pitch. The following passage written for trumpet in F (transposing a perfect fourth up) will give an example of a passage in which the player *had* to have difficulty with at least two pitches and had to alter them to maintain the tempo successfully:

Example IX–7. Bach, *Brandenburg Concerto No. 2*, first movement, mm. 29–30

The F in the passage had to be performed by flatting the eleventh partial, and the A was so badly out of tune that one had to play the fourteenth partial and flatten it.

RANGE

The ranges of each of the brass instruments will be discussed in great detail in the individual sections for each instrument. However, it is most important to remember the following principle in connection with the harmonic series: A wider bore facilitates the production of the lower partials, while a narrow bore is much more expeditious for producing the higher harmonics.

CROOKS, VALVES, AND SLIDES

Brass instruments were originally outdoor instruments used for hunting, military functions, and civil disasters. They were also used in the church, but until the sixteenth century, only for occasions that demanded fanfares. It was not possible to consider these instruments for serious use in composed music until their unwieldy shapes and mechanisms were controlled and altered.

By Haydn's time, a mechanism was invented which allowed the trumpets and horns to go beyond the limits of a single harmonic series. Remember, the pitch of the fundamental depends on the length of the tube. It was found that by adding extra tubing, the player could produce another series on the same instrument. This added pipe, called a *crook*, was U-shaped and inserted somewhere into the original tube.

The composer was then able to decide what series he wanted the instrument to start the piece in, and the player, given a little time, could change the series anywhere in the piece by inserting a crook and then performing in another key. However, he was still limited to the notes in the harmonic series of the new length of tubing.

Both trumpets and horns remained transposing instruments, since it was much easier for the performer to continue to read and finger in C and let the composer (and the crook) take care of the exact transposition. So the following "horn fifths" sound according to their transpositions in this manner:

Example IX–8

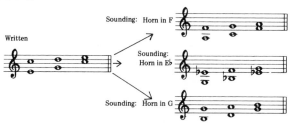

The next improvement in the development of the horn and the trumpet was the invention of the valve (both rotary and piston) early in the nineteenth century, but it was not until the middle of that century that the system was perfected and gained acceptance by the performers.

The principle functions in this manner: Three coiled tubes are permanently attached to the main tube inside the main loop. Each of the attached coils can be activated, or joined, to the main stream of air by a valve which is easily operable by the performer's left hand. In other words, the piston, or lever, activating the extra tubing, accomplishes instantly what the changing of crooks did previously. There are usually three valves on the trumpet and horn. The first valve is the one closest to the player, the middle valve is called the second, and the one furthest away from the player is called the third valve. Tubas often have a fourth valve, which lowers the pitch a perfect fourth. Two or more valves may be depressed at the same time.

By depressing the first valve (alone), the pitch of the whole series is lowered a whole step. Depressing the second valve (alone) lowers the series a semitone. Depressing the third valve (alone) lowers the series a tone and a half. So valves 2 and 3 depressed would equal the lowering of the pitch by a major third, and so on.

This principle has made these two important brass instruments of the orchestra completely chromatic and able to produce all the pitches between the "open" partials of the fundamental series.

The trombone in the fifteenth century closely resembled its modern counterpart. It is completely chromatic, because it permits the player to change the length of the tubing by means of a slide. The instrument is made of two U-shaped pieces, one of which slides into the other. Even though the trombonist still depends on his control of the overtone series, he is able to change the total length of the tube with precision and perfect intonation. There are seven positions of the slide of the tenor trombone, as shown in the following diagram:

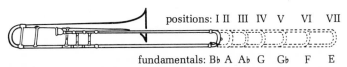

positions: I II III IV V VI VII

fundamentals: Bb A Ab G Gb F E

Positions of the Trombone Slide

These, of course, provide seven different harmonic series as well as seven fundamentals. Remember, the change of position can be accomplished almost instantaneously with practice.

Note how the valves in their various combinations on the trumpet and horn correspond to the trombone positions:

Valves Depressed	*Interval by Which Pitch is Lowered*	*Corresponding Trombone Slide Position*
None	none	first
No. 2	semitone	second
No. 1	whole tone	third
No. 3, or nos. 1 and 2	minor third	fourth
Nos. 2 and 3	major third	fifth
Nos. 1 and 3	perfect fourth	sixth
Nos. 1, 2, and 3	augmented fourth	seventh

FINE TUNING

Each brass instrument has a tuning slide as part of its mechanism to make small pitch adjustments when necessary. Pulling out the tuning slide will add tubing to the instrument and, therefore, flatten the pitch, while pushing the slide in will raise the pitch slightly by shortening the tube. These pitch adjustments by the tuning slide are very slight. If greater discrepancies in pitch exist, the valve slides have to be adjusted.

COMMON CHARACTERISTICS AND EFFECTS ON ALL BRASS INSTRUMENTS

Different Attacks

1. sforzando and the *forte-piano* attack

Example IX–9

2. light, soft, fast tonguing

Example IX–10. Debussy, *Jeux*, 2 measures after 67 to 68

3. double-tonguing, which is executed either *ta-ka* or *te-ka*

Example IX–11. Rimsky-Korsakov, *Scheherazade*, fourth movement, mm. 452–56

4. triple-tonguing, which is executed *ta-ka-ta* or *ta-ta-ka*

Example IX–12. Debussy, *La Mer*, second movement, mm. 104–6

5. fluttertonguing (Notice that the notation is similar to the designation of fluttertonguing for woodwinds.)

Example IX–13. Strauss, *Don Quixote*, Variation II, mm. 18–19

Fluttertonguing is very effective on all brass instruments and is quite easy to produce on all of them.

Breathing and Phrasing

The brass instruments require a great deal more wind than the woodwinds. Keeping in mind that playing these instruments is rather taxing, one should allow frequent intervals of rest for the brass players so their lips can recuperate and they can catch their breath.

Phrasing is very much as it is for woodwinds. If a passage is not slurred, it will be tongued, meaning each note will be articulated separately. On the other hand, all slurred phrases are performed on one breath. In a loud passage one should not phrase too many notes on one breath in a slow tempo, for it does take more breath to play loudly than softly.

Dynamic Range

The brass section of the orchestra has great dynamic power. So much so, in fact, that the orchestrator must always keep the balance of brass versus woodwinds and string in mind, since the full force of a brass section can obliterate the rest of the orchestra. The question of balance will be discussed at greater length later in the book, when combinations of choirs are explored. However, it must be stated here that at the other end of the dynamic scale, the brass section cannot be expected to play as softly as the strings or winds, although the *pianissimo* dynamic of a nonmuted brass section is a unique and most effective orchestral effect.

Example IX–14. Strauss, *Don Juan*, mm. 37–40

Mutes

All brass instruments can be muted. Muting can create a *pianis-simo* that is incredibly soft; however, all mutes change the character of both sound and tonal color quite a bit. There is a variety of mutes for the trumpet and the trombone, but only one that is practical for the horn and one for the tuba. There are also mutes for euphoniums and Wagner tubas. A brass mute is a cone-shaped plug, which is inserted in the bell of the instrument. On its sides there are small blocks of cork which prevent the mute from fitting too tightly against the sides of the bell and make it easy to insert and to remove.

The horn can achieve a muted affect by hand-stopping, that is, pushing the hand tightly into the bell. In that case, the pitch is also raised, and the horn player needs to compensate for that elevation in pitch by fingering a note one half step lower. If the horn uses a commercial mute, the muting becomes nontransposing.

Here are some of the different kinds of mutes available for trumpets and trombones. While trumpet players usually carry several mutes with them, trombonists seldom have but one mute along, since the larger size of trombone mutes make them cumbersome to transport. If a trombonist carries any mute, it will be a straight one. For all other mutes, it is imperative to specify the exact name and any special instructions in the parts as well as the score.

1. Straight Mute

This is the mute that both trumpeters and trombonists use automatically as soon as *con sordino* is indicated in a work. One is able to play both softly and loudly with this mute. It is made of either fiberboard or metal. The fiber mute does not have quite as much "cutting edge" as the very poignant, straight metal mute, especially when playing *fortissimo.*

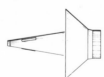

2. Cup Mute

This mute is not commonly used in symphony orchestras, but is associated with jazz. The cup is adjusted to suit the style of the piece being performed. When the whole section plays, the cup is usually open about an inch, while in some solo work or amplified playing, the cup is closed almost against the bell to produce a dark, muffled tone. As a whole, the cup mute can be used to produce colorless, ghostlike nasal sounds.

3. The Harmon or Wa-Wa Mute

This mute is made out of metal, and the end of it can be adjusted to produce a variety of sounds. It is seldom used in the symphony orchestra, except for comic effects, as in Lucien Caillset's arrangement of *Pop Goes the Weasel*, or "wa-wa" jazz effects, as in George Gershwin's *Rhapsody in Blue*. The characteristic sound of a trumpet with a fully assembled Harmon mute is penetrating and has a real shimmer. The mute sounds much duller when inserted in a trombone. The tone can be changed by removing the "cookie cutter" from the stem, extending the stem either halfway or all the way, and using one's hand to open and close the opening to obtain the "wa-wa" effect. In notation, the "+" sign means closing, the "O" sign means opening one's hand.

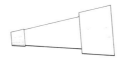

4. Whispa Mute

This is the softest of all the mutes. It sounds as if the instrument were somewhere off stage, so if it is played very softly, it is almost inaudible. The mute is made like the Harmon mute and works on the same principle. The sound is forced through a chamber filled with sound-absorbent material, and small holes allow a little of the sound to escape. It takes more effort to play the instrument, and extreme high notes are most difficult to produce.

5. Solotone Mute

This mute also works on the Harmon mute principle, with all the air passing through the device, none escaping along the sides. The tone is diminished and then reinforced in the first chamber, leaving that chamber through a cardboard tube permanently mounted within. The tone is centered and well focused by a megaphone-shaped cone as it leaves the tube to produce a nasal sound, which seems to be coming through an old-fashioned radio or telephone. Ferde Grofé asks for this mute in the small-orchestra arrangement of the "On the Trail" movement of the *Grand Canyon Suite* (trombone solo).

6. Muting Devices other than Mutes

a. Plunger

This is simply a six-inch bowl with a small handle to muffle the sound or make it "stuffy." One can produce "popping" sounds by holding it very closely to the bell and playing very fast notes.

b. Hat or Derby

This device is usually used in jazz, but can be effectively used in any medium to reduce the intensity of the trumpet or trombone without distorting the sound in any way.

c. Hand over the Bell or Hand in the Bell

This is a way of damping the trumpet or trombone by hand and is not as effective as using mutes, although it can be used to affect pitch variations and muting at the same time, if desired. The composer specifying this device must be conscious of the fact that the pitch is definitely affected by putting one's hand inside the bell.

d. Into the Stand

Again, this is often demanded in jazz playing and can reduce the loudness and brilliance of both the trumpet and the trombone. The player focuses the bell of his instrument about two inches from the stand, thereby lowering the dynamic level.

e. Cloth or Handkerchief in the Bell

A few twentieth-century composers have asked for this device. Charles Ives used it effectively for the trumpet in the *Unanswered Question*. Again, it reduces the volume and brilliance of the tone without causing any fluctuation in pitch and leaves the player in perfect control of his instrument, not having to strain for either high or low notes.

It is imperative to state once again that when muting devices are called for, the instructions to the performer must be explicitly notated in both the parts and the score.

Since mutes change the basic tonal color of each of the brass instruments and do not simply make the instrument softer, the effect of writing *fortissimo* muted passages for the entire brass section can be a most dynamic experience and is encountered quite often, especially in the music of the last hundred years.

Example IX–15. Vaughan Williams, *Symphony No. 6*, fourth movement, mm. 39–42

5. Glissandi

The horns and trumpets can produce a glissando by using a lip slur. These are most effective in the upper register, where the partials are close together; also, they are much easier slurring up- than downward, although jazz trumpeters are able to execute amazing glissandi in both directions. Both trumpet and horn glissandi are sweeping and very exciting gestures without being musically vulgar. The trombone, which is able to play glissandi with relative ease and in both directions, is almost too often called upon to show off this effect, which has by now become a well-worn cliché. Yet when it is appropriately used, it can be most apt. The tuba is able to perform glissandi, but not as easily as its other members of the brass family, and it is advised that the glissandi be upward, which is slightly easier to play than a downward glissando.

Example IX–16

6. Trills and Tremolos

The subject of trills and tremolos on the brass instruments is quite complicated, and therefore it will be dealt with in the individual instrument chapters. Suffice it to say that most brass instruments can perform some tremolos with success, and all are able to execute trills. On some instruments, lip-trills are preferable; on others, the pistons or valves are used; and still other players use combinations of both techniques. Obviously, the trombone player is only able to use lip-trills, sometimes also called lip-slurs.

7. Brass Instruments and the Written Orchestral Score

The arrangement of the brass choir on the orchestral page has some historic peculiarities. The brass section is placed right below the woodwinds on the score page in the following order:

Four Horns
Three Trumpets
Three Trombones
Tuba

Notice that the horns, which are really "the alto" of the brass section, have always been placed above the trumpets. This may be for the simple reason that the horns were regular members of the symphony orchestra before the trumpets; or possibly because, in the Classical orchestra, trumpets were used in combination with timpani and the two were placed in proximity. Both reasons are pure speculation, but seem logical explanations for a rather illogical arrangement.

Usually, horns and trumpets are written without key signatures. Of course, in older music where the trumpet and horn were usually playing in the key of the piece, but notated in C, this was logical. However, this became such common practice that in most scores even today the tradition is observed and all the accidentals marked as they occur, rather than by a key signature. Most performers prefer this manner of notation. Trombone and tuba players are used to reading key signatures, since they have always been notated that way, especially in nineteenth-century scores.

The number of staffs per brass instrument is similar to the arrangement for winds. If there are four horns, use two staffs with first and second on one, third and fourth on the other. There are other special ways to arrange the four horns, which will be discussed in the following chapter.

The three trumpets are also placed on two staffs, with the first and second on one, while the third occupies the second staff. However, if the notation of the three trumpets is too complex to be clear on two staves, each trumpet may occupy its own staff. This practice is followed for horns as well.

The modern symphony orchestra usually has three trombones: two tenor trombones, which are written on one staff and a bass trombone on a separate one.

There is usually only one tuba, and it has its own staff. When there are more tubas, they are usually notated on the same staff, while all euphoniums or Wagner tubas are placed between the bass trombone staff and the tuba staff.

10

Individual Brass Instruments

HORN
Corno (*It.*), Cor (*Fr.*)

Verne Reynolds, horn

In England and America, it has been a practice for a long time to call this instrument the "French horn." Why this nomenclature has been adopted is a mystery, for most of the developments in its construction were accomplished in Germany. The only possible explanation could be that in the earliest orchestral uses of the instrument (around 1710), especially in Germany and England, the horns were marked by the French designation *cor de chasse,* meaning hunting horns, although Bach often uses the term *corno da caccia,* meaning the same thing in Italian. However the designation of "French" horn came about is really not too important, but the term is not a correct one and should slowly but surely be retired.

What is important is that there are two distinct kinds of horns:

1. the natural horn, sometimes called hand horn
   corno naturale (It.); *cor simple* (Fr.); *Waldhorn* (Ger.)
2. the valve horn
   corno ventile (It.); *cor à pistons* (Fr.); *Ventilhorn* (Ger.)

The Natural Horn

As discussed in the previous chapter, the natural horn is an open coil of brass tubing. It is a quarter of an inch in diameter at the small opening where the mouthpiece is inserted and then gently expands to about three inches at the throat of the bell. The bell then flares widely to about eleven inches in diameter. Crooks of various sizes are fitted at the end of the tube near the mouthpiece, or in later years, slid into the place where the tuning slide usually was placed.

The basic horn was an eight-foot-long tube with a fundamental of C and its overtone series. The following crooks, which changed the fundamental and the series, were the most popular during the eighteenth and early part of the nineteenth centuries:

Horn in	Sounding (Transposition)
B♭ alto	a major second lower than notated
A	a minor third lower than notated
A♭	a major third lower than notated
G	a perfect fourth lower than notated
F	a perfect fifth lower than notated
E	a minor sixth lower than notated
E♭	a major sixth lower than notated
D	a minor seventh lower than notated
C *	an octave lower than notated
B♭ basso	a major ninth lower than notated

* Sometimes designated "basso" or C Horn, with crook.

Notice that all horns transpose downward, also that the words "alto" and "basso" appear. *Alto* in this case means high, and *basso* adds an octave to the regular alto transposition of the horn. If the word *alto* does not appear on the score, the transposition follows the table above. Besides the crooks and transpositions mentioned above, there were others less frequently used, such as A basso, G basso, and even B basso (Brahms, *Symphony No. 1*). Of the alto crooks some rare transpositions, such as horn in F♯ (Haydn, *Farewell Symphony*), horn in D♭ (Massenet, *Phaedre;* Bizet, *Carmen*), appear.

Example X–1. Range of the Natural Horn

The fundamental was usually not playable, so the player had eleven good notes available to him out of the possible sixteen partials. The notes with crosses over them were very badly out of tune and had to be adjusted by the hand in the bell if they were flat or by the embouchure if they were sharp. The term *hand horn* came into being because of the skill of the performers to play those partials in the harmonic series in tune by raising the pitches with their hand in the bell or by producing some pitches that did not even exist in the series.

As was mentioned in the previous chapter, most Classical composers seldom asked the horn player to produce any pitch beyond the twelfth partial. From Beethoven on, however, the higher partials were more commonly used. Even when composers such as Brahms and Wagner had access to valve horns, they continued to score for the natural horn.

Since the beginning of orchestral horn playing, the practice of segregating the horns into firsts and seconds has been followed. This segregation is not meant to imply that one player is inferior to the other, but rather that one (the first) plays "high horn" while the other "low horn." Toward the latter part of the eighteenth century, the range limitations of each of these horn parts was temporarily fixed. Following are the approximate ranges of the *cor alto* (first horn) and the *cor basso* (second horn):

Example X–2

The lower horn players often used a larger mouthpiece in order to facilitate the playing of the lower notes.

Before we leave the subject of the natural horn, it is important to mention that the right hand in the bell was of course also used to stop or mute the horn by partially closing the throat of the horn inside the bell. This changed the quality of the sound or tone color of the instrument. It has been stated before that the insertion of the hand into the bell also corrected some pitch inaccuracies in the fundamental harmonic series. With great skill in embouchure control and right-hand manipulation, the hornist could successfully perform a passage such as this one from Schubert's *C-major Symphony*. All stopped notes are designated by placing a cross "+" over or under the note, while nonstopped notes have a circle under them.

Example X–3. Schubert, *Symphony No. 9*, first movement, mm. 1–8

The leading horn players of the late eighteenth and early nineteenth centuries preferred the brighter tone of the F crook compared to the more somber and darker timbre of the Eb and D crooks. This most probably led to the adoption later in the nineteenth century of the basic F horn with valves as the prototype of the first completely chromatic instrument.

The Valve Horn

For a long period of roughly fifty years, the natural horn and the valve horn coexisted. Either composers and performers were prejudiced against the new "mechanical" instrument or they distrusted it; or, as was mentioned previously, the "hunting" outdoor quality of the natural horn was preferred. By the beginning of the twentieth century and especially with the chromatic complexities of music from Wagner on, the valve horn became the standard instrument for all symphony orchestras. Even though many of the beautiful horn passages in Brahms and Bruckner were written for hand horn, they certainly sound better and are more accurately in tune on the valve horn.

Our modern instrument is basically an F horn; however, an even greater improvement has been made, and these modern horns are what we call "double horns." This means that the instrument has two sets of tubing, that of the F horn, which is approximately seventeen feet long; and a trigger worked by the left thumb cuts off four feet of tubing, making it a B♭ alto horn (this is called the *B♭ division*). The double horn is clearly a most practical solution, since composers more and more frequently demanded the higher tessitura of the F horn. It was found that the higher partials were much easier to produce on the B♭ alto, with its shorter length of tubing. (On the B♭ horn the *twelfth* harmonic is the *sixteenth* partial on the F horn.) The composer should be aware of these facts, but does not have to notate for anything but Horn in F, and the performer will choose whether to play on the F or the B♭ part of his double horn.

Example X–4. Range: Horn in F

The modern horn has a very large range, but one cannot caution a composer enough about the great difficulties in producing certain notes. The lower register, especially the pedal tones of the B♭ division, are most difficult to produce and should be avoided in fast passages. These pitches are most effective when they are sustained or played in slow-moving passages. The rest of the range is quite agile, but it is most taxing to play in the higher register all the time, so periodic rests are most welcome.

Example X–5. Register Characteristics: Horn in F (Written Pitches)

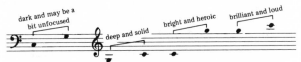

Today the four horns are usually divided in the following manner:

I and III, High Horns
II and IV, Low Horns

This arrangement probably comes from the fact that when four horns were first introduced into the orchestra, each pair was in a different key. When all four played the modern horn and the key for all was the same, the tradition remained. Even when there are three horns in the scoring, the third is placed (pitchwise) between the first and second.

The appearance in the score is almost always as follows:

Example X–6

Before presenting some famous solo passages and some successful harmonic excerpts from the literature, it is important to recapitualate an earlier admonition concerning the difficulty the hornist will experience in executing wide leaps or excessively fast and jagged runs. It must be remembered that the horn player must "hear" and then "find" each note in his mind and in his embouchure.

Old and New Notation

In all new scores and new editions of older scores, the horn in F always transposes a perfect fifth down, whether the part is notated in the treble or the bass clef. In many scores of the nineteenth century, the horn notated in the bass clef transposed a perfect fourth up. Here is how it worked:

Example X–7

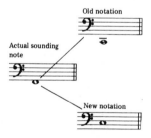

One must be aware of this discrepancy and be prepared to answer questions about one's own notation. Some authorities even feel that a note should be placed at the beginning of the score stating that all horn passages are to be transposed a perfect fifth down. This provides a warning for those horn players who have become accustomed to the old notation, which should no longer be used.

Here are some representative horn passages:

Example X–8. Brahms, *Symphony No. 1*, fourth movement, mm. 30–38

Example X–9. Beethoven, *Symphony No. 6*, third movement, mm. 132–53

Example X–10. Strauss, *Till Eulenspiegel*, mm. 6–12

Example X–11. Ravel, *Pavane for a Dead Princess*, mm. 1–11

Multiple horns in unison:

Example X–12. Strauss, *Don Juan*, mm. 530–40

Example X–13. Mahler, *Symphony No. 1*, first movement, mm. 345–56

See also:

Brahms, *Symphony No. 4*, first movement, mm. 1–4
Dvořák, *Symphony No. 5*, fourth movement, mm. 132–36

Multiple horns in harmony:

Example X–14. Handel, *Judas Maccabaeus*, "See the Conquering Hero," mm. 9–16

Example X–15. Weber, Overture to *Der Freischütz*, mm. 10–25

Example X–16. Humperdinck, Overture to *Hänsel and Gretel*, mm. 1–8

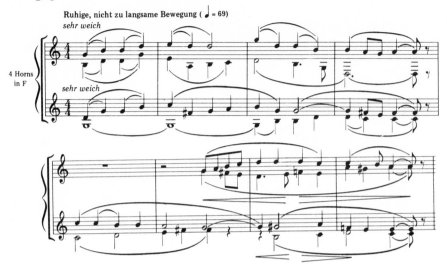

See also:

Mendelssohn, *A Midsummer Night's Dream*, Nocturne, mm. 72–80

Liszt, *Les Preludes*, mm. 69–73

Franck, *Symphony in D minor*, second movement, mm. 62–70

Wagner, *Tannhäuser*, Act I, scene 3, mm. 1–38

Mahler, *Symphony No. 1*, first movement, mm. 32–36

Muted and Stopped Horn,
Chiuso (*It.*), Bouché (*Fr.*), Gestopft (*Ger.*)

When the word *con sordino* is used, the modern horn player puts a mute into the bell. This mute changes the tone color of the instrument, but does not change the pitch. Here are two famous passages for muted horns, one soft and one loud. (The nomenclature for muting is the same as for strings.)

Example X–17. Debussy, *Prélude à l'après-midi d'un faune*, mm. 106–9

Example X–18. Mahler, *Symphony No. 4*, fourth movement, mm. 76–79

As soon as the mute is to be removed, either the term *senza sordino* or *open* must appear.

The *stopped horn* is one that is muted by inserting the right hand as far as possible into the bell to the throat, blocking much of the tone. This results in a soft but nasal and sharp sound. Stopped horn is used for single notes or soft passages. It is also effective when one wishes to have the horn play *sf > p*. The sign, as has been shown before for the stopping of a note, is a cross "+" above or below the note, with a "○" meaning open.

Here is an excerpt from *Capriccio espagnol* by Rimsky-Korsakov, in which he asks that the same passage be played open then stopped.

Example X–19. Rimsky-Korsakov, *Capriccio espagnol*, second movement, mm. 45–48

Another popular effect is called for with the French word *cuivre*, which means "brassy." It is obtained by greater-than-normal lip tension and harder blowing, causing the metal to vibrate.

Example X–20. Bizet, *L'Arlesienne Suite No. 1*, "Carillon," mm. 1–4

Some composers ask that a passage be played "Bells up" or "Bells in the air." In French this is marked *pavillons en l'air*, and in German, *Schalltrichter auf*. When this effect is asked for, the hornist turns the bell upward so the opening faces the audience. He also removes his right hand from inside and holds the bell up with it. Of course, this is for very loud and boisterous passages.

Example X–21. Mahler, *Symphony No. 4*, third movement, mm. 319–25

The glissando is used infrequently on the horn. As has been previously stated, it sounds best in the upper part of the range where the partials are closest together, and then only upward and in loud passages. There are a few examples of glissandi:

Example X–22. Strauss, *Der Rosenkavalier*, Introduction, m. 30

Example X–23. Barber, *Symphony No. 1*, mm. 135–36

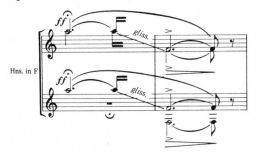

See also Stravinsky, *Le Sacre du printemps*, "Danse sacrale," mm. 152–56.

Phrasing, Tonguing, and Trills

All phrases under one slur will automatically be performed on one breath. As far as single-tonguing is concerned, we should make a distinct difference between two different kinds of articulations. We may call one regular, staccato, or hard-tonguing, and the other, soft- or legato-tonguing. The first would use the syllable *ta* as its tonguing articulation, the other, *da*. There are innumerable examples of these two kinds of single-tonguing. Here is an example of each:

Example X–24. Tchaikovsky, *Symphony No. 5*, second movement, mm. 8–16 (soft-tonguing)

Example X–25. Wagner, *Siegfried*, Act I, scene 2, mm. 1–14 (hard-tonguing)

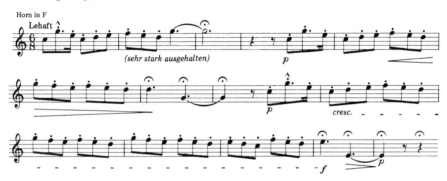

Single-, double-, and triple-tonguing are all possible. The following passage, because of its speed, would probably be double-tongued:

Example X–26. Rimsky-Korsakov, *Capriccio espagnol*, fifth movement, mm. 119–31 (double-tonguing)

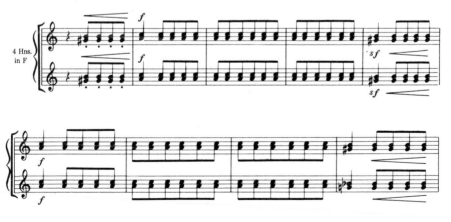

Example X–27. Strauss, *Don Juan*, mm. 501–5 (triple-tonguing)

Next, a rather simple instance of triple-tonguing of repeated notes in a soft dynamic:

Example X–28. Scriabin, *Poème de l'extase*, mm. 181–83

Trills on the horn are produced either with the valve or by the lips alone. They are a bit heavy and sluggish, but can have a comical or sardonic effect. The most successful are regular trills with the major or minor second above or below. Tremolos of intervals larger than seconds are also possible, but extremely difficult and risky. Here are some examples of these effects:

Example X–29. Strauss, *Till Eulenspiegel*, mm. 641–43

Example X–30. Strauss, *Salome*, 360, mm. 1–3

See also:

> Mahler, *Symphony No. 9*, second movement, mm. 13–15
> Chabrier, *España*, mm. 464–68
> Falla, *El Amor Brujo*, "Ritual Fire Dance," mm. 249–54

General Remarks

The horn is an excellent solo instrument as well as a successful doubler. Even though it has a mellower sound than the trumpet, it does possess enough brilliance and carrying power in loud passages to be heard over almost any combination of instruments. On the other hand, because of its velvetlike tone quality, especially in the middle register, four horns make for a wonderful "accompaniment choir" for any solo instrument. It has as much agility as any brass instrument and a distinctiveness of tone color that has always made it a symbol of heroism and individuality for many composers. Before leaving the subject, we should call attention to its dichotomous nature. Many composers have treated the horn as a woodwind instrument some of the time and a member of the brass section at other times. Traditionally it has been a member of the wind quintet as well as the brass quintet in chamber music, and this gives the horn unique status in that genre as well as in the modern symphony orchestra.

TRUMPET
Tromba *(It.)*, Trompette *(Fr.)*, Trompete *(Ger.)*

At first glance, it would seem that the history of the trumpet and trumpet playing closely parallels that of the horn. Like the horn, the early trumpet was valveless, resembling the bugles we know today. Their tone was brilliant, and, of course, the pitch depended on the length of the tube. However, during the Baroque period there was an extraordinary outburst of trumpet virtuosity—what we have come to call the art of clarino playing. The demands made upon the trumpet

The Trumpet family

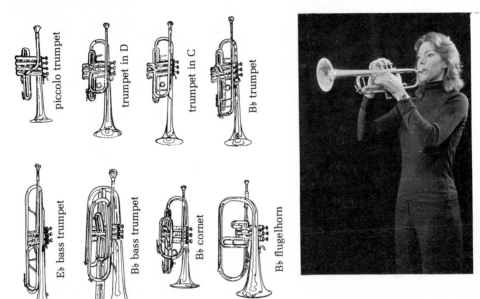

Barbara Butler, trumpet

rivaled those for the oboe and violin. Then, with the rise of the homophonic style in the early eighteenth century, the intricate, showy clarino playing virtually disappeared. In order to perform a diatonic melody required by the new style of the eighteenth century, the trumpet would have to be written in the highest register (the clarino register) and therefore sound extremely piercing and obtrusive. To prevent this unbalance, composers relegated the trumpet to a purely secondary role holding long tonic or dominant pedal notes, or playing in chordal passages during tutti sections. This practice continued into the nineteenth century, until the advent of the valve trumpet. Here is a typical clarino part by Bach and some later trumpet parts of Haydn, Mozart, and Beethoven:

Example X–31. Bach, *Cantata No. 51*, last movement, mm. 5–16

Example X–32. Haydn, *Symphony No. 94* ("Surprise"), fourth movement, mm. 249–68

Example X–33. Beethoven, *Symphony No. 3* ("Eroica"), first movement, mm. 37–45

Example X–34. Mozart, *Piano Concerto* K. 503, third movement, mm. 24–32

In solo literature there are some concertos, such as those by Haydn and Hummel, in which the trumpet's potential is exploited even after the Baroque period.

The range of the natural trumpet presents problems similar to the natural horn ranges. After clarino playing disappeared, the Classical composers seldom if ever wrote higher than the twelfth partial. For all practical purposes, the first two partials of the harmonic series were unplayable on all but the F trumpet, and even there the pitch was quite uncertain. So the composer had the following limited choices:

Example X–35

The seventh partial was always very flat and had to be adjusted by the embouchure, while the eleventh partial really lies between F♮ and F♯, and a major correction was needed. Of course, no "right hand in the bell" adjustment can be accomplished on the trumpet, so all of the pitch corrections depended on the player's skill in manipulating his lips.

Transpositions

The C trumpet is nontransposing and sounds as written. There are no alto-basso designations in the crooks for the natural trumpet, but four of the most popular of these instruments transpose up while three transpose down.

	Trumpet in	Sounds
	F	a perfect fourth up
	E	a major third up
Transposing up:	Eb	a minor third up
	D	a major second up
	C	sounds as written
	B	a minor second down
Transposing down:	Bb	a major second down
	A	a minor third down

As far as we know, these were the only trumpet crooks that were in use. There are works, however, that call for trumpet in G, trumpet in Ab, and others. For these transpositions the most popular crooks were used with adjustments made by the player.

The examples of typical Classical trumpet parts on pages 270–71 illustrate the limitations placed on the instrument by requirements of orchestral balance. Some very strange voice leadings resulted when trumpet notes were unavailable in certain chords, as illustrated by this most "unclassical" leap in the second trumpet part:

Example X–36. Beethoven, *Symphony No. 6*, fifth movement, mm. 219–23

The harmony goes from F major in mm. 219–20, to D minor in mm. 221–22, and to G major in mm 223. The unidiomatic skip of a major ninth is necessary because the C trumpet could not play or double any note in the D minor chord other than the fourth-line D.

On the other hand, Beethoven uses the trumpet most effectively with characteristic gestures, such as these two thrilling passages from the *Symphony No. 5* and that stunning fanfare in the *Leonore Overture No. 3*:

Example X–37. Beethoven, *Symphony No. 5*, second movement, mm. 147–58

Example X–38. Beethoven, *Symphony No. 5*, fourth movement, mm. 1–6

Example X–39. Beethoven, *Leonore Overture No. 3*, mm. 295–99

It is interesting to note that the natural horn was used in the orchestra of the Classical and early Romantic periods much more frequently than the natural trumpet, probably due to the horn's less piercing, mellower quality even in its higher registers. Berlioz in the *Symphonie fantastique* assigns rather uninspiring parts to the two trumpets, but gives rather interesting parts to two cornets, which had valves and were fully chromatic. Also, as shall be established later, these cornets were much mellower than trumpets because of their bore and because they are really descendants of the posthorn family, not the trumpet family.

Other natural trumpet examples:

Example X–40. Tchaikovsky, *Capriccio italien*, mm. 1–7

Example X–41. Mendelssohn, *A Midsummer Night's Dream*, "Wedding March," mm. 1–5

The Valve Trumpet

The earliest valve trumpets made their appearance around the middle of the nineteenth century. They were the old F trumpets, to which three valves had been added. Their playing range was from the third to the twelfth harmonic with all chromatic tones in between.

Example X–42. Range

The instrument has a very large and noble sound and a tendency to dominate the orchestra. This is both a virtue and a flaw, for the melodies written for the instrument by Mahler, Bruckner, Strauss, and others certainly sound most impressive on the F trumpet. Yet its tremendous carrying power tends to unbalance the normal brass section. Therefore, composers of the twentieth century have tended to avoid this "royal" instrument and opt for the smaller valve trumpets in C and B♭.

Here are some excerpts of passages for trumpet in F from the late nineteenth-century literature:

Example X–43. Bruckner, *Symphony No. 7*, first movement, mm. 233–41

Example X–44. Mahler, *Symphony No. 2* ("Resurrection"), first movement, mm. 192–97

Up until the middle of the nineteenth century, composers had notated trumpets in the key of the crooks. Later, most players performed these parts on the valve trumpet in F. Strauss, in his revision of Berlioz's *Treatise on Instrumentation*, suggests that the best procedure to follow in trumpet writing is to notate it in C, letting the player do the transposition on the F trumpet or any other instrument of his choice. Many composers, including Strauss himself, followed this advice. However, as the demand for a higher tessitura increased and the preference for a smaller yet more brilliant tone and greater agility prevailed, the smaller Bb and C trumpets became the standard instruments of the modern symphony orchestra.

The Modern Trumpet

The modern trumpet is a flexible, most agile instrument. It is fitted with three piston valves, not rotary valves like the horn.

Example X–45. Range

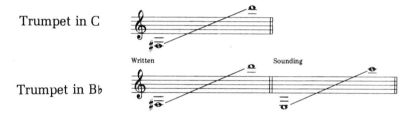

Example X–46. Register Characteristics for both C and Bb Trumpet

The following list shows fingering and easily available pitches in the seven valve positions:

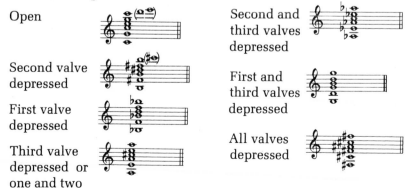

Open

Second valve depressed

First valve depressed

Third valve depressed or one and two

Second and third valves depressed

First and third valves depressed

All valves depressed

On the B♭ instrument these are the written pitches, but they sound a major second lower. All B♭ trumpets were equipped with a small slide to transform it to an A instrument, but it was found that the A slide was very unreliable as far as pitch accuracy was concerned, and therefore it was discontinued.

The C instrument is the smaller of the two standard trumpets of today. Some composers prefer it because it has a more brilliant and more focused sound. The B♭ trumpet is a bit "fatter" and richer and is most commonly used in bands and jazz groups, as well as in the symphony orchestra. In our time, Richard Strauss's admonition still rings true. No matter what instrument you ask for, the trumpeter will choose the one he finds most convenient for his use for a particular work. For instance, many professionals today own D trumpets and prefer to play certain high passages on that smaller instrument. On the other hand, most nonprofessional orchestra players own only B♭ trumpets and therefore have to transpose all their parts for that instrument.

Melodic Writing

The trumpet is the soprano member of the brass family and is often called upon to perform very high passages both loudly and softly. Of course, by its very nature the loud passage is much simpler to play than a *pianissimo* in the extreme high register. In the low register a *pianissimo* is also hard to control, and extremely loud notes, though not easy, are safer than soft ones. The middle register, from middle C to B♭ above the staff, is the most manageable, and all dynamics are possible and effective for professional players. However, a caution is appropriate: the nonprofessional trumpet player will have great difficulty controlling the soft dynamics almost anywhere in the entire range.

Here is a melody encompassing the entire range of the trumpet and showing its characteristics in different situations:

Example X–47. Copland, *Outdoor Overture*, mm. 16–31

See also:

> Schoenberg, *Five Pieces for Orchestra,* No. 2 (*Vergangenes*), mm. 129–31
> Shostakovich, *Symphony No. 5,* last movement, mm. 2–11
> Shostakovich, *Symphony No. 1,* second movement, mm. 113–16
> Bartók, *Concerto for Orchestra,* fifth movement, mm. 201–11

Muted Trumpet

Unless otherwise specified, the orchestral trumpeter will use a straight mute when a mute is called for. Muted passages are effective and very common in the literature. There are no special problems such as the ones faced by the horn. The mutes do not affect transposition, but simply change the tone color of the instrument. They certainly soften the instrument also. Here are some effective muted trumpet passages from the orchestral repertoire:

First, an example of the same passage open and muted:

Example X–48. Mahler, *Symphony No. 1,* fourth movement, mm. 623–25, and mm. 592–94 (the same passage, one-half tone lower and *con sordino*)

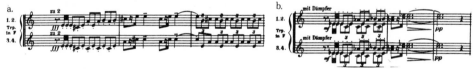

Example X–49. Debussy, *Nocturnes: Fêtes,* mm. 124–30

Example X–50. Gershwin, *Rhapsody in Blue*, mm. 16–19

See also:

> Bartók, *Concerto for Orchestra*, second movement, mm. 90–101
> Stravinsky, *Petrushka*, second tableau, mm. 33–39

Since there is no way the hand can mute the trumpet, horn effects like *cuivre* are quite impossible. The hand is used, however, to produce the jazzy "wa-wa" effect with the mute called by that name, and to manipulate a plunger which softens the instrument greatly. Other trumpet mutes used primarily by dance and theater orchestras are: the Harmon mute, bucket mute, solo tone mute, cup mute, and whisper mute. Many trumpeters have invented their own mutes, so the variants are constantly changing. Sometimes one sees the direction "into the hat" or "into the stand." This simply means that the player points the instrument into a plastic "hand hat" or plays very close to the stand.

The direction for using a mute is usually *con sordino* and *senza sordino* when the mute is to be removed. The German late Romantic composers frequently used the word *gestopft* (meaning "stopped"). The word *offen,* ("open") is a signal to resume the regular sound. The English word *open* has become as popular as the Italian *senza sordino* in recent times.

Phrasing and Tonguing

As in all wind and brass instruments, all slurred notes are performed on one breath, while all separate notes are tongued. The trumpet is no exception to this rule. It has been stated that the trumpet is the most agile of the brass instruments, and now one can add that it is the fastest speaking in the choir. All kinds of fast passages, both tongued and slurred, are possible and most effective; single-, double-, as well as triple-tonguing is in constant use on the trumpet.

Here are some passages to illustrate phrasing and various types of tonguing on the trumpet:

Example X–51. Verdi, *Aïda*, Act I, "Celesta Aïda," mm. 1–13 (triple-tonguing)

Example X–52. Puccini, *La Bohème*, Act II, opening (double-tonguing)

See also:

> Rossini, Overture, to *William Tell*, mm. 226–41
> Ravel, *Daphnis et Chloé Suite No. 2*, 203 , mm. 10–15
> Shostakovich, *Symphony No. 1*, first movement, mm. 1–8
> Bruckner, *Symphony No. 7*, third movement, mm. 77–88
> Dukas, *L'Apprenti sorcier*, mm. 606–15
> Rimsky-Korsakov, *Capriccio espagnol* third movement, mm. 37–41
> Strauss, *Till Eulenspiegel*, mm. 544–64
> Wagner, *Tannhäuser*, Act II, scenes 3 and 4, mm. 72–75, mm. 204–10

Trills

Trills on the trumpet are executed by means of the pistons, although some lip trills are possible in the high register. Some trills are awkward because they involve more than one piston. Those should be avoided if possible:

Example X–53.

Glissandi

The trumpet is sometimes asked to glissando. This is effective only in an upward direction and for the most part in the uppermost portion of the range, where the partials are close together. The player is also able to "bend" a pitch downward by a quarter or a half step. The latter is a new effect required only by later twentieth-century composers.

Example X–54

Auxiliary Trumpets

During this discussion, it has been mentioned that the trumpet in D is returning to frequent use. It is a brilliant, small instrument with a very piercing, bright tone. The technique and range are the same as the C and B♭ trumpets, but the low register (below middle C) is not very manageable. However, one should keep in mind that the D trumpet and its less-known sister, the E♭ trumpet, are usually used in the higher register.

Today, the D and E♭ piccolo trumpets are used to perform the clarino parts in the music of the Baroque masters. They are often joined by the B♭ piccolo trumpet, which transposes a minor seventh up and has an effective range from the B♭ below middle C to the A above the staff.

Example X–55. Range

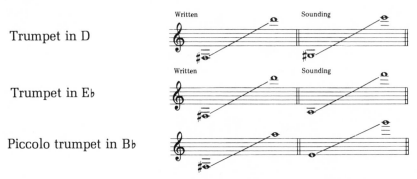

Trumpet in D

Trumpet in E♭

Piccolo trumpet in B♭

Here are some passages for these trumpets:

Example X–56. Stravinsky, *Le Sacre du printemps,* "Jeux des cités rivales," mm. 38–42

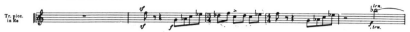

Example X–57. Britten, *Four Sea Interludes,* second movement, mm. 85–89

Example X–58. D'Indy, *Symphony in B-flat,* fourth movement, mm. 336–43

BASS TRUMPET

The bass trumpet is really a trombone with valves. It usually is played by trombone players using a trombone mouthpiece and is written in C, Bb, or Eb. The C and Bb instruments sound an octave or a major ninth lower than written:

Example X–59

The bass trumpet in Eb sounds a major sixth lower than written:

Example X–60

Here are some examples of the use of the bass trumpet:

Example X–61. Wagner, *Die Walküre*, Act III, mm. 12–18

Example X–62. Wagner, *Die Walküre*, Act III, Wotan's aria "Denn Einer nur freie die Braut," mm. 1–4

CORNET

Even though many composers since Berlioz have used the cornet, it has never become a regular member of the symphony orchestra. The instrument looks like a modern trumpet and has been standardized in B♭ (with the same range as the B♭ trumpet), but the tone and construction of the instrument make it a cross between a horn and a trumpet. It has a bore which is two-thirds conical and one-third cylindrical and is played with a cup mouthpiece. The tone is much more mellow than a trumpet, but less brilliant and heroic. It is ideal for folk music and military functions and is used a great deal in nineteenth- and early twentieth-century scores to announce long tunes. The instrument is very secure in pitch and has as much agility as the trumpet, and before the valve trumpet was accepted by composers, they wrote for cornets, which had valves from their inception.

The cornet is a regular member of the band and of many theater orchestras, especially in Europe. The trumpet, with its greater brilliance of tone and its ability to match the cornet in versatility, has for all practical purposes completely replaced the cornet in the orchestra.

Nevertheless, there are some wonderful cornet passages in the orchestral literature:

Example X–63. Tchaikovsky, *Capriccio italien*, mm. 232–40

Example X–64. Stravinsky, *Petrushka*, Ballerina's Dance, mm. 1–28

See also:

> Berlioz, *Symphonie fantastique*, fourth movement, mm. 62–69
> Prokofiev, *Lieutenant Kijé*, mm. 1–5

FLUGELHORN

The Flugelhorn sounds a major second lower than written:

Example X–65. Range

The Flugelhorn is a member of the bugle and cornet family. It is infrequently used in the symphony orchestra, but often in bands, wind ensembles, and jazz groups. The name comes from *Flügelmann* (wing man), the designation of the person who played the instrument and who marched in the front right-hand corner of the German military-band formation. The first Flugelhorns, manufactured in Austria between 1820 and 1830, retain the wide conical bore and the medium-sized bell of their antecedent, the keyed bugle. With the passing of time, however, manufacturers have narrowed the bore so that now the only difference between a cornet and a Flugelhorn is the latter's larger bell.

The most commonly used Flugelhorn today is in B♭ and shares the compass as well as the notation of the cornet. In former years there were Flugelhorns pitched in E♭, F, and C, but these are all outmoded today. The modern instrument has three valves and is played with a funnel-shaped mouthpiece which differs from that of the cornet by its greater width and depth. It has a very mellow and lush sound, perhaps closer to that of the horn than the cornet. As a matter of fact, there is evidence that in the early years of this century the Flugelhorn was at times substituted for the high horn performing the solo in the "Quoniam" from Bach's *B-minor Mass*.

Although the Flugelhorn is not often found in the symphony orchestra, there is a famous place in Stravinsky's *Threni* where the instrument is called for.

Example X–66. Stravinsky, *Threni*, mm. 89–99

TROMBONE
Posaune (*Ger.*)

John Marcellus, trombone

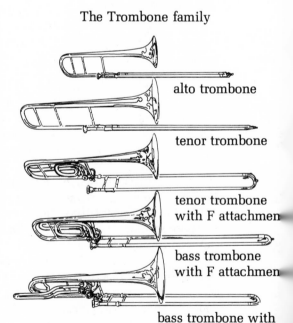

The Trombone family

alto trombone

tenor trombone

tenor trombone with F attachmen

bass trombone with F attachmen

bass trombone with F and E attachments

Although three kinds of trombones are still in general use today—the alto, tenor, and bass trombone—there are no great problems of instrument use and transposition to frustrate the composer or orchestrator. The trombone, as its name implies, is a big trumpet, and first appeared, very much as it is today, way back in the fifteenth century. The unwieldy length of tubing of a bass trumpet necessitated either winding it into coils or cutting some out. The tube was therefore cut into two U-shaped pieces, one of which slides into the other. This mechanism permits the player to change pitches by altering (lengthening or shortening) the length of the tube at will and with a great deal of precision. The reason that three trombones are used in the orchestra is one of compass (range) rather than transposition or construction.

The tube of the trombone is cylindrical for about two thirds of its length and becomes conical toward the bell, which is smaller in alto and tenor trombones and flares much larger in the bass trombone, to facilitate the playing of the lower partials.

Trombones have always been nontransposing instruments. The tenor and bass trombones are notated in the bass clef up to the G above middle C; then, to save ledger lines, the tenor clef is used. The alto trombone parts have traditionally been notated in the alto clef.

TENOR TROMBONE

Of the three versions of trombone, the tenor is the one most commonly used in the modern symphony orchestra. There are usually two tenor trombones in each orchestra, and, until recently, they have performed the music originally written for alto trombone as well as for the tenor. However, the alto trombone is making a comeback and is now being used in some of the nineteenth-century scores which called for it specifically. It is discussed below.

Example X–67. Range

Theoretically, the quarter notes in Example X–67 are possible, and many professional players can play them, but they are difficult and risky.

Example X–68. Register Characteristics

It is important to know the different positions of the slide of the tenor trombone, for each position lowers the pitch one half step from B♭ first position all the way down to E♮, the seventh and farthest position of the slide. In seventh position the slide is all the way out.

Example X–69

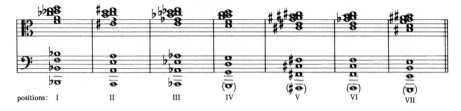

positions: I   II   III   IV   V   VI   VII

The fundamentals of each position are called the *pedal notes*. They are seldom called for in symphonic orchestral music, but do occur in solo trombone literature. Only the fundamentals of the first three positions are good; the others are possible, but difficult to control. In other words, the series for practical purposes begins with the second partial, from which point on, all tones are easily produced.

There are alternate positions available for many pitches; for instance, the D above middle C can be played in the fourth and seventh position, etc., but a few of the lower notes are available in only one position. Therefore, the following passage would be rather difficult at a fast tempo:

Example X–70

It continually alternates between the two extreme positions. It is not impossible but certainly difficult, especially for nonprofessionals.

There is no tuning slide as such on the trombone, but slight intonation adjustments can be made by moving the upper slide on the main body of the instrument.

BASS TROMBONE

The bass trombone is usually the third of the three trombones employed in our standard symphony orchestra. It is pitched a perfect fourth lower than the tenor trombone, so that its first position is the sixth position of the tenor. It is always notated in the bass clef, except for notes way above the staff, in which case the tenor clef is used.

Example X–71. Range

The reason the Bᵇ is in parentheses is that it cannot be played on the regular bass trombone unless the instrument has an E slide or E trigger. Most new bass trombones have this attachment and can therefore play the note. In this connection it is important to point out that the bass trombone is a tenor trombone with extra tubing and a rotary valve mechanism easily manipulated by the left thumb, which activates that extra tubing. This mechanism is called the F *attachment,* since it makes an F instrument out of a B♭ one. In other words, it is a double instrument like the double horn, and with the E trigger can even be thought of as a triple instrument. Many tenor trombones are double instruments and have the extra tubing as well as the F trigger, but the real bass trombones have a wider bell and bore and use a larger mouthpiece. The very newest instruments have a D attachment, which facilitates playing in certain keys even more. These attachments also make certain glissandi possible which were very problematical before the E and D attachments were invented.

Example X–72. Register Characteristics

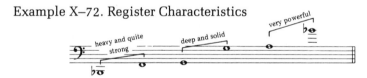

The positions of the bass trombone are:

Example X–73

Each fundamental note given here is the second partial of the series and has an entire harmonic series up to the tenth or twelfth partial above it, as well as an octave pedal note below it. The first four pedal notes are usable; after that, they are available to very few players.

ALTO TROMBONE

The alto trombone was used extensively throughout the nineteenth century, especially by German and Italian composers. It was also a solo instrument during the eighteenth century. Toward the end of the nineteenth century, most composers settled on two tenors and one bass, and the alto fell into disuse. However, many first trombonists today are once again using this instrument to play especially high tessitura parts and to perform the parts originally written for it.

The alto is pitched in Eb, and its first position is a perfect fourth above that of the tenor. It is always notated in the alto clef.

Example X–74. Range

The instrument has a narrower bore than its two cousins, and therefore the notes from 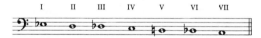 downward are weak and of poor quality. However, the high notes are pure, mellow, yet brilliant, although not as piercing as those of the tenor trombone. Here are the seven positions, with the first note again being the second partial of the series. The fundamental or pedal notes are not very feasible on this instrument, and of course the regular harmonic series to the tenth or twelfth partial is possible above the fundamental.

Example X–75

Phrasing, Tonguing

All tonguings, single, double, as well as triple, are possible and effective on all three trombones. One thing must be kept in mind: because the mouthpiece is large, fast tongue strokes are a little more difficult than on the trumpet. However, today we have such excellent performers that this is much less of a problem. The size of the instrument makes the articulation of the extreme low register a bit sluggish and a bit heavy.

A perfect legato can only be attained between two notes in the same harmonic series, but trombonists have perfected the coordination of soft-tonguing with change of position to give an almost per-

fect impression of legato playing. Even though Mozart did not
orchestrate the *Requiem*, we know that he liked the sound of the
trombone, and his pupil Süssmayr assigned the beautiful legato solo
in the "Tuba mirum" to a trombone. A skilled player can make it
sound like a cello.

Example X–76. Mozart, *Requiem*, "Tuba mirum," mm. 1–18

Here are some other characteristic examples of the orchestral uses
of one, two, three, or more trombones, using various articulations:

Example X–77. Beethoven, *Symphony No. 9*, fourth movement,
"Seid umschlungen," mm. 1–9 (1 trombone)

Example X–78. Berlioz, *Hungarian March*, mm. 96–105 (3 trombones)

Example X–79. Brahms, *Symphony No. 1*, fourth movement, mm.
47–51 (3 trombones)

See also:

Bach, *Cantata No. 118,* "O Jesu Christ, meins Leben Licht," mm. 1–8 (3 trombones)
Schumann, *Symphony No. 3,* fourth movement, mm. 1–8 (3 trombones)
Strauss, *Till Eulenspiegel,* mm. 546–53 (3 trombones)
Wagner, Overture to *Tannhäuser,* mm. 37–53 (3 trombones)

Glissando

The one effect still to be mentioned in this connection is the glissando. For the trombone the glissando is a "natural," for like a string player's glissando with one finger on one string, the trombone player quickly moves the slide between two notes. No purely slide glissando can be larger than a tritone, for that exhausts the positions.

Besides the slide glissando, there are two other types: the lip glissando and a combination slide and lip glissando. Thus, many glissandi which look improbable may be produced by one of these means.

The following glissando, first for the bass trombone, then for the tenor, is perfect, since it extends from seventh to first position.

Example X–80. Bartók, *Concerto for Orchestra,* fourth movement, mm. 90–91

The effect is humorous and bizarre and should be used sparingly in orchestral music, for it has become a cliché by now. However, there is another kind of glissando which is similar to that executed by the horn over the overtone series. It has not been used too often and is quite effective.

Example X–81. Bartók, *Violin Concerto,* third movement, mm. 593–600

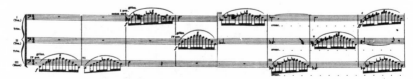

Mutes

There are several different kinds of mutes for the trombone (see pp. 250–52). Here are two examples from twentieth-century literature in which the muted trombone color is used. As with the horn and trumpet, the trombone mute changes the tone color of the instrument besides enabling the player to play very softly. The Sessions example is rather straightforward, but it is interesting to note that in the Berg *Violin Concerto* the trombones are doubled by cellos and basses playing the same notes *col legno*.

Example X–82. Sessions, *Symphony No. 2*, fourth movement, mm. 68–69

Example X–83. Berg, *Violin Concerto*, first movement, mm. 45–51

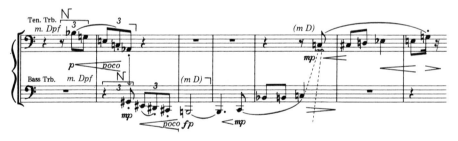

CONTRABASS TROMBONE

Wagner, Strauss, and Schoenberg are among the few composers who have called for the contrabass trombone pitched in B♭, an octave below the tenor trombone. Verdi, especially in *Falstaff*, also calls for such an instrument; however, in Italy it was a valved instrument, and, as with the "contra" parts by the German composers mentioned above, these are now played by the tuba. The contrabass trombone is much too taxing on the performer, and one is advised not to write for it anymore.

VALVE TROMBONE

This is an instrument that was built to apply the valve system rather than the slide system to the trombone. It made very little impact on the orchestra, but it did have some success in bands. It is actually a large trumpet, but the valve system presents severe intonation difficulties, and what a valve instrument might offer in facility and agility it loses in character. Today's composer is urged not to write for this instrument, since very few orchestral musicians own one.

General Remarks

The trombone as an orchestral instrument is extremely versatile. It can be used for solos, as well as to provide a warm harmonic background. As has been illustrated by the examples, it also works well as a contrapuntal partner both with other instruments and with other trombones. In subsequent chapters, we shall discuss its multiple uses as a doubler where its mellow tone and large dynamic range are exceptionally useful. All tonguings and articulations work well, and skips, no matter how wide, may be difficult, but are playable and most effective.

TUBA

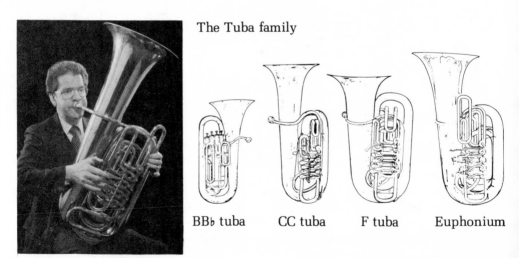

The Tuba family

BB♭ tuba   CC tuba   F tuba   Euphonium

Cherry Beauregard, tuba

The tuba as we know it today was not introduced into the symphony orchestra until around 1875. It was Richard Wagner who conceived of and wrote for an instrument which would have the sound characteristics of a horn yet be able to provide bass support for the trumpets and trombones. This instrument was to replace the ophicleide and a smaller tubalike instrument that had been used since the beginning of the nineteenth century. Wagner never did anything in a small way; instead of scoring for one bass tuba, he wrote for a whole family of them in *The Ring*. The tenor tubas were in B♭ and E♭, while the bass tubas were in F and double B♭ (an octave below the tenor in B♭). Not many composers other than Wagner, his contemporary Bruckner, and his disciple Richard Strauss adopted the family of tubas. Gradually, the bass tuba became a standard instrument in the modern symphony orchestra.

The modern performer may choose from five or six tubas which range from the B♭ tuba through the F, E♭, C, to the double B♭ tuba. The ones in C and double B♭ are the favorites of most symphonic tuba players today because they are comfortable with the fingering and are able to produce all the required pitches of the symphonic tuba repertoire.

All tubas are nontransposing, and the key or pitch designations only refer to the range, the fundamentals, and pedal notes. The instruments employ either piston or, more commonly, rotary valve systems and are constructed with a wide conical bore and a very wide bell. The player plays into a very deep cup mouthpiece, which facilitates sounding the low notes as well as the pedal tones.

The valve system is of the usual design with an added fourth valve which lowers the fundamantal a perfect fourth. There are tubas which have a fifth and even a sixth valve; however, these are rare. The tuba is always notated in the bass clef.

Example X–84. Range

It is important to reiterate that any tubist in any modern symphony orchestra will be able to perform within this rather large range. Many tubists own more than one instrument and will change to the instrument appropriate for the particular music they are called upon to play.

Example X–85. Register Characteristic

The tuba is the true bass of the brass choir and shares some of the characteristics of the double bass and contrabassoon. It gets much thinner and loses some of its characteristic quality as it goes toward its extreme upper register. The very low register is said to be weaker than the strong middle, but it has been this author's experience that if the low notes are used as slow-moving bass notes, they can be very well controlled, and they will be effective at any dynamic from *ff* to *pp*. Because of its size, the instrument speaks a bit sluggishly at the bottom of its range, but is refreshingly agile from its middle register to the uppermost notes.

It takes a great deal of breath to play this largest of all brass instruments, and special care must be exercised not to tire out the performer. Frequent rests are strongly recommended between passages.

The tone quality is very smooth and round, and because of the conical bore and the deep mouthpiece, it is not very piercing, and resembles that of the horn. The tuba blends well with the three trombones and provides an excellent bass for them. Further, it mixes beautifully with the trumpets and, of course, the horns. The power of its attack can best be understood by considering the following type of passage:

Example X–86

The next excerpt, from the beginning of Wagner's *Faust Overture*, exemplifies the opposite facet of the instrument's character. Here we see it capable of a smooth, lyrical, soft sound:

Example X–87. Wagner, *Faust Overture*, mm. 1–3

Naturally, it is more difficult to play softly in the higher register, but the next examples, though not extremely high, will show how well the tuba sounds in its middle to upper register.

Example X–88. Mahler, *Symphony No. 1*, third movement, mm. 15–23

We have already spoken of the tuba's surprising agility considering its size. Here are some samples of fast passages as well as one that asks for wide skips, which are as feasible on the tuba as on any other bass instrument.

Example X–89. Respighi, *The Fountains of Rome*, "La fontana di Trevi," mm. 28–35

Example X–90. Ravel, *La Valse*, mm. 3–14 after [68]

See also:

Strauss, *Till Eulenspiegel*, mm. 553–58
Shostakovich, *Symphony No. 7*, second movement, mm. 198–216

Now to one of the most famous solo tuba passages in all of the symphonic literature, which features the upper range of the tuba so very effectively.

Example X–91. Mussorgsky-Ravel, *Pictures at an Exhibition,*
"Bydlo," mm. 1–10

Trills have thus far seldom been used in symphonic literature for
the tuba; they are, however, very effective and can be manipulated
by the valves.

Example X–92. Wagner, Prelude to *Die Meistersinger,* mm. 158–65

As has already been shown in the examples above phrasing and
tonguing are similar on the tuba to every other brass instrument.
Slurring is obviously done on one breath, while single-, double-, and
triple-tonguing are all possible. Not much use has been found for
double- and triple-tonguing as yet in the standard orchestral literature. Fluttertonguing is also available, and this unusual example
shows a muted tuba executing very soft fluttertonguing:

Example X–93. Schoenberg, *Erwartung,* m. 426

A single type of mute is available. It is a bit awkward to put into
the bell and to remove. Time must be allowed for the player to
accomplish this Herculean feat. Here is a passage for muted tuba:

Example X–94

The tuba is a great doubler and can help reinforce the bass part both at a loud and soft dynamic. We have already seen many loud passages. Here is a soft one in which the tuba approximates a double-bass pizzicato:

Example X–95. Mahler, *Symphony No. 8*, first movement, mm. 250–52

In this century the tuba has been used in many capacities and has proven to be successful as a solo orchestral voice as well as in combination with other instruments. Many composers have written scores involving two tubas (Stravinsky, Schoenberg, Harris, etc.), usually to strengthen the bass of an oversized horn and trumpet section. Another reason for using two tubas in some of these scores is not to overtax the single tubist; therefore, one plays the high tessitura while the second covers the lower register. In bands, the Sousaphone with a strangely rearranged bell is popular, but since it is never used in a normal symphony orchestra, it will not be discussed here except to say that it is able to play all parts originally written for tuba.

EUPHONIUM OR TENOR TUBA

The euphonium has replaced Wagner's tenor tuba, and the parts originally written for the Wagner tubas are usually played on the euphonium, at least in America. In contrast to the Wagner tenor tuba, which was a transposing instrument, the euphonium is nontransposing and notated in the bass clef. When reading Wagner tubas in the treble clef, the player must transpose, because the pitches sound a major ninth below the written notes.

Example X–96. Range

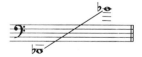

As can be seen, the euphonium has the same range as the bass trombone, but is constructed like a miniature tuba with a conical bore and a flared bell. It has four valves. The euphonium has a very mellow and smooth sound, and none of the pitch problems which for some reason always plagued the Wagner tubas. As yet, the euphonium is only used as a replacement for the tenor tuba, and very few orchestral composers have written specifically for it. On the other hand, it appears extensively in the band and wind ensemble literature, where it is used with or as a substitute for the baritone.

Here is a passage which, in this country at least, is performed mostly on the euphonium. It must be remembered that the transposition is a major second lower than written.

Example X–97. Strauss, *Don Quixote*, mm. 140–42

BARITONE

The baritone is strictly a band instrument; however, since it is so closely related to the euphonuim and sometimes substitutes for it, a general description is included here.

It has the range of the tenor trombone and manipulates its pitches with three valves.

Example X–98. Range

The baritone is very facile and blends well with all other instruments in the band. Some examples will be given in the chapter related to band scoring.

OPHICLEIDE

The tuba has completely replaced this instrument, which performed the bass brass parts throughout the nineteenth century. Mendelssohn, Schumann, Meyerbeer, Verdi, and many other composers used it. One of its last appearances was in Wagner's *Rienzi*. Besides the tuba, the bassoon or contrabassoon may at times be assigned the ophicleide parts.

As a matter of fact, this obsolete instrument resembled a metal bassoon, except that it had a conical tube which flared widely into a bell with a diameter of about eight inches across. The tube was pierced with large holes, covered by padded discs operated by keys similar to the bassoon. The mouthpiece was a bit more cupped than the horn's, and is said to have sounded quite mellow, similar to the modern euphonium. It was nontransposing and notated in the bass clef, so that its parts could easily be played by tuba or bassoon.

11

Scoring for Brass, and Brass Combined with Strings and Winds

The brass choir of the modern symphony orchestra contains some of the oldest instruments in existence, yet is the last of the major choirs to be fully emancipated. This is mainly due to the reluctance of many nineteenth-century composers to accept the mechanical advances in the construction of the trumpets and the horns. We can only speculate that Wagner and Brahms, who did use valve trumpets and horns in some works, preferred the sound of the natural instruments. Nevertheless, since the latter part of the nineteenth century, the brass choir has certainly gained wider acceptance, and the novice must be warned not to overuse this most powerful sound resource, for it can easily overshadow the rest of the orchestra. In order to learn how to use the brass section of the orchestra to greatest advantage, let us look at a series of examples illustrating its development from a solo choir in the Renaissance through its more selective uses in the Baroque period, its discreet appearance in the Classical and

300

early Romantic orchestra, and finally the late Romantic to twentieth-century's total liberation. Before we begin exposing the pragmatic history of the brass choir, let us cover some essential preliminaries.

It is not possible to establish any kind of pattern before the Classical period, in regard to number or kinds of brass instruments in common use. The doublings of the instruments depended on the size of the room and the availability of players in the Renaissance. In the Baroque, two or three horns were usually used, most often with three trumpets, and almost always coupled with timpani; the trombones were used in threes. This sounds like a large complement, but, except for some "battle pieces," outdoor works like Handel's *Water Music*, and a few operatic scenes, the brass were rarely if ever used all together. We have instances of them being used in the same work but usually in different movements. If one hears a Baroque work with trumpets, horns, and trombones playing in unison or octaves, it is probably an arrangement, not an original.

Once the orchestral section was established in the late Classical period, two horns, two trumpets, and three trombones were the norm, with the tuba added just a bit later. Then the section grew to four horns, with the rest of the complement remaining the same. This meant that a brass chord could contain nine different notes. When the brass section· expanded to four horns, three trumpets, three trombones, and tuba, as is usual today, eleven notes are available. In simple four-part chords, that means doubling. One way of viewing this doubling question is worth remembering: when the dynamic is *mf* or less, each brass instrument may be assigned a separate pitch and perform it successfully, depending on the register placement. If the dynamic is louder than *mf*, it is advisable to double the horns, meaning that two horns in unison equal the power of one trumpet or one trombone. That does not hold true if the trumpet is in a low register, but it is generally a good rule to keep in mind. Here are some successful chords scored for brass. The techniques of juxtaposition, interlocking, enclosure, and overlapping which were discussed in Chapter VIII (on pp. 219–22) also apply to the scoring of brass chords.

All the notes are at concert pitch:

Example XI–1

The major uses of the brass choir in the orchestra are:

1. as a homophonic unit;
2. to strengthen and clarify the harmony (The pedal technique of the Classical period is included under this rubric);
3. to state a melody;
4. as melodic doublers;
5. to build climaxes;
6. as independent voices in a contrapuntal setup;
7. for special effects (muted, jazzy, band, more contemporary sounds).

Before we discuss any of these normal orchestral functions, let us look at some typical Renaissance and Baroque uses, keeping in mind that the clarino style of trumpet playing was very much in vogue during these periods, as was the high register of the horn.

The interlude from *In ecclesiis* by Giovanni Gabrieli (1557–1612) was probably performed by three trumpets and three trombones. These may have been doubled and played from both balconies at St. Mark's in Venice.

Example XI–2. Gabrieli, *In ecclesiis,* mm. 51–67

A more "orchestral" example from the Baroque period is this noble opening of the *Fireworks Music,* by G. F. Handel. This is purely homophonic and resembles the Gabrieli, but with the three horns doubling the three trumpet parts. Later on in the work the two groups of brasses are used antiphonally in chorale style, similar to the opening. In this score all instruments are in C, but originally both horns and trumpets were in D and played in octaves, not unison.

Example XI–3. Handel, *Royal Fireworks Music*, Overture, mm. 1–19.

At the height of the Classical period, trombones were not included in most symphonies, although they were still standard in the opera and church orchestra. Beethoven waits until the final movement of the *Fifth Symphony* to introduce the trombones, which contributes to a tremendously climatic feeling. This is certainly a most effective use of the brass choir. When the brass is scored in this kind of a bombastic way throughout a work continuously, the resulting sound gets very tiresome, and robs the climactic passages of their full power and majesty. Notice how much more versatile the trombones are than the horns and trumpets, which get stuck on the tonic and dominant notes once the initial fanfare chord is over.

Example XI–4. Beethoven, *Symphony No. 5*, fourth movement, mm. 1–8

THE BRASS CHOIR AS A HOMOPHONIC UNIT

Now some passages to demonstrate the brass choir used homophonically both by itself or in combination, that is, doubled by the other two choirs.

First, we shall study two passages which present the brass in unison and octaves, a very strong and penetrating device.

In the third movement of Hindemith's *Nobilissima visione*, we have a most powerful presentation of the passacaglia theme by four horns (in F) with two trumpets (in C) in octaves, and three trombones doubling in unison. It is a "dark" doubling, since neither the trumpets nor the horns ever go too high. Only the trombones reach their upper range, which adds to the strength and nobility of the sound. Of course, the placement makes a difference. If Hindemith had wanted an extremely bright sound, he could have transposed it up a third or a fourth and had the trumpets and the horns at an extremely high register. The brilliance of this passage as it is scored comes from the unison of the horns and trombones rather than of blaring trumpets. In subsequent repetitions of the theme, Hindemith sometimes doubles the brasses with other members of the orchestra to give new colors. He saves the tuba to give fresh color in its presentation of the theme two octaves lower for the second variation at 34 .

Example XI–5. Hindemith, *Nobilissima visione*, third movement (Passacaglia), mm. 1–6.

In this original version of Bruckner's *Seventh Symphony*, a huge climax is reached in the last movement with the brass almost in unison with the rest of the orchestra, and lending tremendous weight. Notice how from mm. 188–212 the brass choir is doubled very irregularly by the strings or the woodwinds. When one hears the passage, the homophonic brass seems to be its major component, with the other instruments coloring some but not all the pitches. At m. 212 then, one measure is still in quasi-unison to recall the entire passage; thereafter, in m. 210 we finally build the climax with octaves. Study these measures carefully and remember that the tenor tubas are written in the "old-fashioned" system and therefore must be read: Bb tenor tubas a major ninth below, F tenor tubas a perfect twelfth.

Example XI–6. Bruckner, *Symphony No. 7*, last movement, mm. 188–235

Let us now examine some typical homophonic passages from the
literature. When any choralelike works are studied, the spacing,
voice leading, and doublings should be carefully noted. It is helpful
to use different colored pencils to note the doublings, and also, of
course, to make a piano reduction of a large brass ensemble in order
to ascertain which pitches are the essential ones and how these have
been doubled. Always be aware of the melody or melody notes the
composer wishes to stress, and *why*, as well as *how* these are made
to dominate.

In Stravinsky's *J. S. Bach Choral Variations*, a twentieth-century
master orchestrates a Bach Christmas carol.* The voice leading,
which is partially Bach's and sometimes Stravinsky's, is extraordinarily interesting. This is an example of extremely thick brass writing, perhaps simulating a combination stop on an organ. If played
well, it is most effective, but one has to take care that the last phrase
is not muddy. We shall look at another example from these variations later on, because if a composer is asked to transcribe music
from the Baroque era, he should realize, as Stravinsky did, that he
must think, feel, and hear his way back into the idiom.

* The choice of instruments for the chorale is reminiscent of the seventeenth-cen-
tury brass *Turm-Musik* by people like Pezel.

Example XI–7. Stravinsky, *J. S. Bach Choral Variations*, mm. 1–8

For a most impressive coda to "W.M.B." from Elgar's *Enigma Variations*, the brass again predominate in this powerful, choralelike ending. Study the doublings carefully and notice the octave and double-octave doublings so very effective in obtaining a massive sound such as this.

Example XI–8. Elgar, *Enigma Variations*, "W.M.B.," mm. 24–32

This is the famous opening of the last movement of *Pictures at an Exhibition,* "The Great Gate of Kiev." The important fact to notice here is that Ravel fills out and doubles the bass parts with two bassoons and a contra, leaving trombones I and II to play in their more brilliant range. Look at the original piano part, and see that the grace notes, which give greater emphasis to the bass of the piano, are disregarded in the orchestration, for they are superfluous given the strength of the tuba and contrabassoon. Strangely enough, the timpani, which usually supports the roots of the chords, gives us almost a pedal on Bb instead. This is an interesting detail and lends an introductory flavor to this chorale which is resolved when the winds come in at m. 13 and Eb is predominant.

Example XI–9. Mussorgsky-Ravel, *Pictures at an Exhibition,* "The Great Gate of Kiev," mm. 1–17

COMBINATIONS FOR MELODIC PRESENTATION

There are, of course, hundreds of examples in which brass instruments are used as soloists either alone or in combination. Some of these solos were excerpted in the previous two chapters, but we shall look at a few combinations that will implant new sounds in the orchestrator's ear. These are colors he may use whenever he wishes.

In the chapters on individual brass instruments, we saw some examples of a melodic nature for multiple trumpets, horns, and trombones. The presentation by four horns in unison, which is usually a brilliant, high concept, has become a favorite since Wagner, Mahler, and Strauss. At this point, we will quote the advice of that excellent composer and orchestrator, Gunther Schuller, himself a horn player. Often we curse the horn players for cracking at the climax of a wonderful passage. Here are two paragraphs from a fine little book, which shed some light on this problem:

> When more than one player attempts a high passage at a loud dynamic level, unless their intonation is perfect, a curious phenomenon takes place. The fractional intonational differences set up intense vibrations, vibrations so intense in the immediate vicinity of the players (they lose in impact at a wider range, which is why very few conductors become aware of this problem), that it becomes virtually impossible for any one of the players to sustain his note. That is the reason why one hears so many cracked notes in high register unison horn passages. It is therefore advisable to orchestrate such passages, whenever possible, for first and third horn alone, or to reinforce the two horns with one trumpet.
>
> The acoustical explanation of this disturbing phenomenon is that high notes on a horn create such intensely vibrating air columns, that another player's lips and instrument, if in the immediate vicinity, are *physically* affected. If the same unison passage were attempted with each player sitting ten feet apart, the problem would (for all practical purposes) be eliminated.*

On to some combinations:

1. Usually the horn and cello double on long sustained melodies. In Example XI–10 (p. 312), the solo cello is given added articulation by the horns doubling the single line. The staggered effect of the four horns adds four personalities to the solo cello. Notice that the horns are in F, but the notation in the bass clef is old-fashioned, meaning the written pitches sound a perfect fourth higher.

2. Example XI–11 (p. 313) illustrates the very common combination of trumpets doubling oboes or vice versa. Both have a sharp edge to their tone, and even though everything, including an organ, is playing, this doubling is powerful enough to break through.

3. In Example XI–12, we have a most popular doubling of trombones with bassoons, violas, cellos, and double basses. The trombones contribute great power to this tutti, and at the same time, by dropping out two trombones and leaving only the third to bolster the lower strings, Schubert orchestrates a beautiful diminuendo.

---

*Gunther Schuller, *Horn Technique* (Oxford University Press, 1962), pp. 82–83.

Example XI–10. Strauss, *Don Quixote*, mm. 189–93

Example XI–11. Weinberger, *Polka and Fugue*, mm. 185–91

Example XI–12. Schubert, *Rosamunde*, Entr'acte I, mm. 106–23

4. Another most powerful combination of trombones, horns, bassoons, and lower strings to present the "national anthem" against a very heavy orchestration of the counterpoint.

Example XI–13. Tchaikovsky, *1812 Overture*, mm. 386–98

5. This excerpt could also have been presented with the contrapuntal examples, but it is felt that the effectiveness of the canon is due more to the color contrasts than to any other musical parameter.

Example XI–14. Berlioz, *Roman Carnival Overture*, mm. 298–331

6. Here is an interesting strengthening or darkening of the bass by the tuba to give a heavy feeling to this unusual beginning of the third movement.

Example XI–15. Prokofiev, *Symphony No. 5*, third movement, mm. 1–3

7. This mysterious opening presents a tuba solo doubled by bass clarinet and bassoons, but with two different articulations. While the winds are slurred, the tuba is asked to articulate every note.

Example XI–16. Wagner, *Siegfried*, Prelude to Act III, mm. 1–7

8. Tuba plus trombones, bassoons, cellos, and basses constitute one of the most powerful combinations in the symphony orchestra.

Example XI–17. Liszt, *Les Preludes*, mm. 405–10

9. Before leaving the question of combinations, let us look at an extraordinary spot in *Lohengren* where the strings at first double the "chorale" in the trumpets, trombones, and tuba, then the winds take over the doubling, leading to a diminuendo and a gorgeous *pianissimo*.

Example XI–18. Wagner, *Lohengrin*, Prelude to Act I, mm. 50–58

Some other interesting combinations can be found in Prokofiev's *Lieutenant Kijé*, "Troika," ⑤1, mm. 1–8, Stravinsky's *Pulcinella*, ⑧5–⑨4, Copland's *Appalachian Spring* ⑤9–⑥1, and many others.

CLIMACTIC USE OF THE BRASS

Everyone is familiar with the use of brass as an element of climax, but composers have used a variety of ways to achieve this ultimate climactic entrance of the brass. Study the following examples carefully to learn the various techniques:

1. One of the most successful ways of building climaxes is by holding back in order to save a certain color for a specific event. We have already discussed this in previous chapters. In this marvelous example, Schubert uses the trombones to introduce the closing theme, leading to the development section, and again to close the recapitulation and lead to the coda. Up to this truly mysterious moment the task of the trombones has been to double lines or to sustain chords. Here they offer an entirely new sound color, adding clarity to the moment and to the entire form of the movement.

Example XI–19. Schubert, *Symphony No. 9*, first movement, mm. 198–231

2. Here we have a situation where the alternation between choirs leads to a climax not by the brass but by the rest of the orchestra plus horns in their woodwind capacity. Franck calls for trumpets as well as piston (valve) cornets, but the latter are usually performed on trumpets in the modern symphony orchestra.

Example XI–20. Franck, *Symphony in D minor*, third movement, mm. 74– 88

3. Tchaikovsky was a master climax builder; although many criti-
cize him for often overdoing this effect, he knew the technique, and

Example XI–21. Tchaikovsky, *Symphony No. 4,* first movement,
mm. 277–90

we should profit from this. He has already reached a big climax in m. 278, where he reintroduces the opening flourish for the third time, except with a new agitated string counterpoint. This suddenly breaks off, and the strings dwindle down to the cellos and basses only. Suddenly a huge tutti begins the recapitulation of the movement, and the composer adds, besides the timpani roll, a powerful new thematic element (*cantus firmus*) against other previously heard contrapuntal fragments.

There are almost as many instances of this effect as there are works in the orchestral repertoire, and we shall examine some others in Chapter 14.

CONTRAPUNTAL BRASS WRITING

We turn now to some examples of contrapuntal brass writing. In Renaissance music and in the works of some later composers (Handel and Berlioz, in particular), the antiphonal effect was often used, but we shall limit ourselves to other kinds of imitation and freer contrapuntal writing.

1. In Variation IV of this work, Stravinsky orchestrates with trumpets, trombones, flutes, and bassoons in a simulation of the Baroque style, while the violas, cellos, and bassoons double the chorus. Even though the trumpets are not too high, they play a clarino-type part.

Example XI–22. Stravinsky, J. S. Bach *Choral Variations*, Variation
IV, mm. 1–6

2. Here is a most effective fugato for the entire brass choir, which
ends with the brass punctuating the theme as presented by the timpani. Notice that all the instruments are in their very best registers,
so that the subject comes through clearly every time it is played. The
punctuation at * is a most common use of the brasses, a favorite
device of Hindemith and many other composers as well.

Example XI–23. Hindemith, *Symphonic Metamorphoses*, second
movement, mm. 158–88

3. One of the best known and most quoted brass passages in twentieth-century orchestral literature comes from the first movement of this work. The fugato is presented by the trumpets and trombones, then inverted by the horns plus the entire choir. Here again, as in many examples that we have studied, the composer equates the strength of two horns in unison with that of one trumpet or one trombone. The effect of the stretto from m. 363 to m. 386 is especially thrilling.

Example XI–24. Bartók, *Concerto for Orchestra*, first movement, mm. 313–87

4. We end this section on the brass choir with an incredible passage from the first of Schoenberg's *Five Pieces*. All brasses are muted (straight mutes), and all are expected to play loud, except for the *ffpp* at m. 73, culminating in the fluttertongue. Notice the wonderful independence of the trombones against the trumpets and winds and the exuberant horn calls. The fluttertongue at the end is quite a surprise after all that counterpoint.

Example XI–25. Schoenberg, *Five Pieces for Orchestra*, No. 1, "Premonitions," mm. 57–77

Schoenberg was an extraordinary orchestrator who gave very significant parts to previously neglected members of the orchestra, such as the tuba, double bass, contrabassoon, even mandolin. In studying orchestral techniques of our century, no one should overlook such valuable scores as Schoenberg's *Gurrelieder,* the opera *Erwartung,* and certainly the *Five Pieces for Orchestra.*

JAZZ EFFECTS AND NEW TECHNIQUES

Again, as in the discussion of the other choirs, we come to that open-ended portion of brass-choir effects that are rather new and even more personal than the mere selection of an individual instrument. Let us examine three pieces which use rather common jazz elements in the orchestra and a rather recent work that utilizes the Harmon mute in a contemporary orchestral setting.

1. This is so well known that it needs little comment, save to say that the wa-wa mute is used for trumpet as well as trombone.

Example XI–26. Gershwin, *Rhapsody in Blue* (original version for the Whiteman Band), mm. 131–37

2. Gershwin's major contribution was in the field of jazz, and when he wrote music for the concert hall, he naturally transferred his ideas to his legitimate scores. In Example XI–27, we have a solo by the trumpet to be played "In hat with felt crown." Notice also the *sf* ⟩ *p* muted effect that introduces the solo and is so common today.

3. Example XI–28 contains an effect which comes from jazz but is often used in contemporary scores to point up a final *sff.* The way it is performed is for the players to "lip and tongue hard" into the note with a slight slur from below. At this point it makes the common attack on the next note a real *forte* after the excitement of the *sff.*

Example XI–27. Gershwin, *Concerto in F*, second movement, mm. 31–44

Example XI–28. Gould, *Interplay*, fourth movement, 5 mm. before 21

4. A great deal of new brass technique can be learned from this brief excerpt. The composer uses two symbols for the mutes: ⋀ = straight mute, ⏀ = harmon mute. The ○ means an open harmon mute, while + is the sign for closing it with the stem. We also see the n at the beginning of a pitch; this means that the composer wishes to have the note begin from *niente* (nothing), or in some cases go to n, *niente*. Notice that some instruments are open and some closed. This score is meticulously marked, and that is exactly what one must do, especially if the players have a great many instructions with which to cope. The brass and the other choirs are treated with equality, and the writing in this work is a testament to the complete emancipation of the brass choir in our time.

Example XI–29. Druckman, *Windows*, mm. 4–10

12

The Percussion
Ensemble

The range and variety of percussion instruments in use today defies description or categorization. Composers invent new effects, and as fast as they can describe them, percussionists with uncanny skill build an instrument capable of producing them. The present state of the percussion ensemble is, therefore, an open-ended matter.

Percussion instruments have been with us since the dawn of mankind, especially in the highly developed folk cultures of the Far East and Africa. Only in the past century has the composer of concert music become aware of their expressive potential. During the seventeenth and eighteenth centuries, a few percussion instruments stemming, as one author puts it, from "Turkish military music," were extensively used in operatic scores. These included snare drums, triangles, cymbals, and small gongs, plus castanets and tambourines adopted from the Mediterranean region. A few other instruments put in rare appearances in toy symphonies, and Bach includes a bell as the symbol of the tolling death knell in his cantata *Schlage doch gewünschte Stunde.** The timpani became fashionable in King Henry

---

* According to the musicologist, Gerhard Herz, this cantata is not by Bach, but by Melchior Hoffman. Since music publishers have not kept up with music scholarship, we retain the old attribution for ease of access to the score.

Some of the prominent members of the percussion family.

VIII's time, and Purcell was the first major composer to realize the possibility of using cavalry drums for orchestral purposes. These drums had been imported from Germany for army use, and eventually became the basis for the modern timpani or kettledrums.

REVIEW OF CATEGORIES

There are several ways of catagorizing this large "kitchen" of instruments: by the way they produce the sound; by the material of which they are made; or by their native origins. For our purpose, we shall follow the first alternative along the lines suggested by Kurt Sachs in his history of musical instruments. The four categories are: idiophones, membranophones, chordaphones, and aerophones. Each broad group will then be divided into:

1. instruments of definite pitch;
2. instruments of indefinite pitch;
3. instruments which, even though considered of indefinite pitch, can be tuned to approximate pitches.

I. *Idiophones* produce their sound by the vibration of the entire body of the instrument. Triangles, cymbals, wood blocks, etc., are such instruments, but there are some, like marimbas, vibraphones, and chimes, which are constructed of several vibrating bodies combined into one instrument. In order to produce a sound on an idiophone, any one of a number of techniques may be employed: They may be struck, scraped, shaken, or stroked.

II. *Membranophones* produce their sound by the vibration of a skin or membrane tightly stretched and fastened over a resonating shell or tube. The resonator may be open at one end (bongos, tambourine, etc.) or completely closed, as in the case of the timpani. Some mebranophones, such as snare, tenor, and bass drum, have two membranes. One of them is struck while the other vibrates "in sympathy." Membranophones are also usually struck with some kind of a beater or by the hand to produce the vibration, hence the sound.

III. *Chordaphones* produce their sound by the vibration of their strings when struck. The sound is amplified by a resonator, which may be a case, a board, a box, or a combination of these. All chordaphones are tuned instruments. The piano, harpsichord, etc., will be discussed in a separate keyboard chapter, although they are usually considered percussion instruments when used in the modern symphony orchestra as members rather than soloists. On the other hand, the cimbalon, which does not exactly conform with the other keyboard instruments, will be covered in this chapter.

IV. *Aerophones* produce their sound by causing an air column to vibrate within an enclosed body, like woodwind and brass instruments. All kinds of whistles, sirens, and machines (like the wind machine) are included in this category. While all have definite pitch, their pitch is not always specified.

Today, electronic techniques and instruments are used to amplify and distort many percussion instruments, such as the echoplex, and even synthesizers are considered part of the percussion ensemble. These will be discussed briefly at the end of this chapter.

Idiophones and membranophones will be subdivided into pitched and nonpitched classes, but it is very important to understand the concept of definite pitch in relation to all percussion instruments. The dividing line between definite and indefinite pitch is not at all well defined. The inharmonic (meaning discordant) partials and the noise factor of a definitely pitched percussion instrument are at times so pronounced that our ear often tolerates deviations from the prescribed pitch which we would never accept from other instruments of the orchestra. Richard Strauss, in his revision of Berlioz's *Treatise,* calls attention to several "out-of-the-harmony" pitches assigned to the timpani by such composers as Beethoven and Verdi, where retuning to the correct pitch was impossible because there was not enough time. Nonetheless, if the pitches were close to the "required" one (a second away), the entire chord was played over the "wrong" timpani note. Although neither Strauss nor any of us today would advocate this practice, especially on the precisely tuned contemporary timpani, it proves how deceptive the actual pitch of a definitely pitched percussion instrument can be. On the other hand, the nonpitched instruments and those with approximate pitches, such as high, medium, and low, blend in with the definite pitches around them in the orchestra, pick up fundamentals which make them consonant contributors to the chord, and give the lie to the notion that nonpitched percussion instruments are simply "noisemakers."

Notation

Even though many attempts have been made to standardize percussion notation or even to agree on a symbolic designation for each of the many instruments, such agreement has not as yet been reached. A helpful suggestion would be that the notation should show in the clearest possible manner what the performer is to play. If symbolic designations are contained in a score, the composer must explain these both in the score and at the beginning of the part, so that the player can easily identify them. Otherwise, it is incumbent on the composer to label the various instruments as they occur in the work by their full names or appropriate abbreviations. In this rather brief study of the great variety of percussion instruments, the symbol for each will be given, and a short example provided to illustrate the notation.*

Number of Percussion Players

In symphonic circles the timpani are considered separate members of the percussion section. The reason for that is probably the longevity of the timpani as a regular member of the orchestra and the fact that the timpanist always plays that instrument only. The other percussionists play a variety of instruments, and there is usually one "chief percussionist" who will assign the parts. Those of us who are not percussion players often misunderstand what it takes to "choreograph" a piece so that all the instruments are covered and no human clashes or accidental noises mar the performance. To decide whether one, two, three, four, or even five percussion players are needed to perform a work, one should first write it all out and then make that decision based on several questions:

---

*For the best possible thinking on the subject, see Kurt Stone, *Music Notation in the 20th Century* (W. W. Norton, 1980), pp. 205 ff.

1. Is there enough time for one player to "cover" several instruments at a time? For example, if this one player has to switch from a mallet instrument to one with wooden sticks, does he have enough time?

2. How many percussion instruments can one person play simultaneously? Could one of these players cover two or more instruments at a time?

Try to be as economical of personnel as possible, but consult often with an experienced percussion player before making a decision, remembering that the timpanist should not be counted on to take over any percussion parts other than his own, even though he may have time to do so.

General Remarks

Each instrument of the percussion ensemble will be briefly described and the method of performance presented. Then one or two passages will be provided which show its notation and basic playing characteristics and techniques. A picture will also be provided for each instrument, and those most commonly used in the symphony orchestra will receive a little more in-depth treatment. At the end of the chapter, an extensive list of works that use a great variety of percussion instruments will be included, while an exhaustive list of books dealing with these instruments can be found in the appendix.

One word of caution before proceeding with our discussion. There are many percussion instruments, especially the mallet, pitched idiophones, which are manufactured in various sizes and therefore have different ranges. The composer should always choose the size he needs and leave the procuring of the proper instrument to the performing organization. Within reason, percussionists, being the newest members of the "orchestra club," are usually most happy to oblige the composer.

IDIOPHONES

Instruments of Definite Pitch: Mallet Instruments

XYLOPHONE (XYL.) X

The xylophone was the first mallet instrument to find a permanent place in the orchestra. It consists of a set of wooden bars of varying lengths arranged in the form of a piano keyboard. Up until recently, xylophones had no resonators below each of the wooden bars. Today most of them have these resonators to give added body to the very dry, hard, brittle sound of the instrument. The single notes are of a very sharp articulation and have very little sustaining power. If a note is to be sustained, the player must roll it with two mallets. The most successful passages are therefore rapid or single notes, which give a sharp edge of brilliance to similar passages played by other instruments in the orchestra at the same time. These effects are like sharp *pizzicati*. Trills, *arpeggios*, and *glissandi* are also extremely effective.

Xylophone parts are notated on a single staff in the treble clef. Some composers prefer to write xylophone parts at pitch, while others notate them an octave lower than they sound. An indication of the procedure followed should appear in the part. There are several models of the instrument with the following ranges: (All three sound an octave higher than notated.)

Example XII–1

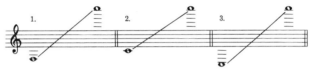

The last model is not always available, but the player can compensate by transposing the notes not found on a given instrument into another octave quite successfully.

Mallets

Usually only two mallets are used by the xylophonist, one in each hand. For loud playing, hard wooden, ebonite, or hard rubber and plastic mallets are used; for soft playing, yarn mallets are used. The instrument is most brilliant and piercing in the top register, but has great power to cut through the orchestra at all registers if the right mallets are used. While the composer should specify the type of mallets by the words "hard, medium, soft" for all mallet instruments, the actual type and construction material of the mallet should be left to the choice and discretion of the performer.

Example XIII–2

MARIMBA (MRB.) M

The marimba is a direct descendant of the xylophone. Though sounding an octave lower than the xylophone, it has the same compass of four octaves and looks very much like its ancestor. The rosewood bars are of course graduated, but thinner, longer, and wider than the xylophone's, and the resonators have always been part of its construction. The playing technique is exactly like the xylophone's, but its mellower, deeper sound has generated a different kind of music. Most marimba players use two mallets in each hand (a few even manipulate three in each hand), which makes it rather easy to roll the larger chords characteristic of the marimba repertoire. Composers have written extensively for this instrument only since 1950, but it is now coming into its own as part of the contemporary orchestra.

The size and range of the marimba is fairly standard, and there are no transposition problems. The music may be notated on one or two staffs, in either the treble or bass clef. All the mallets that are successful on the xylophone can be used on the marimba.

Example XII–3. Range (sounds as written)

(The range of some marimbas goes down to A or even F.)

The lower register of this instrument is unique, and especially beautiful, while the farther up one goes, the closer the marimba tone resembles the xylophone.

Example XII–4

VIBRAPHONE (VIBS) V⊐

The vibraphone is essentially an American invention, vaguely related to the glockenspiel because of its metal bars. It is the only mallet instrument that uses vibrato or tremolo produced by an electrically driven series of fans located on top of the resonator tubes.

The graduated metal bars are arranged in keyboard fashion and can be played with the motor on or off. If the motor is off, there is no added vibrato, and the tone sounds very much like a struck tuning fork, pure and metallic, with a limited sustaining span. When the motor is on, the pitch vibrates and comes alive with a great deal of sustaining time. The motor's speed can be controlled so that a tone can vibrate very slowly or very quickly. There should be precise instructions regarding the motor—off, on, speed—in both the score and part.

Another device that helps sustain and then dampen the pitch is a pedal operated by the foot. When it is depressed, the tones ring; when it is released, the pitches are dampened. The composer should indicate his intentions for the use of this pedal by writing *l.v.* (let vibrate) over a note or chord and show how long it is to be sustained. Chords of four or even six notes are possible; trills, glissandi, and fast passages are, of course as effective on the vibrophone as on the xylophone and marimba; however, the nonrolled sustained pitches or chords give this instrument its unique sound.

Example XII–5. Range (sounds as written)

There are three sizes of vibrophones, the first and third of which are available in most professional organizations.

A variety of mallets is available, including hard and medium chord mallets; plastic and wooden mallets are used rarely, but yarn mallets are common for soft passages, and wire brushes are very effective in glissando effects.

Example XII–6

ORCHESTRA BELLS (O.B.) G

The German name for this instrument is the one most commonly used. The glockenspiel consists of two rows of steel bars arranged in a keyboard. These highly tempered steel bars are mounted on a frame and attached to a portable case. It is the oldest of all the mallet percussion instruments, and we find numerous passages in nineteenth-century music.

It is a transposing instrument always sounding two octaves above the written pitch unless otherwise specified, but there are some composers (Schoenberg, for one) who insist on notating it at pitch. The glockenspiel comes in only one size.

Example XII–7. Range (sounds two octaves higher than written)

This instrument is usually played with only two mallets, although some performers use a two-mallets-per-hand technique. The glockenspiel is the only instrument for which a brass mallet should be used. This gives the loudest and most sonorous results. Other mallets, such as wooden, plastic, or hard mallets, give less of a ringing and more of a "clicking" sound, while the harder yarn mallets enable the performer to play quite softly. The glockenspiel has the power to be heard above a whole tutti orchestra, especially in its upper register, and even though it has the capacity to sustain pitches longer than the xylophone and the marimba, one can slow the process of decay and add a bit of vibrato by waving one's hand back and forth close to the bars after they are struck.

Example XII–8

CHIMES (CHM.) ⫿⫿⫿

The chimes of the orchestra are often called tubular bells. They are a series of cylindrical brass tubes of varying lengths hung on a wooden or metal rack and arranged chromatically. Some come in sets of eighteen, but most American orchestral tubular bells consist of twenty bells. They sound as written.

Example XII–9. Range

The sound simulates that of a church bell and has the same "out-of-tune" quality. The set has a sustaining pedal, which is operated by the right foot. Chimes are effective in soft as well as loud passages. If a soft sound is desired, the player uses a rawhide mallet and may even cover it with a cloth. For louder sounds the rawhide mallet, which actually looks more like a hammer than a mallet, as well as wooden and metal mallets are used. Faster passages convey the impression of many church bells ringing at once, especially if the sustaining pedal is depressed. The glissando is also practical but should not be overused. It is good policy not to write more than two simultaneous pitches at once, although some composers have asked for two players, each of whom plays two notes to form a four-note chord.

Example XII–10

CROTALES

Crotales are a set of small metal discs, three to five inches in diameter. They may be mounted on a wooden board shaped like a piano keyboard or held by a leather strap. A metal mallet is always used to play them, but when hand-held, they may also be struck together like cymbals. These pitched discs should not be confused with finger cymbals, which are idiophones of the indefinite pitch variety. The crotales are thicker and are tuned in a chromatic scale. As far as available pitches are concerned, two kinds of crotales exist. The lower set, which is rare, ranges from middle C to the B♮ above. The more popular set contains the pitches from fourth-space C to the C above the staff. All pitches sound two octaves higher than notated; in other words, the transposition resembles that of the glockenspiel. It is significant to note that crotales actually sound very similar to the glockenspiel, but have a less piercing and more defused sound when struck together. When struck by a metal mallet, the tone quality greatly resembles that of the glockenspiel.

Example XII–11. Range

A metal mallet is used for best effect, but wooden and plastic models can also be used, although they do not have as great a sustaining power. The practice of waving one's hand to and fro over the disc to sustain the sound is sometimes used; also, when the discs are held by their leather handles after they have been manually struck together, they can be shaken to keep the sound alive.

Example XII–12

General Remarks

Before proceeding to some instruments which are important but rarer than the principal idiophones of definite pitch already discussed, here are a couple of techniques which are now employed and are very effective:

1. Use a cello or bass bow for the performance of the vibraphone (on the end of the key) and the crotales (on the edge). The vibraphone sound is especially effective with the motor on and the sustaining pedal depressed.

Example XII–13

2. While there are innumerable techniques with different mallets, the "dead sound" which can be achieved on the xylophone, marimba, and vibraphone by striking the bar and leaving the mallet

on it is most interesting. This gives a nonvibrant (muffled staccato) color and is especially useful when one of these instruments is featured as soloist or is lightly accompanied.

Example XII–14

MUSICAL SAW

For a long time this was a folk instrument made from an ordinary saw. Now it is manufactured with a finely tuned steel blade, without teeth, fixed to a wooden handle. The instrument is held between the knees; the left hand holds the extremity of the blade, while a violin bow is drawn across the edge to produce the sound. The player has no fingering to fall back on; he simply curves the blade in a certain way to obtain the pitches. There is a very pronounced vibrato to every pitch and a glissando between all the pitches. The musical saw is most suited to singing, sustained lines, and even though not as focused, the sound is very much like that of a bowed vibraphone with the motor tuned up to the highest degree of vibrato.

Example XII–15. Range

Example XII–16

FLEXATONE

This instrument sounds very much like the musical saw, but works on a slightly different principle. A thin, triangular-shaped blade is fixed at its base into a metal frame with a handle. The unattached end of the blade is near the handle, so it can be flexed by the thumb to adjust intonation. Curved steel springs are fixed to each side of the blade with a soft ball fastened to each of the free ends. When the player shakes the instrument, the ball strikes the blade and makes the sound which is adjusted by the thumb. It is a high-pitched sound with much tremolo although single shorter sounds can be produced. It is best not to specify exact pitches, but let the instrument "fit into" the approximate ones.

Example XII–17. Range

Example XII–18

CRYSTAL GLASSES

The musical saw, the flexatone, and crystal glasses all have a kind of "electronic" sound and have been very successfully used since World War II by such composers as Crumb, Schwantner, Mayuzumi, Kagel, and Haubenstock-Ramati. These glasses are simple crystal goblets of various sizes which produce beautifully pure pitches. They can either be struck or more commonly stroked around the rim with wetted fingers to give a long, singing tone. The practice of using glasses as musical instruments is quite old. It goes as far back as Gluck, and its close relative, the glass harmonica, an instrument made of glass bowls, was of great interest to Mozart and Beethoven.

Some composers today, instead of requiring set pitches for the glasses, simply ask for low, medium, and high, or in the case of Haubenstock-Ramati's *Les Symphonies de timbres*, four glasses—soprano, alto, tenor, and bass. In addition to glasses, porcelain bowls, glass bottles, and flasks have all been utilized.

Example XII–19

STEEL DRUMS

This is a misnomer, for a steel drum is not a drum at all, but the top portion of a large oil can—a metal head on a metal shell. It is a beautiful-sounding instrument of Caribbean origin. The top is heated until it is slightly concave; then it is incised into sections, each of which is tuned to a different pitch by hammering to the appropriate indentation. The sound is produced by striking the different pitches or sections with a soft mallet. It resembles a metallic, ringing marimba, and a number of these instruments are usually played by a group of players called a steel band. One may play the melody while the others provide the harmony. Not too many composers have as yet availed themselves of this instrument, except to invoke folk life in the Caribbean.

Example XII–20

Instruments of Indefinite Pitch: Metals

CYMBALS (CYM.)

Pair of Cymbals ⧓

Suspended Cymbal ⊥ or ⌐

Hi-Hat Cymbals ⇌

The cymbal, an old Turkish instrument, is a curved metal plate with a raised cup or bell in the center. It is important to know the nomenclature of the three parts of the bell in case a composer wishes to specify where a certain sound should be produced.

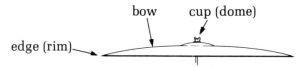

Cymbals are made in at least three different sizes, but if a composer asks for more, the percussionist can usually find them. The standard sizes are 10 to 14 inches, 15 to 18 inches, and 19 to 24 inches.

There are three basic playing methods:

1. Pairs of cymbals are held by leather straps fastened at the cup.

 a. These may be clashed together *forte* and then held high over the player's head. If the stroke is fast, they can be clashed and immediately dampened against the player's chest. Soft strokes, of course, are very effective.

b. One cymbal may be swished across the other to give a hissing effect.

c. A roll, which is not too satisfactory, may be created by rubbing the plates together with a fast rotary motion.

Example XII–21

2. A cymbal may be suspended from a strap on a stand and struck with either a wooden drumstick, which gives a well-articulated stroke, or marimba yarn mallets, timpani mallets, or wire brushes for softer effects. All these sticks and mallets can be used to effect rolls on the various sizes of suspended cymbals. A triangle beater is sometimes used to strike the instrument or scrape it. This gives a truly metallic sound. There are differences in the sound of striking or rolling at the edge, the bow, or the cup, and it is best to specify the exact point of articulation if relevant. If it is not specified, the performer will usually strike and roll toward the edge.

Example XII–22

3. The Hi-Hat cymbals are not often used in the orchestra unless a composer wishes to simulate the drum set of jazz combos. This instrument consists of two cymbals facing each other, mounted on a metal rod and crashed together by a foot pedal. When crashed, it produces a dry, nonsustaining click so typical of drum set parts, or a slightly clattery, soft crash when allowed to vibrate.

Example XII–23

4. The Sizzle cymbal is the newest member of the cymbal family. It comes in a variety of sizes, and is played with the same beaters as for the suspended cymbal. The sizzle cymbal is also suspended by a

strap or attached with a metal clamp to a vertical rod stand. It produces a sizzling, hissing sound when struck or rolled because it has holes drilled around its circumference, which have little metal rivets in them. When the instrument is played, these rivets bounce and produce a unique sound.

Example XII–24

FINGER CYMBALS

Finger cymbals consist of a pair of small metal plates about two inches in diameter, having no definite pitch. They are struck together, and while each one would of course produce a definite pitch, two struck together obscure each other's pitches and easily blend into any pitches around them. Besides being struck together to produce a high metallic sound not unlike the triangle, they can also be struck by a metal, wooden, or plastic beater. They must not be confused with the much higher-caliber crotales, which do have definite pitch. They were often used as rhythm instruments in Medieval music.

Example XII–25

TRIANGLE (TRGL.) △

The triangle is one of the oldest nonpitched percussion instruments in the orchestra. It is also most probably of Turkish origin and was favored as an instrument in early opera. The triangle became a regular member of the symphony orchestra in the nineteenth century after Beethoven (*Ninth Symphony*, Finale). It is essentially a round metal rod bent into the shape of a triangle. There are several sizes available: three basic ones—6 inches, 8 inches, and 10 inches— give a gradation of high, medium, and low. The triangle has a crystal-like, pure, high timbre that can be used as a solo sound, but in combination with other instruments it gives luminescence to a large orchestral chord. It is played with a small metal beater and can be struck or rolled. A roll or trill is produced by striking two sides of the triangle in one of the corners. Softer sonorities are really more effective than loud ones, which tend to get tiresome and obtrusive. The instrument blends beautifully, especially with strings and winds in the upper register, but also renders good contrast to bass instruments. It has a good sustaining time, and the l.v. (let vibrate) symbol is often used. One must be careful in scoring for triangle to specify exactly how long the sound should last.

Example XII–26

ANVIL (ANV.)

This instrument simulates the sound of a blacksmith's anvil. It was used quite a bit in the late nineteenth century, especially by Wagner in *Das Rheingold* and also by numerous twentieth-century composers like Varèse, Bloch, and Foss. It is a large steel block struck by a metal hammer. Any like object, such as a small section of railroad track, can be substituted for it if an orchestra does not provide the manufactured anvil.

Example XII–27

COWBELLS △

In Europe the real thing is frequently used, especially for such passages as in the Mahler *Sixth Symphony* (first movement, mm. 198–216). In this country cowbells are manufactured in various sizes from about three to ten inches in a somewhat triangular form. They are usually bronze-plated. The pitch of the low, medium, and high sizes does not vary greatly, and they are used in Latin American dance bands as much if not more than in symphony orchestras. They are struck with a snare drumstick and give a clanging sound.

Example XII–28

TAM-TAM (T.T.)  AND OTHER GONGS ⊙

The tam-tam is usually considered the largest gong, but this is a dangerous assumption, for most gongs are tuned to a definite pitch. Yet it does look like a gong made of a heavy metal, struck with a large device called a tam-tam beater. A differentiation should be made between the nonpitched gong family, of which the tam-tam is the largest member, and the authentic oriental gongs, which do have specific pitches. This subject is one on which even the experts do not agree. We shall therefore supply pictures of both nonpitched gongs and "nipple gongs" with definite pitch and also show an example of how they are used in music. By these means, this important group of instruments will be introduced in a purely musical manner. While the tam-tam is struck with an especially large beater, the other gongs are usually played with a timpani mallet or a slightly thicker beater.

Example XII–29

OTHER AVAILABLE INSTRUMENTS

Example XII–30. Sleigh Bells   —∞ or ⬭

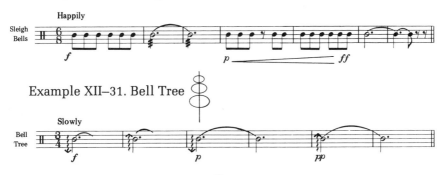

Example XII–31. Bell Tree

Example XII–32. Brake Drum. (These are automobile brakedrums, and come in various sizes.)

Example XII–33. Thunder Sheet.  (This is a large sheet of metal suspended or shaken.)

WIND CHIMES (W.CH.) 𝕿𝕿

There are three kinds of wind chimes:

1. Bamboo Wind Chimes.
2. Glass Wind Chimes.
3. Metal Wind Chimes.

All wind chimes are based on the same principle: the suspending of various sizes of bamboo sticks, pieces of glass, wood, or metal, similar to a mobile. The chimes are struck by the hand and jangled until they are stopped by the hand. Bamboo and wooden chimes can also be stroked by a small wooden stick or grasped together suddenly to emit a dry sudden sound similar to "chock." The sound of the wooden and bamboo chimes is loud when they are "chocked" together, but otherwise they emit a small, hollow, brittle rustling. The wooden chimes are much higher pitched than those of bamboo, while the glass chimes emit a very high, delicate, soft jingling, and the metal chimes, a bit more blatant yet not very loud sound. Here is a passage demonstrating the sound of all the different wind chimes:

Example XII–34

Instruments of Indefinite Pitch: Wooden

WOOD BLOCKS (W.BL.) ▭

Wood blocks come in sets of three to five sizes. They are rectangular pieces of hard wood, and even though they are considered nonpitched instruments, the different size blocks produce a variety of nondefinite pitches in a spectrum from low (the largest block) to high (the smallest block). Drumsticks, marimba, wooden, plastic, or rubber mallets are all effective beaters. The sound is incisive, pene-

trating, and very dry, and these blocks are valuable and exciting
playing a single *secco* sound, rolls, or fast passages for which they
are especially well suited.

Example XII–35

TEMPLE BLOCKS (T.BL.) ⊖

The temple blocks are a graduated series of five clam-shaped
wooden blocks mounted on a stand. They are usually lacquered red
and are of Far Eastern origin. The technique of playing and the beaters are the same as for the wood blocks, but the sound is quite a bit
more resonant, more mellow, and more hollow. The music for temple blocks is also similar to that for wood blocks with special emphasis on *secco* single strokes, rolls, and fast passages.

Example XII–36

CLAVES (CLAV.) ▬▬

This is an instrument of Latin American origin consisting of two
round pieces of hard wood, each approximately one inch in diameter and approximately six inches long. One of the claves is lightly
cradled in one hand on the fingers of a loose fist and struck incisively by the other clave held in the other hand. The cupped hand
acts as a resonator. The sound is like striking the highest wood block
very hard, but it has slightly more resonance and "ping." It usually
plays ostinati (the "key" rhythm) in Latin American rhumbas, congas, and sambas, but it has also been used in orchestral music to
reinforce *secco* chords or as an alternative to wood or temple block
sounds.

Example XII–37

CASTANETS (CAST.) ●━━

Castanets are probably of Mediterranean origin and have been in existence for hundreds of years. There are even concertos for castanets and strings by some Spanish and Italian composers of the seventeenth and eighteenth centuries. Often they are used in the orchestra to suggest Spain or Spanish subjects, and a famous passage for castanets—the "Habañera" from Bizet's *Carmen*—comes to mind immediately. But today, composers use them to emphasize rhythms and reinforce sharp attacks as well.

The instrument is made of a pair of small, hardwood, spoon-shaped shells which are struck together. There are three kinds of orchestra castanets:

1. Hand castanets: usually two pairs, one held in each hand. These require considerable skill to play and are rarely found in the orchestra.

2. Paddle castanets: a pair of castanets mounted, one on each side of a wooden paddle. These are easy to play and can have a very loud dynamic.

3. Concert castanets are mounted on a board. The lower castanet is stationary and connected to the upper one by a spring. The upper castanet is clicked against the lower with a finger or a drumstick. This castanet machine is the newest of the three ways of performing on this instrument, and the most commonly used in the orchestra.

Example XII–38

SAND BLOCK [SANDPAPER BLOCK] (S.BL.)

This always sounds like a "soft shoe" dance and consists of two small blocks covered with sandpaper on the bottom side. The sandpaper surfaces are brought together and rubbed against each other. There can be simple, coarse, short strokes, rhythmic passages, or rolls. If one wishes an especially harsh sound, one should specify that the sandpaper be especially coarse. If the opposite effect is desired, fine or medium sandpaper should be requested.

Example XII–39

MARACAS (MRCS.) O—

The maracas are another Latin American instrument and usually come in pairs, although if they are played in a non–South American context, one will often suffice. The instrument is made of a gourd or wood or plastic shell filled with pebbles or seeds. In Latin American dances they usually play ostinto patterns, but in orchestral situations the sizzle of the maraca has always had a special charm. It may be shaken or slowly twirled (stirred). This latter is very effective, especially written as a *pianissimo* roll (solo). Also, simply tapping the maraca with one hand to get a short-note effect is possible.

Example XII–40

JAWBONE

(The new manufactured instrument is called the vibraflap) This is also a Latin instrument related to the maracas, since it also rattles. It looks like the jawbone of a donkey. The player holds it in one hand and strikes it toward the top with the fist of his other hand, making "loose teeth" rattle. Usually one writes only single strokes for this instrument, since each will buzz for a time commensurate with the force of the blow.

Example XII–41

GUIRO ⌒⌒⌒⌒

This is a large gourd in the shape of a bottle with a serrated side on which one scrapes back and forth with a wooden stick or scraper. Naturally it is used a great deal in Latin American dance bands, but many composers have used it instead of the European ratchet or rattle. Single strokes as well as rolls are possible.

Example XII–42

RATCHET ⊟—

This instrument simulates a child's ratchet, and it is constructed in a similar manner: a hard tongue of wood or metal is held in a frame so that when the "wheel of teeth" is rotated against it by a handle, these teeth catch and make a loud clacking sonority. The instrument is best used in a loud dynamic and for rolls, since single strokes are risky and would work much better on the guiro.

Example XII–43

WHIP [SLAPSTICK]

In Europe this instrument is usually called a whip, while in America we call it slapstick. Its construction is much closer to the latter term, for it is made up of two strips of thin hard wood tied together into a paddle held by a string. It can produce only a single very hard stroke when the two pieces of wood are clapped together. The use of this instrument is usually to emphasize a sforzando effect.

Example XII–44

LOG DRUM 🔲 AND SLIT DRUM 🔲

These are Mexican-Indian and African instruments respectively. The log drum is simply a hollowed-out log plugged up at each end. A slit is made along the entire surface on one side; then two "tongues" are cut in, dividing the wood into two different lengths producing two different "pitches" when the wood is struck on the two different sides of the opening. Several sizes of the log drum can be required, and they will produce pitches according to their size and thickness. One can even specify well-defined pitches.

Slit drums are similar in construction, but look a bit more sophisticated. The sound is produced by hard marimba mallets striking the drums on either side of the slits. The intervallic relationships, depending on the thickness of the drum, can be a third or most often a perfect fourth or even fifth. They can easily take the place of wood or temple blocks but have a darker sound.

Example XII–45

2 log, then
2 slit drums

ff

MEMBRANOPHONES

Instruments of Definite Pitch

TIMPANI (TIMP.) ♀

The oldest regular percussion members of the symphony orchestra are the timpani or kettle drums. Until this century the total range of the timpani was ⟨notation⟩ . Now, however, we have a series of interlocking drums that give us a much larger range. Four sizes of timpani are commonly available in all orchestras: 30-inch, 28-inch, 25-inch, and 23-inch. If a piccolo timpani, 21 inches in diameter, is not available, a tuned tom-tom or roto tom may be used in its place.

Example XII–46. Ranges

The tuning of the timpani until earlier in this century was accomplished by tightening or loosening the calfskin head membrane of the drum by means of the screws placed around the perimeter. Much time was needed to change the tuning of the instrument; therefore, only limited functions were assigned to the timpani. Today the drums are fully mechanical, with a foot pedal on each drum to change pitches very quickly and easily. This innovation has greatly enhanced the function and potential of the instrument.

During the Classical period only two drums were commonly used in the orchestra, usually 28-inch and 25-inch. The role of the timpani was to strengthen the tonic and dominant bass notes and participate in strong tutti passages, especially in consummating climactic cadence points. Occasionally they were called for in quiet passages to create a special atmosphere, such as in the Haydn *Drum-roll Symphony.* Not until Beethoven's time did the timpani become a solo instrument. The standard coupling with the trumpets was still very prevalent in the symphonic scores of Haydn and Mozart, so that when Beethoven, in his last two symphonies, had the two timpani tuned in an octave F, and in the sardonic scherzo of the *Ninth* used solo timpani, it was quite a shocking innovation. Berlioz, who even used two or more sets of drums and two or more players in some works, was the first to develop timpani writing which expanded to three then four or more drums in our own time.

Usually, special timpani mallets are used. These come in hard, medium, and soft varieties. Other mallets, such as wooden drumsticks, or simply the handles of the timpani mallets, etc., can be used for special effects.

The timpani are extremely versatile. They can play single notes, rolls, and, with our mechanical aids, can easily do glissandi. The single notes can be slow or fast, and the dynamic range of the timpani is exceedingly great.

The timpani tone is affected not only by the kind of mallet used, but also by the place on the head where the mallet strikes the drum. Usually, the player strikes the head about six inches in from the rim. A beautiful *pianissimo* can be achieved by playing even closer to the rim. A very thick, thudlike sound which obscures the pitch somewhat is obtained by hitting the center of the head.

Muting is made possible by placing a cloth to cover part or all of the head, and today some composers have asked the timpanists to place cymbals, tambourines, maracas, and other percussion instruments on the head, letting them ring sympathetically when the drum is struck. The side of the drum, the bowl in other words, is sometimes used as an unpitched percussion instrument played with wooden sticks, as is the rim.

The timpani part must be carefully prepared to show dynamics and the exact duration of each note; for instance, where a roll or trill is to end, how long a note may ring, etc. A roll may be notated in one of two ways:

Example XII–47

A longer roll should be notated:

Example XII–48

A tremolo on two different drums should be notated to indicate whether it is measured or unmeasured.

Example XII–49

Two or more notes can be played at the same time. Here is a passage which is possible on a four-drum set:

Example XII–50

It is advisable to mark changes in tuning, especially if it must be accomplished rather quickly. This is done in the following manner:

Example XII–51

Here are some examples of timpani usage from the orchestral literature:

Example XII–52. Beethoven, *Symphony No. 9*, second movement, mm. 261–73

Example XII–53. Berlioz, *Symphonie fantastique*, fourth movement, mm. 83–90

Example XII–54. Bloch, *Schelomo*, mm. 170–71

See also:

Harris, *Third Symphony*, mm. 421–25
Bernstein, *Jeremiah Symphony*, second movement, mm. 288–301
Bartók, *Music for String Instruments, Percussion, and Celesta*

ROTO TOMS

An American manufacturer (Remo) recently developed a series of roto toms (tom-toms) that are tuned by manual turns of the shell on a frame. They come in seven sizes and have a pitch compass as follows:

Example XII–55. Ranges

These drums are now made with a timpani-style bowl resonator, and they sound very much like that instrument except for the fact that their pitch is clearer and more articulate. The potential range of the timpani is greatly extended by use of the roto tom, which uses the same beaters and has a compatible sound. When timpani and roto toms are used in combination, it is helpful if a different-shape notehead is used for each. Roto toms blend beautifully with all kinds of instruments and create excellent contrast for the repetition of timpani passages at higher pitches. It is also possible to play a slow melody on a drum. The following notation is suggested:

Timpani: regular notation

Roto toms: ⊗   ⊗   x   x

Example XII–56

All timpani techniques can be applied to roto toms.

Regular roto toms are now obsolete and are replaced by the drums described above; yet many organizations still have them. The regular roto toms come in three sizes: 10-inch, 8-inch, and 6-inch, with the following ranges:

Example XII–57. Ranges

These are tuned like the Remo toms, by rotating the head clockwise to tighten, counterclockwise to relax. They are simply plastic heads stretched over a metal rim fastened to a base. Their sound is much dryer and of much less sustaining quality than the timpani or the Remo toms. All kinds of wooden sticks, wood, plastic, or rubber mallets, and even chord mallets are affective:

Instruments of Indefinite Pitch

SNARE DRUM (S. Dr.) ▱ with snares; ▭ without snares

The snare or side drum is another instrument that has long been a member of the symphony orchestra and even longer in the opera orchestra. The instrument has two heads: the top and playing head is called *batter*, while the bottom one, which has the snares (cat gut, wire, or nylon) stretched across it, is referred to as *snare*. The snare drum has a switch on the side which, if loosened, shuts off the snares and makes the instrument sound like a tom-tom. With the snares on, the instrument has a crisp, sharp sound and is excellent for playing concise rhythmic patterns. There are four basic strokes besides the single left-right stroke:

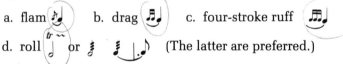

a. flam   b. drag   c. four-stroke ruff

d. roll   or   (The latter are preferred.)

In the first three strokes the grace notes precede the accented note unless otherwise specified.

Besides the "snares off" color change, one may place a cloth on the batter head and mute the instrument. One should designate this effect as "cover head." Another effect quite frequently used is the rim shot, a very sharp sound produced by placing one stick on the head and rim and then hitting it in the middle with the other stick. The instruction to the player should read: r.sh.

Wooden sticks are the normal beaters for the snare drum, although wire brushes are used for soft effects, especially in jazz. Here are some examples of snare drum passages:

Example XII–58

Notation of a trill is possible, but the 𝄐 is preferred.

TENOR DRUM (T.DR.) ☐

The tenor drum is found quite frequently in bands and orchestras. It has a deep and resonant sound and shares the basic snare-drum techniques, although it has no snares. Wooden sticks serve as beaters, though timpani mallets and marimba mallets are also effective.

Example XII–59

FIELD DRUM (F.DR.)

This is a deeper shell snare drum (with snares) than the tenor drum, which has the same circumference but no snares. The field drum, seldom used in orchestras, has a darker, less crisp sound than the snare drum and is played with large snare drumsticks. The same techniques apply to both, however.

Example XII–60

Field Drum

BASS DRUM (B.DR.)

"If you hit the bass drum hard, it does not make any difference what the chord is above it; if you roll *fortissimo* on the bass drum, the rest of the orchestra can quit playing." This is what Walter Piston once said to his orchestration class, and it accurately describes the tremendous power of the instrument and the care one must take in using it. Its response is a bit slower than the smaller drums, but it is very effective in relatively slow-moving repeated notes as well as *secco* fast isolated strokes.

The instrument has two heads, both of which can be used for playing if the instrument is standing upright on its side (⬭). The bass drum can also be laid flat (⊖). It is effective in soft passages and adds tremendous weight to the percussion section in loud dynamic situations. One should remember Piston's admonition and not overuse it. It may be used to close off a short-note percussion passage or to begin such a gesture with a single stroke (Copland, *Third Symphony*, second movement, beginning and ending). It can also simulate distant thunder or evoke a feeling of impending doom with a *pianissimo* roll. In older symphonic literature it was often used to recall war or belligerent hostility.

Usually, a mallet resembling a timpani mallet but a bit larger, softer, and with a little more felt on the head, is provided for the bass drum. Wooden sticks are also used for strokes and rolls.

Example XII–61

Adagio

1st *f* ; 2nd *p*   3

Example XII–62

Happily

mf

1st time with regular mallets; 2nd time with wood of mallets

TOM-TOMS (T.T.) □

These are the membranophones which occupy that grey area between definite and indefinite pitch, for the tom-toms can be tuned to approximate pitches if desired. They come in two pairs of four varied-size drums. The pitch may be divided like four voices—soprano, tenor, alto, bass—and tom-toms may be notated on the four spaces of the staff. The drums themselves resemble smaller tenor drums with no snares; many have only one head. There is another set available, called two-headed tom-toms, which is even more like the tenor drum. These are most often used in jazz bands, but if the composer so specifies, they can be available in a symphony orchestra. The single-headed tom-toms are crisper and more articulate, while the double-headed ones have greater sustaining power and are deeper and more somber in sound.

Yarn, chord mallets, or regular snare drumsticks are the most common beaters used, and the technique is similar to the drum technique. Much of the music also incorporates the gestures otherwise written for wood blocks and temple blocks, with which tom-toms often carry on a dialogue in the orchestra. By the way, the two kinds of tom-toms, one-headed and two-headed, are interchangeable, and most listeners cannot tell the difference between them.

Example XII–63

TIMBALES (TIMB.) ⌐

The timbales come in pairs fastened to a metal stand similar to the one-headed tom-toms. As a matter of fact, these drums are too often mistaken for tom-toms. However, they are of Latin American origin and come in only two sizes: 13 inches and 14 inches in diameter, one a high drum and the other low. Like the tom-toms, they are one-headed drums but have a metal shell of about snare-drum depth, and therefore a more metallic and piercing sound. There are several ways of playing them:

a. with timbale sticks, which are wooden dowels, thinner and lighter than snare drumsticks;
b. with marimba mallets;
c. with one's hands;
d. with any kind of mallet or stick on the rim, in the center of the drum, or in a rim shot.

Example XII–64

BONGOS ⌐

The bongos always come in attached pairs and are single-headed drums of Latin American origin. There are primitive bongos which are simply skin over shell and cannot be changed in tuning. They are indefinitely pitched—low, high, higher, and highest. The professional bongos have a tightening apparatus on the rim. Usually they are adjusted so that they are a perfect fourth or fifth apart. Most musical organizations have only one set of bongos, but several sizes are manufactured, and a composer is safe writing for two sets, which means four drums of unequal tuning.

Bongos are traditionally held between the knees and played by hand. However, they can be mounted like timbales and played by hand or with snare drumsticks, any kind of mallet, and even very softly with brushes. There is a very special technique for bongo playing, and the professional bongo player has developed finger muscles and callouses on his hands so that he can perform extraordinary feats on the instruments. The ordinary percussion player cannot be expected to be proficient in that type of specialized playing, but typical tom-tom type music can be performed without a problem.

Example XII–65

CONGA DRUM (C.DR.) ()

This is the Latin American bass drum instrument quite often used today in the symphony orhcestra. It stands about thirty inches high, and its single head is about eleven inches in diameter. The typical conga drum has a reverse hourglass figure. The drum is best played with the hands, but all types of mallets may be used. By striking the head near the rim, one can get a higher pitch than by hitting the center of the head; therefore, one should specify what kind of "pitch" one desires. Usually it is notated on two lines or in two spaces to indicate the pitch difference.

Example XII–66

TAMBOURINE (TAMB.) ↶

The tambourine, as is the case with many of these percussion instruments, has ancient origins, and we find mention of it in the Bible. It evokes thoughts of Spain, but is used for all kinds of music today. The instrument is basically a shallow drum consisting of a single-head skin fastened over a wooden hoop. Around the frame there are several slots with pairs of small disc cymbals, which jingle when the instrument is struck or shaken. Since there are several sizes of tamourines, one should specify whether one wishes a large 15-inch, medium 10-inch, or small 6-inch model. If there is no particular specification, the player will usually use the 10-inch instrument.

There are several playing techniques:

a. striking the instrument with one's knuckles;
b. playing it softly with one's fingers;
c. shaking it (notated like a roll), usually used for loud rolls;
d. a thumb roll excellent for soft rolls (must be spelled out in the part);
e. all kinds of sticks and mallets, if the instrument is placed on a stand or chair;
f. placed on other percussion instruments like timpani, snare drums, bass drums, and played with a mallet.

Example XII–67

BEATERS

Since in our discussion of the percussion instruments the graphic notation has been given whenever possible, it is most important to give the symbols for all beaters. These symbols are now almost universally accepted, and even if the instruments are included on a score, those symbols should be used throughout and explained in a guide to the notation at the beginning of the score and parts. It will save a great deal of time and clarify the intentions of the composer or orchestrator.

Hard sticks (wood or plastic heads)	Bass drum stick
Medium sticks (rubber heads)	Heavy beater (for tamtam etc.)
Soft sticks (lambswool or soft felt heads)	Two hard sticks in each hand
Metal sticks	Two soft sticks (l.h.) and two hard sticks (r.h.)
Wire brushes	Two soft sticks in each hand

There are of course many other percussion instruments, but the ones discussed in this chapter are by far the most frequently used in the modern symphony orhcestra, band, or wind ensemble. Many instruments which were omitted can be found in the books mentioned in the Appendix. Instruments like the Indian and Arabian tablas need more specialized study than this discussion can provide, so it was left to the composer or orchestrator to find more authentic sources for these rare and exotic instruments.

CHORDOPHONES

CIMBALON

The cimbalon is the most highly developed of the ancient dulcimers. More and more in American folk music, the Appalachian dulcimer has reappeared. However, the Hungarians developed their dulcimer (the cimbalon) early in this century for use in the symphony orchestra. The cimbalon is usually trapezoid-shaped; it is similar to a piano without a keyboard, having a multiple of strings for each pitch. The instrument is laid flat and struck in various ways on its metal strings with a leather or sometimes a wooden mallet. The modern cimbalon is equipped with a foot-operated damper pedal and has a compass of four octaves with all chromatic tones.

Example XII–68. Range

The instrument is used beautifully by Bartók, Kodály, and Stravinsky, in rapid and florid passages. Like the marimba, the notes to be sustained are usually rolled.

Example XII–69. Kodály, *Háry János*, fifth movement, mm. 87–93

The piano, harpsichord, harmonium, and organ will be discussed in the following chapter, despite the fact that the piano as well as the harpsichord are chordophones and are often designated as percussion instruments in a symphony orchestra.

AEROPHONES

WHISTLES

Whistles of all kinds are used for various effects, especially in late twentieth-century scores. The kind of whistle required should be carefully indicated in the score: bird whistle, police whistle, slide whistle, tin whistle, train whistle. If no specific pitches are desired, there should at least be an explanation of exactly what the whistle is to do.

Tunes should be exactly notated. In *Billy the Kid*, Copland asks for a tin whistle to play this tune:

Example XII–70. Copland, *Billy the Kid*, "Street in a Frontier Town," mm. 1–4

SIRENS

Many twentieth-century composers have used sirens, especially Varèse, Antheil, and Hindemith, to paint a realistic picture of modern society. If one wishes to use sirens, the volume and the type of siren, such as high, shrill, ringing, etc., should be designated. The notation is not standardized, but could be on one line, showing the duration and dynamic.

MOTOR HORNS

Motor horns of all kinds have been used, especially in early twentieth-century pieces (Gershwin, *An American in Paris*) in which urban life was to be evoked. All these effects must be used very carefully, for most of them have by now become clichés.

13

Keyboard Instruments

Many books are available which deal with the repertoire, technique, and construction of some of the instruments to be discussed in this chapter, especially the piano, harpsichord, and organ. This chapter is not intended to dwell on these aspects of the instruments, but rather discuss their use as orchestral colors. The Keyboard instruments are more familiar to students and composers than a good many of the other instruments of the orchestra, but their use as non-solo members of the ensemble places them in a completely different context, one which has taken on great importance during the past hundred years.

PIANO
Pianoforte (It.), Klavier (Ger.)

Example XIII–1. Range

The piano is perhaps the best known of all musical instruments, but its inclusion in the ranks of the symphony orchestra is a rather recent phenomenon. One must conclude from studying the usage of

The Piano

the piano as an orchestral instrument that it was a French innovation, since it is in the scores of D'Indy, Debussy, and Stravinsky that
it first appears.

In relationship to the orchestra, the piano may be viewed in the
following capacities:

   1. as the solo instrument in a piano concerto;

   2. as the executant of an obligato in orchestral works, such as
Bloch's *Concerto Grosso No. 1,* D'Indy's *Symphony on a French
Mountain Air,* De Falla's *Nights in the Gardens of Spain,* Stravinsky's *Petrushka,* and others (Saint-Saëns's *Carnival of the Animals*
uses two pianos obligato.);

   3. as a purely orchestral instrument, in such works as Debussy's
Printemps, Martin's *Symphony No. 4,* Shostakovich's *Symphony No.
1,* Copland's *Symphony No. 3,* Prokofiev's *Symphony No. 5,* Sessions's *Symphony No. 2,* Colgrass's *As Quiet As,* and many others.

The piano is usually used to double a passage or emphasize a *secco*
chord or note, with its extreme registers employed more often than
those at the middle of the instrument. Occasional solos are assigned
to the piano for contrast, and since the instrument is usually placed.
somewhere in back of the orchestra, these featured passages do not
convey the impression of a solo in a particular work. Contemporary
composers often use it as a percussion instrument. The piano is a
substitute for or a contrast to the xylophone, marimba, or vibraphone
and at the bottom of its range can also reinforce the timpani or bass
drum. Combination doublings with strings, woodwinds, and brass

are of course also successful. There are instances where the piano is used instead of a harp, playing arpeggios in *fortissimo* passages where the latter would be completely obliterated. In this connection one should remark that, of necessity, many nonprofessional and school orchestras use a piano to minimize the "holes" that exist in the organization, since there may be no oboe, bassoon, or viola. This is something that is purely pragmatic and will be discussed in a much later chapter.

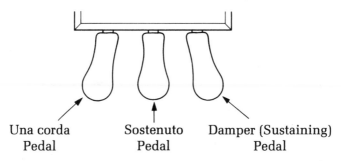

Una corda Pedal	Sostenuto Pedal	Damper (Sustaining) Pedal

The Three Piano Pedals

The most frequently used of the three is the damper pedal which lifts all the dampers and permits the strings to vibrate even after the key has been released. The *una corde* pedal is the next most important. *Una corde* means one string, and describes the action of this pedal on a grand piano: when depressed, it moves the hammers into a position where they can strike only one or in some cases two of the three strings of one pitch. On an upright piano, this pedal moves the hammers closer to the string. Both actions are designed to soften the tone of the instrument. The center pedal is the most problematical. It is correctly called the sostenuto pedal and sustains only those pitches that are depressed at the same time the pedal is put into action. It is most useful for pedal points, for one can depress a pitch and at the same time the sostenuto pedal, thereby sustaining that pitch only, while playing other passages over it. Other pedals may be used at will without affecting the pedal-point note. Unfortunately, many European pianos and a great majority of uprights do not have this pedal, so it is a risk to write for it. Nevertheless, orchestral pianos are usually nine-foot grands and would most certainly have all three pedals.

Often, because of the rather novel nature of the middle pedal and its infrequent use, the right pedal has been called sostenuto; however, that is not correct; the names given above are the ones to be used. However, in English, if one refers to the sustaining pedal, one usually means the right or damper pedal, simply describing its action. This term is acceptable.

The contemporary composer often extends the techniques of the piano such as:

1. Prepared piano is indicated, meaning that the strings are prepared with various objects either on top of them or stuck between them.

2. The piano strings are struck with various beaters or brushes to sound like mallet percussion or dulcimers.

3. The piano strings are plucked either *secco* or let vibrate.

4. Roaring bass tremolos, which simulate a whole battery of bass drums, can be performed by depressing the sustaining pedal and playing a tremolo with both hands on the lowest strings.

5. Some composers (i.e., Bernstein in *The Age of Anxiety*, Copland in *Billy the Kid*) ask for upright pianos to suggest the "local color" of the barroom or music hall.

6. Toy pianos have been employed for special effects.

Before illustrating some successful uses of the piano in its various functions as an orchestral instrument, it is important to call attention to some extraordinary works where multiple pianos and percussion take the place of an entire orchestra. Two of the most important of these are Stravinksy's *Les Noces* and Orff's *Catulli carmina*.

Orchestral Uses of the Piano

Piano as a doubling instrument:

Example XIII–2. Stravinsky, *Petrushka,* "Danse russe," mm. 1–9

Example XIII–3. Shostakovich, *Symphony No. 1*, second movement, mm. 113–18

See also Copland, *Symphony No. 3*, second movement, mm. 115–20.

Incidental solos:

Example XIII–4. Stravinsky, *Petrushka*, second tableau, mm. 19–32

See also Berg, *Lulu Suite*, "Ostinato," mm. 37–45.

As an accompanying instrument:

Example XIII–5. Bernstein, *On the Town*, "Times Square," mm. 1–5

See also: Stravinsky, *Petrushka*, second tableau, mm. 62–67
      Stravinsky, *Oedipus Rex*, |19|, mm. 1–11

CELESTA
Célesta (Fr.)

Example XIII–6. Range (sounds one octave higher than written)

    The celesta is a steel-bar piano, looking like a miniature version of that instrument and sounding very much like a glockenspiel. The mechanism of the celesta works in the following manner: felt hammers strike steel bars, which lie across a small wooden resonator box. The tone is soft and delicate, and even though it has quite a bit of penetrating power because of its high frequencies, it is by no means as piercing as the glockenspiel. The instrument has a damper pedal, and the notes do not sustain too long; but since they are produced by striking metal bars over a resonator, there is no true short staccato. Melodic lines, chords, and arpeggios are all most effective on the celesta, which is usually played by the pianist of the orchestra or a percussionist who happens to play the piano. Besides solo celesta passages, some of the most exciting pages of music for this instrument occur when it doubles the strings, the harp, the piano, soft woodwinds, and gives a "silver lining" to the overall sound. The celesta is probably used more frequently in the orchestra than any other keyboard instrument.

Here are some outstanding examples of celesta passages:

Example XIII–7. Tchaikovsky, *The Nutcracker*, "Dance of the Sugar Plum Fairy," mm. 5–12

Example XIII–8. Strauss, *Der Rosenkavalier*, Act II, Octavian's aria "Mir ist die Ehre," 25 , mm. 1–6

See also Shostakovich, *Symphony No. 5*, first movement, last 4 mm.
    Berio, *Concertino*, mm. 1–6
    Foss, *Time Cycle*, second movement, mm. 171–75
    Bartók, *Music for String Instruments, Percussion, and Celesta* third movement, mm. 34–41

HARPSICHORD

Cembalo (It. and Ger.),
Clavecin (Fr.)

Example XIII–9. Range

    The harpsichord is really a plucked stringed instrument: instead of being struck by hammers, the strings are plucked by crow quills or leather tabs. Usually five to eight pedals or hand-pulled pistons operate register stops, and since the big harpsichords have two keyboards, there is a coupler to combine the registrations on the two. This affords a great deal of variety in the tone quality and adds strength to the instrument by joining the keyboards together.

    During the Baroque era and even in some of the early Haydn symphonies, the harpsichord was always present in the orchestra to realize the continuo parts. When the style changed and the orchestra expanded, there was no longer a need for the instrument as an integral part of the ensemble, and because of its relatively small sound, it was replaced by the piano as the keyboard solo instrument. Some harpsichords, called pedal harpsichords, have a full organ pedal keyboard. These are rare, and one has to request them specially. For the last fifty years at least, there has been a renewed interest in building harpsichords and in using it as part of the orchestra. Composers have seen fit to use it in the orchestra for color, but care must be taken that this rather delicate instrument is not overwhelmed. It is advised that it be heard alone or in combination with instruments capable of playing quite softly. Some composers have written for amplified harpsichord (Penderecki, *Partita*); in those cases the harpsichord is not so much at a disadvantage. Some successful uses of the harpsichord today are in the following works: De Falla's *El Retablo de Maese Pedro*, Martin's *Petite Symphonie Concertante*, Strauss's *Dance Suite after Couperin*, Carter's *Double Concerto*, Powell's *Miniatures for Baroque Ensemble*.

Example XIII–10. Powell, *Miniatures*, fourth movement, mm. 1–5

HARMONIUM
Organetto (It.)

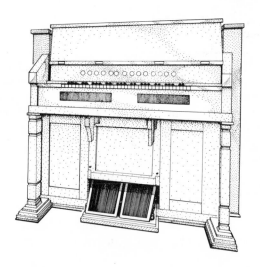

The harmonium is a small pump organ, sometimes called a reed organ. It has either one or two keyboards and a range of five octaves:

Example XIII–11. Range

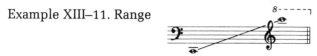

Some harmoniums have as many as fifteen organ stops, which change the tone quality and extend the range an octave below and an octave above. These instruments are rare in our time when the harmonium is infrequently used. The player pumps two pedals below the keyboard, which set the air in motion to work the bellows inside the instrument; these, in turn, activate the reeds when the keys are depressed. Relatively few works use the harmonium, although it did have a renaissance during the 1920s and seems to be coming into vogue again today. The parts usually resemble substitute organ parts.

Example XIII–12. Strauss, *Ariadne auf Naxos*, mm. 80–89

See also Webern, *Five Pieces for Orchestra*, Op. 10, No. 5, mm. 9–
10, m. 15, m. 21.

ORGAN
Organo (It.), Orgue (Fr.), Orgel (Ger.)

Example XIII–13. Range

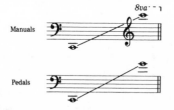

The early history of the organ (also called "The King of the Instruments") in the orchestra is a very long one, predating the Baroque
period. It was indispensable as a continuo instrument and also as a
frequent soloist with orchestral accompaniment. Once again, as in
the case of the harpsichord, when the style changed and continuo
became an antiquated technique, the organ was relegated to the

church and disappeared as an integral member of the orchestra. It did retain its position in the opera house, where it was called upon from time to time to simulate a religious scene. Meyerbeer in *Le Prophète*, Gounod in *Faust*, Halévy in *La Juive*, Verdi in *Otello*, and Wagner in *Lohengrin* were some of the composers who used the organ successfully to portray religious feelings in their operas. Solo music for organ was quite popular especially at the beginning and middle of the nineteenth century with Mendelssohn, Schumann, Brahms, and Reubke. Not until Saint-Saëns's *Symphony No. 3*, however, was there a major concert work written with organ since the Baroque and early Classical periods. After that, Mahler (*Symphony No. 8*) and Strauss (*Also sprach Zarathustra*) must have convinced twentieth-century composers of the feasibility of the organ as an orchestral instrument. Quite a few organ concertos have been written in the past fifty years, and solo music from France, Germany, England, and the United States is voluminous. The great attraction of the organ as an orchestral instrument is its ability to sustain pitches for an indeterminate period, and also that there are many combinations available to complement or contrast the orchestral colors. Unfortunately, many concert halls do not have a pipe organ, and often an electronic organ or a small positiv organ with insufficient power and color is substituted for a large pipe organ which the composer had in mind.

Example XIII–14. Saint-Saëns, *Symphony No. 3*, first movement, mm. 350–65.

See also Strauss, *Also sprach Zarathustra*, mm. 19–21.

14

Scoring for Percussion with Keyboard Alone and in Combination

This chapter will be divided into two parts. The first is an extension of the previous two chapters and will cover the major problems of score placement as well as special notation for percussion and keyboard instruments. The second part will deal with the tremendously varied use of the percussion-keyboard ensemble in combination with other choirs of the symphony orchestra.

ARRANGEMENT IN THE SCORE

The percussion and keyboard section is traditionally placed between the brass and the strings on the score page, with the timpani appearing first. Since there are at most three to four percussion players in a symphony orchestra, not including the timpanist and keyboard player, and since these few percussion players are asked to perform on a multitude of different instruments, it is imperative that the composer or orchestrator arrange the percussion section of the score very carefully and that the notation be instantly legible.

There are many schools of thought concerning score setup. There is even a "cop-out" school that says, "Place the instruments any old way and let the players figure it out for themselves." This is certainly not the way to solve the problem. Let us find an approach that is clear and logical:

1. Order in which keyboard instruments appear in the score: highest one at the top, then in descending order:

> Glockenspiel
> Xylophone
> Vibraphone
> Marimba
> Chimes
> Celesta
> Piano
> Harpsichord
> Organ

Of course, not all of these instruments are used in every score, but when any of them do appear, they should be arranged in this sequence in the score. All these instruments are usually placed *below* the timpani and the nonpitched percussion instruments. If harps are called for, they should be placed *above* all the keyboard instruments. Let us say that the percussion section at a particular spot in a large work consists of the following instruments: timpani, harp, xylophone, and celesta; the setup would be:

> Timpani
> Harp
> Xylophone
> Celesta

2. Order of nonpitched percussion:
   a. The high to low principle should be observed.
   b. Another principle of organization of this group is by materials:

> I. Metal
> II. Wood
> III. Membrane

Since there are so many nonpitched instruments, let us take only a few of the most common and set them up in suitable score sequence, remembering that as a group they are placed immediately below the timpani. We will rearrange the following instruments: snare drum, bass drum, triangle, tambourine, sleigh bells, wood blocks, tenor drum, temple blocks, cymbals, and a tam-tam. According to our guidelines above, here is the order in which they would appear in the score:

Triangle
Sleigh Bells
Cymbals
Tam-tam
Wood Blocks
Temple Blocks
Tambourine
Snare Drum
Tenor Drum
Bass Drum

Of course, it is unusual to find all these percussion instruments playing at the same time in an orchestral work. The assignment of a particular group of instruments to any one particular player is not of great importance unless:

1. The physical disposition of the instruments is predetermined;

2. Two instruments must be played at the same time, in which case

    a. the player will use a different beater in each hand;

    b. the player will use the same beater(s) for both instruments or each instrument will be played with one hand only.

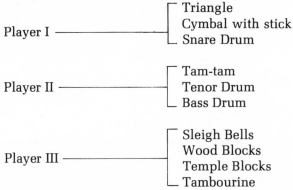

Player I
    Triangle
    Cymbal with stick
    Snare Drum

Player II
    Tam-tam
    Tenor Drum
    Bass Drum

Player III
    Sleigh Bells
    Wood Blocks
    Temple Blocks
    Tambourine

Player I could strike two of his instruments at the same time. Players II and III would also be able to do the same thing by having a different beater in each hand.

Here is where notation is very important. We need not discuss the notation for the pitched percussion instruments, for they present no particular problem, except that we must be warned that all instruments, no matter where they are placed on the score, must be diligently labeled.

1. Nonpitched percussion with no variation in sound (i.e., maracas, claves) may be notated on a single line, which may be either a one-line staff or a line or space within a five-line staff.

Example XIV–1

Notice that the "percussion clef" ‖ is used on the single line or centered on the third line of a five-line staff.

Let us suppose we have one player playing snare, tenor, and bass drums. We may use either of two methods: one line for each instrument, or the five-line staff, as follows:

Example XIV–2

The stems of the tenor drum may go up or down, but either way, these would certainly be clear and concise ways of notating the three instruments. Both methods of notation are equally valid if three different players are performing the three different parts.

2. Nonpitched percussion with pitch variations:

When three wood blocks, five temple blocks, three timbales, or four cymbals of different sizes are used, there are again two accepted methods of notating clearly. Either the one- or two-line staff or the five-line staff may be used, in the following manner:

Example XIV–3

or

There are many instances where a composer wishes to have a player perform on two instruments in very close proximity, and often this is notated on one line.

Example XIV–4

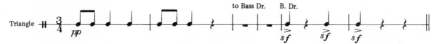

This is certainly a space-saving solution, especially if there is only one percussion player or if there is very little written for the percussion section in the work. But one further refinement would make this notation even clearer: the bass-drum stems should go down instead of up to differentiate further between the two instruments.

Example XIV–5

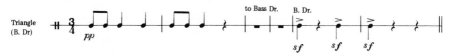

One crucially important fact must be kept in mind whenever one player is called upon to switch from one instrument to another: one must allow enough time for the player to change sticks. It is not so bad between triangle and bass drum, for example, for the player can hold a triangle beater in one hand and a bass drumstick in the other. However, if the switch were between a triangle and a snare drum, the performer must put down the triangle beater and ready the two snare drumsticks in order to play on the latter instrument.

There is another notation problem that concerns switching from a nonpitched to a pitched percussion instrument printed on the same line and played by the same performer. Here are two clear ways of solving this particular problem:

Example XIV–6

or

Notice again that some time has to be allotted for the player to switch from mallets to sticks, unless the composer wishes both instruments to be performed with xylophone mallets. Certainly this is possible, and less time will elapse between the performances of the two instruments, for the player will position them in such a manner that he is able to play them both at the same time.

Here are some percussion placements on scores from orchestral works using large percussion sections:

Example XIV–7. Mozart, Overture to *Die Entführung aus dem Serail*, mm. 1–9

Example XIV–8. Shostakovich, *Symphony No. 6*, opening

Example XIV–9. Orff, *Carmina burana*, No. 14, "In taberna quando sumus," mm. 83 –96

Example XIV–10. Stravinsky, *Les Noces*, second tableau, mm. 163–73

PERCUSSION SECTION SETUP

Unless a particular effect is called for (as in an antiphonal work) or the composer/orchestrator has had first-hand experience with the problem of choreographing this very complex section, it is best to leave the physical setup to the players themselves. Most professional percussion sections have developed their own favorite, sometimes idiosyncratic setups. It is best to list all the percussion instruments clearly at the beginning of the score, as well as in the percussion parts, and leave the assignment and placement up to the section leader. If three or four players are demanded, be sure that they are able to handle all the instruments required in the score at any given moment in the piece, and that enough time is allowed for each player to be able to go to his next instrument or group of instruments. It is better to ask for an extra player in a work with an extremely active percussion section than to demand that too few percussionists cover a multiplicity of instruments.* Be aware, however, that orchestra managers don't like to hire extra players and that, as Bernard Rogers so wisely said, "In writing percussion, the sanctified tradition is 'The less, the better.' "**

Here are some examples of a few percussion-section placements suggested in scores by contemporary composers.

Example XIV–11. Kotonski, *a battere*

batteria I
3 piatti (alto, medio, basso)
hi-hat
2 cymb. antiques (in Si e Si♭)
4 cow bells
tam-tam (medio grande)

batteria II
3 piatti (alto, medio, basso)
cow bell
triangolo
Almglocke (la più grossa)
gong giavanese (o gran tam-tam)
piatto (posto orizzontalmente sul timpano a ped.)

batteria III
3 piatti (alto, medio, basso)
hi-hat
4 Almglocken
2 cymb. antiques (in Mi e Fa)
chitarra
cembalo
viola
violoncello

---

*There are extreme examples of huge percussion sections before our own time. Respighi in *Feste romane* asks for fourteen different percussion instruments, ten of which play at one time in a section of the work. No orchestra is going to hire ten players, so some will of necessity be left out, at least in American orchestras.

**Bernard Rogers, *The Art of Orchestration* (New York: Appleton-Century-Croft, 1951), p. 76.

Example XIV–12. Crumb, *Echoes of Time and the River*

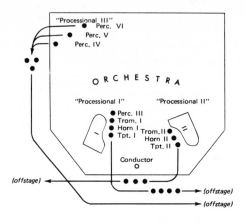

Example XIV–13. Diagram by R. Smith Brindle

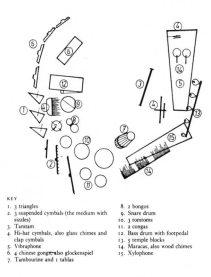

KEY

1. 3 triangles
2. 3 suspended cymbals (the medium with sizzles)
3. Tamtam
4. Hi-hat cymbals, also glass chimes and clap cymbals
5. Vibraphone
6. 4 chinese gongs, also glockenspiel
7. Tambourine and 1 tablas

8. 2 bongos
9. Snare drum
10. 3 tomtoms
11. 2 congas
12. Bass drum with footpedal
13. 5 temple blocks
14. Maracas, also wood chimes
15. Xylophone

Example XIV–14. Berio, *Circles*

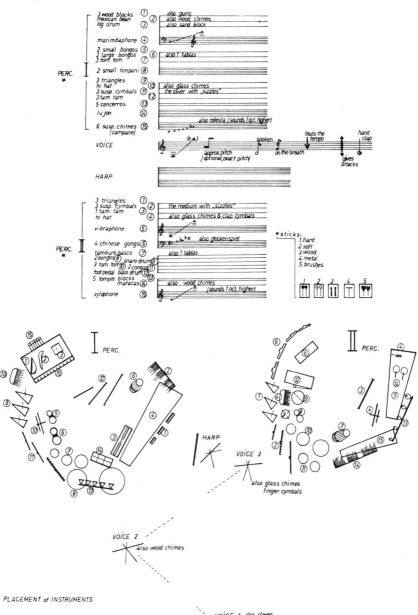

PLACEMENT of INSTRUMENTS

USES OF THE PERCUSSION SECTION

1. Historically, the percussion section has been used to simulate march music (i.e. *à la Turque*) or to lend an ethnic flavor. (This does not apply to the early timpani.)

2. The percussion section serves to emphasize accents and general rhythmic activity.

3. It is used to build or to "cap" a climax. Under this category we may also include the shock value of a cymbal struck at the very beginning of a work (Prelude to Bizet's *Carmen*, for instance).

4. It may also color certain pitches or entire passages by doubling other instruments in the orchestra.

Of course, there are many other uses for this most colorful section of the modern orchestra, but these are the most important. Lately, given the expansion of the percussion section and the extraordinary technical skill of our performers, composers have been using percussion, especially pitched percussion, as an independent section, often alternating with another choir of the orchestra.

Let us look at some examples from the great orchestral literature. Since we are concerned with orchestral literature rather than chamber or percussion repertoire, we shall omit works such as Varèse's *Ionization*, which of course is for percussion alone. In our discussion we shall include the harp and keyboard instruments, since these are most often placed together with the percussion group.

March and Ethnic Music

An example from Beethoven's *Ninth Symphony* typifies the marchlike percussion group so popular with Classical as well as the early Romantic composers for conjuring up the spectre of marching soldiers, wars, or any other kind of strife. Notice that the timpani are not used, for they were not considered part of this particular percussion group which, as mentioned before, was usually called the "Turkish instruments." The variation begins with the bass drum only, giving an accent to the bassoons and the contra. Then it is joined by the triangle and cymbals when the tune enters in the winds and horns. There is a gradual crescendo in the score, as if a band were coming toward us from afar.

Example XIV–15. Beethoven, *Symphony No. 9,* fourth movement, Alla marcia, mm. 1–33

Example XIV–16. Rimsky-Korsakov, *Capriccio espagnol*, fourth movement, mm. 79–98

(continued on next page)

Rimsky-Korsakov, *Capriccio espagnol:* The combination of tambourines and castanets to suggest Spain became a cliché with composers of the eighteenth and nineteenth centuries. However, one must not condemn it, for it does conjure up the Iberian peninsula with reliable immediacy. The same instruments are used to suggest any region around the Mediterranean, since they often appear in "Italian" and even "Moroccan" pieces

Rhythmic Emphasis and Accents

The second common usage of percussion instruments is for rhythmic emphasis or sharp accents. Let us examine several places in the same work that illustrate the imaginative use of different instruments for that purpose. We shall draw our examples from Copland's *Appalachian Spring.*

1. Xylophone reinforces every high accent, while the tabor (or long drum) lends support to the stopped horn (low accent).

Example XIV–17. Copland, *Appalachian Spring*, mm. 46–54

2. The piano gives emphasis to the *sfp* effect in the strings.

Example XIV–18. Copland, *Appalachian Spring*, mm. 55–61

3. The wood block supports the off-beat accent.

Example XIV–19. Copland, *Appalachian Spring*, mm. 225–28

4. The triangle adds to the excitement and buildup of the run leading to a sharp accent; then the snare drum, first with a brush, then
with a stick on the rim, gives added emphasis to the off-beat in order
to create a lighter downbeat impression.

Example XIV–20. Copland, *Appalachian Spring*, mm. 229–44

5. A very dry wood color, the claves, strengthens the high accents at this rhythmically exciting spot. Notice that when this music returns at the end of this section, Copland adds xylophone and strings, finally crowning the climax with a series of solo timpani strokes aided by bass pizzicatos.

Example XIV–21. Copland, *Appalachian Spring*, mm. 375–82

Climactic Effects

Using the percussion section to build a climax and then help to sustain it is a stunning device employed by many of the great masters. The percussion may sometimes aid in this buildup with an ostinato or other kinds of repeated gestures. Alternative is to hold back the percussion until the climactic moment. In this portion of the chapter, we shall look at a number of examples of successful climaxes which will give us hints on how to use the percussion most effectively in those situations.

Debussy, *Fêtes,* from *Nocturnes:* At [10], an extremely soft steady beat begins in the timpani, supported by harps and pizzicato strings. The beat continues under the theme until [11], when the timpani changes the ostinato to single strokes on the first and second beat. Still, melodic fragments are heard in the winds and horns, and there is a steady crescendo to [13], when the timpani ostinato becomes the "theme figure" ♪♫ ♪♫ and keeps driving toward the climax at [14]. Interestingly enough, the climax is broken off suddenly, and the beginning material of the piece returns, making the form crystal clear. The timpani receives some help from two other members of the percussion section when the snare drum enters at two measures before [13], and the cymbals join in at [13].

Example XIV–22. Debussy, *Nocturnes: Fetés,* from [10] to [14]

Warren Benson, *Symphony for Drums and Wind Orchestra:* This is an unusually fine example of a sustained climax kept alive by the percussion section only, while the rest of the orchestra cuts off at N. Notice the great effectiveness of the ostinato parts, which have been heard in this movement before. Also, the composer uses variations of the repeated figures just before the climax. Then this material becomes an ostinato at $\boxed{N}$. The device of letting a movement "die out" with percussion is certainly a contemporary one, and this particular lengthy "demise" is most powerful.

Example XIV–23. Benson, *Symphony for Drums and Wind Orchestra*, third movement, 3 before $\boxed{M}$ to end

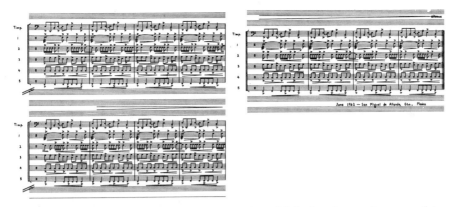

Next, we shall look at an excerpt in which the timpani are used in moving toward the climax, but another instrument is effectively introduced to reinforce the final moment.

One of the most carefully and masterfully planned climaxes occurs at the end of Brahms's *Symphony No. 2.* Very little need be said about it except that Brahms's restraint in using the timpani is rewarded by one of the most thrilling and powerful endings in the symphonic literature. Of course, the excellent brass (trombone, tuba) writing helps, but it is the entrance of the timpani that makes this climax work.

Example XIV–24. Brahms, *Symphony No. 2,* fourth movement, mm. 392–end

Before continuing, we must mention that there are many instances of such climaxes; therefore, the student should study some others. To mention but a few: Wagner's *Overture to Rienzi*, mm. 47–65; W. Schuman's *New England Triptych*, first movement, mm. 235–69; J.

Schwantner's *And the Mountains Rising Nowhere*, mm. 91–120. These will serve to demonstrate some of the different ways in which the task of building climaxes with percussion is accomplished.

We have mentioned before that a dramatic moment may come at the very beginning, and that a percussion sound is a great "ear-opener." In this regard, the Prelude to *Carmen* by Bizet was cited: here are several other effective percussion beginnings:

Example XIV–25. Rossini, Overture to *La Gazza ladra*

Example XIV–26. Beethoven: *Violin Concerto*, first movement

Example XIV–27. Tchaikovsky, *Symphony No. 4*, fourth movement

Example XIV–28. Shostakovich: *Symphony No. 5*, fourth movement

Notice that the percussion does not have to be loud to be effective!

Coloring Pitches or Passages

Here is an entire section of a work colored by timpani, bass drum, and tam-tam to give a heavy "cortège" or procession effect.

Example XIV–29. Stravinsky, *Le Sacre du printemps*, "Procession of the Sage," mm. 1–14

On the other hand, the ethereal quality at the ending of the following piece is greatly enhanced by the introduction of the antique cymbals (crotales), doubling a "dissonant" note of the chord at first, and then actually playing a solo at the end.

Example XIV–30. Debussy, *Prélude à l'après-midi d'un faune*, mm. 94–110

(continued on next page)

In the next excerpt, taken from De Falla's *Three-Cornered Hat*, the xylophone, timpani, and piano, as well as the harp, color the notes accompanying the high woodwinds.

Example XIV–31. De Falla, *The Three-Cornered Hat,* "Dance of the Miller's Wife," mm. 12–16

Leslie Bassett uses three keyboard instruments to color each change of chord in the upper strings.

Example XIV–32. Bassett, *Variations for Orchestra*, 1 before PP to
4 after PP

The versatility of the percussion section is virtually limitless.
However, it is often overused by the inexperienced orchestrator, in
an attempt to cover up weak places in the composition. By studying
the scores of the masters both past and present, we should be able to
learn the virtues of restraint and caution, for even more than the
entire brass section, a loud bass drum or cymbal roll can obliterate
the entire orchestra, no matter how loud the tutti may be playing.

In dealing with any instrument, choir, or section, we must recognize one fundamental, underlying issue: whatever instruments are
used must be an organic part of the composition; they must sound
inevitable. The *idea* of the composition must govern the selection of
any instrument or group of instruments in order to serve the music
and present it in the most effective manner possible.

To conclude, let us look at a rather marvelous example of inevita-
bility as far as the percussion section is concerned. In this seven-
measure excerpt the timpani are used to emphasize the double bass
pizzicato. The snare drum is employed throughout the composition
but never again in the manner in which it is played in measure seven.
The wood block becomes an integral part of the theme, and because
of its sparing use, its importance is heightened, since each time this
introductory theme returns, the wood block is used right along with

the plucking of the strings. Then at m. 821 its part is expanded, and the wood block solo lends its support to a most satisfying conclusion. In this little dance variation the entire percussion section is used with the greatest ingenuity and taste.

Example XIV–33. Bernstein, *Fancy Free*, "Danzon," mm. 737–43

Example XIV–34. Bernstein, *Fancy Free*, "Danzon," mm. 820–30

ORCHESTRATION

15

Scoring for Orchestra

This book is cumulative; now that we are familiar with the ranges, register characteristics, and combinatorial possibilities of all the instruments in the symphony orchestra, we are prepared to consider special problems in handling the entire orchestra as one large instrument.

The art critic Jacques Maroges once said, "The greatest colorists have always obtained the maximum brilliance and vibration with a minimum of color." This is an important maxim to remember as we study and analyze the use of the entire orchestra. The inexperienced orchestrator may either use the entire body for too long an unrelieved stretch, or utilize such a great variety of different effects that the structure of the work is put in jeopardy by the constant flux of color and texture. Balance of colors and discriminating handling of the musical elements in the orchestration will enhance the clarity of the music and therefore yield the very best orchestral sound. The great orchestators of the past and present realized that one can tire very easily of the tutti sound of the orchestra and that using all the choirs together for too long a time is tedious and monotonous. Therefore, in this chapter we will examine how some of these great masters have used the orchestra for the handling of foreground, middleground, and background material; how to score the most effective tutti; how to handle a purely polyphonic section; and how to deal with newer techniques such as *Klangfarben* orchestration, texture orchestration, and other special devices.

It must be emphasized yet again that the orchestration should support the form of the work; conversely, no matter how imaginative and colorful the orchestration, it cannot save a badly composed piece of music. In the words of Rimsky-Korsakov, "Only that which is well written can be well orchestrated."*

There is no universally accepted system of analyzing the orchestration of a work, except by isolating its major elements and examining their orchestral settings after one has analyzed the structure of the work as a whole. For our purposes, we shall excerpt small sections of a work to see how the composer has handled the material orchestrally, but the student is urged to become thoroughly familiar with the major themes or main gestures, whether melodic, secondary, rhythmic, or harmonic, before attempting to analyze the orchestration.

THE UNISON-OCTAVE TUTTI

Before we begin our discussion of this textural genre, we must clarify the word tutti. This Italian word, when used in connection with the orchestra, generally means the simultaneous use of all of the instruments. In this case the word *all* is relative, for one must not take it literally to mean every single instrument, although in certain instances this may indeed be the case. Perhaps it would be profitable to describe tutti sections in two ways: 1) the *partial tutti*, using most of the instruments at hand; and 2) the *full tutti*, where every instrument is playing simultaneously.

Here are some examples of effective unison tutti. Each one will be analyzed separately so that we may acquire the various skills in handling this very powerful device. Very few actual unison tutti exist because of the range limitations of some of the instruments, but the following are two very successful ones.

All the instruments are in unison, and the composer wisely omits the upper woodwinds because their ranges do not extend down far enough to play the entire passage. Trumpets could have been used, and one may speculate that a contemporary composer would have

---

*Preface to *Principles of Orchestration*, trans. Edward Agate (New York: Kalmus, n.d.), p. vii.

Example XV–1. D'Indy, *Istar*, mm. 206–16

scored them even if that is not their best register. Notice that the trombones are marked *ppp* so as not to dominate the entire orchestra. Even though the double basses could play most of the notes, they would not contribute significantly to the sound, so the composer has left them out. The performance of the passage on the G-string for the violin is another strengthening device. Here again, a contemporary composer might have used the oboes to emphasize the *sf* in the fifth full measure and perhaps a muted trumpet to give that accent a special flavor. It is interesting to note the various articulations calculated to give the unison a certain tension. To the smooth slurred winds and horns is added a nonslurred articulated line in the strings and trombones, plus a curious tremolo from the violas. In other words, there is an imaginative undercurrent of activity adding subtle flavor to the otherwise single-minded statement.

Example XV–2. Barber, *Symphony No. 1*, mm. 128–36

Here we have a different kind of tutti unison (actually octaves) occurring at the climax (end) of the first section of the symphony. Barber orchestrates a crescendo by adding the brass instruments and timpani in octaves on a single pitch, and then the germinal idea of the section is played in a multi-octave spread. The timpani repeats the idea constituted of different colors to still another unison at 15 , followed by an orchestral glissando. Barber very subtly enlarges the doubling slightly in every measure in order to exploit varied timbres each time the little germ motive is played. Notice four more details:

1. Barber does not write octave skips from m. 129 to m. 130 in the horns, trombones, or tuba, perhaps because that would make the gesture too heavy and pompous and risk losing its brittle quality.

2. He wisely cuts out the piccolo and flutes before the glissando so they won't be forced to drop out before the last notes.

3. The trombones and tuba are also omitted in m. 136, because that would make the glissando too heavy and deemphasize the high D, which is so poignantly supported by the high horns.

4. The entrance of Trombone III, tuba, and timpani on the low B♭ really reinforces the finality of the phrase.

Example XV–3. Mozart: *Symphony No. 40,* fourth movement, mm. 125–32

The orchestral unison spread over several octaves has always been popular and has been used very frequently either to introduce a new idea, summarize an old one, or state a major melody or gesture before it is contrapuntally developed. The latter is the case here, and Mozart uses a partial tutti since the horns could not play many of the notes. What is most interesting about the spacing of this octave tutti is its variety. At first, Violins I and II and the flute plus the two oboes play in unison, while the octave immediately below is rather sparsely scored with the violas only; the octave below that is more heavily scored for the cellos and both bassoons, supported yet an octave lower by the double basses. Notice, however, that from m. 128 on, Mozart divides the orchestra differently; from the heavy scoring in the middle register, one suspects that he wants the listener to understand the theme to be:

with the flute and oboe added simply for sheen and brilliance. By this subtle turn in the scoring, we can certainly learn a great deal about orchestration as the means for clarifying one's intentions. If, for instance, Mozart had kept the unison of the flute and the violins, he would have had to drop the flute out for the final note of the passage, and it would have added nothing to the heavy string scoring. Similarly, the oboes would have had to be dropped since they cannot play the last note, although they would have added a raucous quality to the low C♯. They fill out the space much better exactly where they are written and the flute is not left alone in its upper reaches. In other words, the composer wants every note in this passage played effectively by every instrument that he uses, yet wants his gesture to sound as written in the example above; therefore, he chose this distribution of pitches and octaves in the instruments.

Example XV–4. Beethoven, *Symphony No. 9*, first movement, mm. 16–21

Here is a full orchestral tutti beset with problems of instrumental limitations or practices characteristic of the trumpets, horns, flutes, and violins of that time. This most powerful passage probably would have been scored differently (not *better*, mind you) today because a piccolo could have played the upper-octave D anacrusis so that the all-important falling fourth would be emphasized. The first violins would probably have been placed an octave higher, and for that matter, the first flute might have been asked to play the top D, which is possible on today's instruments. Of course, the trumpets and all four horns would be able to perform the entire passage in octaves with the rest of the orchestra. One may even say that five timpani could be assigned to play the entire passage with the tutti. Beethoven did not have most of these options, yet wrote a remarkable climax. The limitations of the instruments are converted into assets, for the emphasis on the D and the A provided by the horns (III and IV), trumpets, and timpani give an open feeling to the whole statement and lend even greater power to the final D. Notice some of the excellent doubling and nondoubling. It is significant that Beethoven superimposes an octave on the high octave of the violins, oboes, and clarinets, with only two flutes. This is real contemporary orchestral thinking, for this high octave in the flute is so piercing it need not be doubled by any other instrument to cut through.

Study every instrumental line separately to ascertain exactly why it deviates (or has to deviate) from the melody as played by the strings, the bassoons, first oboe, first clarinet, and second horn, and you will unlock many of the reasons for the various uses of these instruments in Beethoven's time. Beethoven teaches us some most valuable lessons concerning strengths and weaknesses in certain registers of these instruments, such as the doubling of the flutes from m. 18 on, the voicing of the oboes and clarinets (the clarinets could certainly have remained in octaves, but apparently the composer did not wish to strengthen that octave), the limitation of the Bb horn in this key, and so on.

Example XV–5. Smetana, Overture to *The Bartered Bride,* mm. 1–12

This final example in the study of unison or octave tutti is somewhat different from the others and a good bridge to the next texture we will discuss—melody and accompaniment—since the sustained chords act like an accompaniment to the lively melodic figure. Sustained notes or chords are the adhesive that provides cohesion in a tutti passage. Even without the sustaining brass, the winds and strings would sound spritely and exuberant, but the bright brass sound enhances those qualities. The atmosphere is rendered even more like a celebration, and a certain "roundness" of tone is added by the sustaining brass. What would a contemporary composer have done? Well, we could speculate that he might have scored the trumpets and horns in unison and octaves with the winds and strings. But this would have added too much weight to the eighth notes and taken the lightness out of the passage. He could have simply removed the sustaining notes and left out the brass altogether. This would have given the passage a more brittle quality. Finally, he might have added xylophone to give added "ping" to the fast notes; however, that certainly would be out of style for Smetana's orchestra of 1866. Smetana's solution is perfect, for it gives the very agile instruments an opportunity to show off in their best registers. In addition, the harmonic implications of a run realized by sustaining brass, makes for a thrilling opening of the work.

FOREGROUND AND BACKGROUND

It is more accurate to identify this texture by a more abstract label than "melody and accompaniment," because there will be so many occasions when just two elements are present, neither being exactly melody or accompaniment, but two separate and distinct musical ideas. The simplest example is, of course, a melodic foreground with a strictly harmonic background.

Example XV–6. Tchaikovsky, *Francesca da Rimini*, mm. 325–49

This is the most obvious kind of scoring and is very effective. The melody is introduced *a cappella* in the clarinet and after its introduction flows right into a tune with string accompaniment. It should be mentioned forthwith that the most striking accompanying color is usually in contrast to that of the solo (melody) instrument, although there are many instances where successful accompaniments are played by instruments that are the same or similar to the solo carrier. The pizzicato adds to the contrast and, by comparison, makes the clarinet sound even warmer. The *con sordino* designation means little here, for pizzicato is not affected very much by mutes. The mutes are put on for the next passage, which is the continuation of the clarinet melody by the violins (in octaves), accompanied by sustained lower strings, bassoon, and timpani, a wonderful contrast to the clarinet presentation. Timing and placement or assignment of color should be mentioned in connection with this example. An anacrusis or a rest before a certain color enters are two excellent ways of introducing new elements and making sure they are clearly perceived. (This will be especially true in polyphonic textures, discussed later on.) In the Tchaikovsky example, the introduction of the clarinet all by itself is a bit extreme, but it does illustrate this point well.

There are thousands of examples of foreground–background orchestrations, many of which have been mentioned previously when discussing the choirs separately. Here are two more, which involve much of the entire orchestra:

Example XV–7. Weber, Overture to *Der Freischütz*, mm. 1–18

The four horns are beautifully accompanied by the strings. The string texture is both arpeggiated in the first and second violins and sustained in the lower strings. Notice that here the accompaniment begins first, and the entrance of the two horns sounds very fresh.

Example XV–8a. Mahler, *Kindertotenlieder*, "Nun will die Sonn'," mm. 58–61: Piano Version

b. Orchestral Version

In order to understand the complex scoring of this most incredible example of orchestral thinking, we must first look at a piano version of the music. Notice there are only two components: an eighth-note foreground in the right hand and an eighth-note background in the left hand. This is a kind of first-species counterpoint: two distinct parts, note against note. A third element might possibly be an implied D pedal; at least a pianist playing these few measures would pedal as if there were. Mahler indeed does utilize a soft pedal note in the fourth horns and at the beginning in the bass clarinet. The other two parts are distributed among the instruments in chamber-music fashion. There are no two instruments with identical parts for more than a few notes. Almost every pitch is colored differently; one may even say that this foreshadows the practice of *Klangfarben* orchestratioń, made popular by the expressionists. (We shall learn more about that later on in this chapter.) One further observation which is important in our contemporary thinking for orchestra: while from Wagner and Mahler to the present time composers have availed themselves of the huge orchestral forces developed through-out the nineteenth century, composers today often avoid writing for a large orchestra, or if they do, emphasize the importance of single instruments and their characteristic sounds rather than the "fat" combinations favored by earlier masters. This must not be consid-ered a value judgment; as a matter of fact, some people believe that this chamber treatment of the large orchestra is a trend away from effective orchestration. Both points of view are valid, provided the orchestra is used with great imagination and skill; if the music is good, the results either way will be most satisfying.

Study this Mahler excerpt very carefully, and make a list of the doublings of each gesture—or even each note—so that these com-posite sounds will be well ingrained into the ear for your own even-tual use.

HOMOPHONIC TEXTURE

Let us divide this section into two parts:

1. chords;

2. harmonic (homophonic) writing, in which one element is given to the entire orchestra to play together. In connection with this topic, we shall discuss voice leading as well as doubling.

Chords for Full Orchestra

We have already discussed the problem of spacing chords for each individual choir; now let us examine some successful orchestral chordal scoring.

It would be best to set down some overriding considerations:

1. The melody notes should be more prominent than the harmony notes.

2. Care must be taken to assign pitches to the instruments in their best registral positions so that the notes may be performed at the desired dynamic.

3. When considering doubling notes, try to find instruments that have an acoustic affinity for one another. This is especially impor-tant when doubling at pitch.

We have already spoken of the three major spacings of chords—juxtaposed (or superimposed), interlocked, and enclosed. Usually these techniques are mixed when we deal with a full orchestra. Here are some examples:

Example XV–9. Beethoven, *Missa Solemnis,* chords from m. 1 and m. 21

The tonic chord in the first measure of the work emphasizes the tonic note D most prominently; it is a rather open sound, with all the strings plus the trumpets, three horns, and timpani on D, and both flutes sounding the higher octave. Only the remaining woodwinds play the chord tones, as if they were ' "realizing" the first few overtones of the D fundamental. The chord in m. 21, on the other hand, is a full chord in which all the sections play all the notes in the tonic chord. The dynamic after a rest is a sudden *forte,* and the chorus enters, supported by the organ to make the sound quite heavy and full. Notice that in the first doubling, the flutes were given the octave above the first violins, while in the big chord the first flute doubles the first violin at pitch, and the second flute plays the A above the staff alone. It is a most effective spacing.

Example XV–10. Weber, Overture to *Der Freischütz,* m. 284

This is the climactic chord of the main section of the overture. It is a brilliant and crystal-clear tutti chord, with the strings and timpani adding power by their tremolo and roll respectively. It is important to study the exact makeup of the chord. The strings are simply "stacked" or superimposed from the lowest C to the high G. The bassoons and the third trombone take care of the octaves below the double basses. The brasses are also juxtaposed, and only the oboes and clarinets are interlocked. Weber must have felt that the second oboe doubled by the first trumpet is a more sympathetic doubling acoustically than a clarinet-trumpet combination. It is also interesting to note which instruments are not doubled at pitch, since the composer obviously felt that these were in such a good registral position that they would be more effective alone. They are: Oboe I, Horns I and IV, Trombone II and Bassoon II. Consider this chord carefully, and remember its spacing when a brilliant chord is in order.

Example XV–11. Schumann, *Symphony No. 1*, first movement, mm. 3–4

It is important to study this chordal progression for two reasons: first, to ascertain how the composer emphasizes the melody, and second, to observe how he handles the voice leading of the harmonic progression. Schumann uses double- and triple-stops to obtain a sweeping sound in the strings *non divisi*. This adds to the ringing effect of these chords. All the string notes are doubled in the juxtaposed woodwinds, while the horns and trumpets, both in Bb, play the only notes they can in this situation—the "horn fifths."

Example XV–12

The voice leading of the chords is absolutely "according to the book" and should be studied carefully. All sevenths (Eb) resolve downward; all dominant notes (F) remain as common tones, except those involved in the "horn fifths." All pitches are doubled at least once, and it is interesting that Schumann holds back on the use of trombones and timpani in order to build an even heavier chord in the next phrase.

Example XV–13. Brahms, *Symphony No. 3*, first movement, final chord

We must label this a "dangerous" chord, because the articulation and dynamic are difficult to achieve. Many Romantic composers love to end movements in this way, and one must expect the flutes to overpower the structure because it is simply very difficult to play *piano* that high. This chord always sounds louder than it should, although it is a beautifully luminous sound. Actually, it would be easier to control if the strings had the top octave doubled by the winds at the octave below, but that would have been impossible in this situation.* The spacing of the chord as written is certainly beau-

---

*The flute was already holding the top pitch, and the strings were otherwise involved.

tiful, and the stacking effect gives it a very warm hue. Notice the doubling of the first and second trombones with the violas; this emphasis, and the low notes of the strings with the first and second violins doubled an octave higher by the winds, contribute to the separation of high and low perceived by the ear.

Example XV–14a. Brahms, *Symphony No. 3*, first movement, mm. 183–87: Reduction

b. Full Score

Here are a reduction and full score of this passage. It is advisable for the student to make a reduction of the wind and brass chords as well, in order to find out exactly what is doubled and how the voice leading operates. This is certainly brilliant scoring, but it neither overwhelms nor overshadows the tune of the first and second violins; they are in their best register, and the high flutes help by emphasizing the first melody note in each measure. Notice that each chord is fully represented in all the choirs and in every octave.

Example XV–15. Mahler, *Symphony No. 1*, fourth movement, mm. 123–27

A most brilliant sound aided by string tremolos, rolls in the timpani and triangle, plus a cymbal crash. It is important to notice that all the upper octaves are completely filled in; only the lowest octave, played by the cellos, double basses, tuba, third trombone, and timpani, is left bare. The high brass doubled an octave higher by both violins and upper wind makes this an overwhelming chordal structure, with one section completely juxtaposed upon the other.

Example XV–16. Debussy, *La Mer*, last measure

It is imperative to study a chord that is "under control," meaning that it is articulated as a *fortissimo* sound and then must diminuendo to *pianissimo*. The composer, therefore, has to distribute the pitches among those instruments that can easily control the notes and accomplish the dynamic requirement. Debussy does so brilliantly. The two highest notes (A♯) are assigned to the first violin and the piccolo. The violins, of course, are able to play softly on any note high or low, while the piccolo is in its least exposed register and can keep this note, written ♭ under perfect control. The harp simply provides a loud or soft "ping" for the top pitches. Again, there is a big gap between the low C♯ and the rest of the chord, which is juxtaposed in every choir. The melody note (E♯) in the two trumpets comes out brilliantly in this register; and it is doubled by the two oboes and at the octave by the English horn. This E♯ and the high A♯ are the only notes doubled at pitch, so that all the other chord tones are much softer and retain their own individual colors.

Before we proceed to homophonic passages from the literature, let us summarize briefly the whole question of doubling. There are basically two reasons for doubling:

1. for dynamic tonal strength or power;
2. for subtle coloristic tonal effects.

It must not be forgotten that doublings at pitch usually result in the loss of the individual color characteristics of both instruments. Further, sustained doublings tire the ear. Often octave doublings give much clearer and more brilliant results, especially if the purpose of the doubling is for tonal power.

Unison doubling or blending of the same instrument gives a peculiar weight to the tone, but because two, three, or four like instruments cannot always play in tune with each other, many of the upper overtones are cut to give a "flatness" to the strength of the pitches. Many composers consciously seek this effect, as in this example from Mahler's *Fourth Symphony*:

Example XV–17. Mahler, *Symphony No. 4*, first movement, mm. 125–41

Here four flutes play a "shrieking" melody that is both heavy and powerful (also always slightly but beautifully out of tune). This passage would be just as loud with one flute playing it, but that would be too clear and transparent for Mahler's purpose.

How and what to double is always a matter of personal preference, but it must be a conscious matter, in which all these facts are taken into consideration. Beethoven, for instance, most often uses octave doublings for added power. Mozart, Mendelssohn, Debussy, and Ravel prefer unmixed pure sounds for melodies, but they also use octave doublings and sometimes very subtle blends. Rimsky-Korsakov favors tone mixings and big combinations of unison doublings. All these must be studied so that the orchestrator can make choices after having examined the various combinatorial possibilities in the best scores of the past and present. To show one excellent example of doublings for the sake of power, consider this example from Tchaikovsky's *Romeo and Juliet*. The trumpets play a2 at pitch, while the accompanying chords are all doubled throughout the orchestra for a most powerful "punctuation" effect. Here the power of the whole chord is the issue, not its tone color: brilliance versus subtlety.

Example XV–18. Tchaikovsky, *Romeo and Juliet*, mm. 334–37

We shall, of course, continue to examine this problem, but the considerations discussed above should be kept in mind at all times so that the choices concerning doubling can be made from a position of knowledge, experience, and strength.

Examples of Homphonic Texture

Example XV–19. Schubert, Symphony No. 8, first movement, mm. 170–76

This very simple example begins as a unison (octaves) over a dominant and tonic pedal. After m. 173, the melody is carried on by the strings, while the rest of the orchestra builds two chords. The transition from unison to a thicker harmony is facilitated by the sustained tonic pitches in the brass and the dominant pitch in the timpani. Notice the wide separation between the flutes and the strings. Notice, too, the reluctance of the strings to break into harmony. This color division makes it much easier for the ear to separate melody from the harmony (background from foreground) and the result is a most successfully scored passage.

The ear is able to separate two ideas presented simultaneously if they are scored with opposing timbres and differing designs. This is an important principle to keep in mind for emphasized clarity in orchestration whenever a variety of ideas is present at any given time.

Example XV–22. Mahler, *Symphony No. 4*, fourth movement, mm. 106–11

Example XV–20. Mahler, *Symphony No. 4*, fourth movement, mm. 36–39

Example XV–21. Mahler, *Symphony No. 4*, fourth movement, mm. 72–75

The exquisite passage which recurs three times during the course of this movement is scored very differently each time it appears in partial tutti. The "heavenly" quality is effected by modern organum chords, parallel-motion triads with contrary or similar motion in the bass. Examine the highly successful combinations of instruments in each of the three scorings. Mm. 36–39: The strings are reserved for the final open fifth sound, while the harmony is given to the flutes, horns, and harp to play chords under the singer's line. Notice that the third horn doubles the singer's pitches an octave below. Mm. 72–75: This version features the strings as the main accompanist, and it is the softest scoring with a beautiful assist from the piccolo. The harp writing is interesting, first in thirds, then in octaves, to add to the smooth unison writing in mm. 73–74. The softness of this version is aided by a full D-major chord in the fourth measure rather than the stark open fifth sound of the previous version. Mm. 106–11: The final repetition of the phrase is extended and colored in two very distinct ways: first, by very soft brasses with harp; then by a lovely, rather rare combination; flutes, clarinets, and muted double basses, with the harp acting as the constant. This kind of partial tutti, colored differently each time, illustrates an essential aspect of great orchestral thinking: Even though great color variety is provided, the recognizable texture and similar chord structure that mark the passage prevail to give a great sense of unity to the form of the movement.

Example XV–23. Wagner: Prelude to Die Meistersinger, mm. 1–9

The noble beginning of this Prelude illustrates the technique whereby a dark yet loud and majestic color is created through vital semi-independent parts for the different instruments. The first chord is immediately noteworthy. The strings play only a big chord, while the melody is given to the trumpets, doubled by their best "affinity instruments," two oboes and two clarinets at pitch. This certainly creates the heavy, dark color often associated with band music. Curiously enough, Wagner does not continue the melody in this combination but has the violins take over the tune. One may speculate that possibly he did not trust the valve trumpets to carry on the stately melody, but it is much more likely that he did not want the first statement to be quite so climactic, for he does give the entire theme to the trumpets later on in the work. The violins (first and second) add a grandeur to the initial statement, and their *non divisi* double stops add power to the sound, while the oboe and clarinet doubling gives them a sharper edge. The inner harmony is filled out by the two bassoons, four horns, and the first two trombones, with a bit of assistance from the violas. The color resulting from this combination is very warm and most appropriate to the sombre, organlike beginning. A strong bass line is entrusted to a very powerful combination: third trombone, tuba, cellos, and basses in octaves. This is, all told, beautifully balanced homophonic phrase. It is important to note that the trumpet, which might alter the balance once it has stopped playing the melody, is given a secondary role in the harmonic structure in a register where it cannot disturb the quality of the established hue. Since this is such a popular work, the student should be able to study a bit more of the score to see how Wagner holds back "the highs" so cleverly and how they lighten the entire atmosphere and build the crescendo as upper octaves gradually double the violins after m. 18.

POLYPHONIC TEXTURE, OR FOREGROUND—BACKGROUND–MIDDLEGROUND DISTRIBUTION

We have already discussed the handling of polyphonic textures in the individual choirs; we have further observed some superb scoring of three diverse elements in the second movement of Beethoven's *Seventh Symphony*. This skill is difficult to master, and it is hoped that the next few examples will provide insight into some of the most successful solutions by masters of the orchestral repertoire. We shall not spend too much time on fugal writing, because it is the most obvious type of polyphony and is becoming less and less useful nowadays. While we will not ignore this genre, we will concentrate more on handling three or more important elements sounding simultaneously to create sophisticated polyphonic situations.

Example XV–24. Mozart, Symphony No. 41, "Jupiter," fourth
movement, mm. 368–424.

The end of the *Jupiter Symphony* is one of the monumental examples of polyphonic writing in the history of music. This is a quintuple fugue where each subject is exposed by itself and then utilized throughout the development section in various combinations with the other themes or elements. The reason for calling them elements is to emphasize that they are all rather short fragments, not long subjects as are found in many (not all, of course) Baroque fugues. Here are the five themes (or elements) that make up the melodic material of this finale:

Example XV–25

We notice immediately that each of the five gestures has its own characteristic rhythmic makeup. In other words, each is recognizable separately. The first theme is a kind of *cantus firmus* which is at the same time a unifying element for the entire symphony, since it appears in the first as well as the third movement. The others all have their own profiles which make them distinct. This is essential in a multi-element orchestral texture if one wants the listener to follow the different gestures. Of course, the individual elements also work together in quintuple counterpoint, quite a feat in itself.

Now let us go to the score. From mm. 372 to 388, Mozart doubles only the *cantus firmus*–type first theme, while the other tunes are brought in, played by different sections of the string choir. It is important to note that each rendition of the first theme is colored somewhat differently and supported by one member of the string choir: (a) bassoons, horns, cellos; (b) flute, oboes, violas; (c) flute, oboes, second violins; (d) flute, oboes, first violin. As the texture thickens, the third theme is strengthened by coupling the violas and second violins in sixths in mm. 383–84, in mm. 387–88, and by adding the preliminary four notes to the theme. These, of course, add weight to the harmony. Mozart and many of his countemporaries were not prone to write independent double-bass parts, but in this contrapuntal texture the double bass is a completely independent member of the ensemble. Once the web of counterpoint becomes truly involved, combining the first four elements, Mozart shows us an important technique, namely, to keep an established color intact long enough to carry out its assignment. The listener must not be overburdened with shifting colors in which the main musical ideas may be lost and secondary color considerations become the point of focus. From m. 389 to m. 400 the following colors are constant:

1. first violin doubled by flute at pitch (third theme);
2. second violin doubled by first oboe at pitch (third, fourth, then second theme);
3. violas doubled by second oboe at pitch (fourth, second, then first theme);
4. cellos doubled by first bassoon at pitch (second, first, then third theme);
5. double basses doubled by second bassoon at the octave (first, third, then fourth theme);
6. horns, trumpets, and timpani providing the cohesive tonic-dominant, nonthematic pedal notes.

Suddenly at m. 400, a tremendous climax, which has been building, shakes up the colors for four measures and introduces the fifth element for the final part of the coda. This closeup section is mostly harmonic, but the fourth element is emphasized when it is played three times in its entirety (both in unison and harmonized). In all the doubling here, Mozart's primary concern is tonal power; each theme must be heard at good strength. He relies on the rhythmic-melodic characteristics of each element to differentiate it clearly, assigning each a strong and sympathetic color combination to aid this purpose.

Example XV–26. Wagner, Prelude to *Die Meistersinger*, mm. 158–61

This is an example of three distinct musical elements or themes most successfully combined. They are so clearly perceived because they are assigned to very distinctive color combinations. The two main elements are the bass and the first violin tunes; the arpeggio theme is the third, but less "thematic" element. Of course, anything that outlines a chord is important, since the first or main theme is built on one, so the arpeggiated gesture takes on significance in that way also. As in the Mozart example, Wagner's three elements are rhythmically very independent, and have been exposed separately before this combination occurs. This fact, added to the very clever color variance among the three elements, gives clarity and great excitement to this exquisite passage.

First theme: double basses, tuba, two bassoons (double basses an octave lower)

Second theme: Violin I, Clarinet I doubled at pitch; octave-lower cellos plus Horn I doubled at pitch

Third theme (or counterpoint): made up of three harmonic voices doubled at the octave, Violin II and viola, plus two flutes, two oboes, Clarinet II, Horns II, III, IV, and occasionally the Trumpet II

Two more important observations:

1. The color of each theme is made up of a combination of at least one string, one woodwind, and one brass instrument.

2. One of the factors that differentiates each theme besides its individual rhythmic characteristics is its specific and unique articulation.

The next few examples deal with works in which three or more

Example XV–27. Rimsky-Korsakov, *Scheherazade*, fourth movement, mm. 482–93

elements not necessarily of equal thematic importance are combined. These instances of foreground, middleground, and background combinations occur frequently in orchestral literature.

A most poignant combination of cello in its highest, most piercing register, doubled at pitch by the first two horns and again by the two clarinets an octave higher, plays the main theme. The clarinets are also in an excellent register to be heard most distinctly.

The middleground, which we might call the "dance figure" accompaniment, is provided by the piccolo, two flutes, and the two violin sections playing staccato and spiccato respectively.

The background, sustained harmony of the passage is supplied by oboes, bassoons, Horns III–IV, violas and double basses. The harp adds a bit of color, setting off both the first phrase and its repetition in addition to supporting the final cadence.

The great nineteenth-century orchestrators teach us that if we want to emulate their "big" orchestral sound, whether the dynamic be *forte* or *piano*, it is essential that the doubling be of a mixed color. Further, in order to insure clarity, the rhythms of the elements must be distinct. Finally, varied articulations will help the listener immeasurably to distinguish the different elements in a complex orchestral texture.

Example XV–28. Holst, *The Planets*, "Jupiter," mm. 140–56

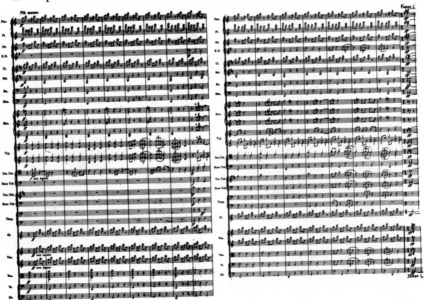

Building to the enormous climax at m. 156 is accomplished by the combination of three elements. The foreground or main theme is played at first by the four trumpets, then repeated by tenor trombones, tenor and bass tubas, violas, and cellos.

The middleground or subsidiary theme is first sounded by the two tenor trombones, and its repetition by the six horns in unison.

The background or harmony with figuration is scored for the rest of the orchestra. Figuration gives a wonderful buoyancy to this passage. Two piccolos, two flutes, three oboes, three clarinets, plus the two violin sections, are supported by the glockenspiel to provide this sparkle, and during the big tutti (m. 148), two of the trumpets join this melodized harmonic background. The *secco* chords in mm. 140–48 and the heavy bass notes supporting the harmony from mm. 150 to 156 give stability to the rhythm and enhance the flow of the passage. The chord at m. 156 is not only glorious because of the surprising modulation, but also because all motion ceases, and we await with expectation the next event—the brass fanfare.

This excerpt from the cello concerto *Schelomo* is similar to the Holst in that it presents two distinct ideas plus a harmonic background, but the two main elements here are much more complex.

Example XV–29. Bloch, *Schelomo*, mm. 228–43

All the ideas have already been stated separately, so the listener is well aware of them. Again, each has its own distinct shape and rhythmic characteristics. Let us quote the two major elements, and one other that is only touched upon briefly:

Example XV–30

Bloch, like Holst, does not do too much in the way of coloring pitch or passages by combining the different choirs. He is already

---

*This quote, from the beginning of the concerto, becomes background here and eventually, at 31, the harmonic chords inherit from this figure the straight triplet for their continued articulation.

much more concerned with choir separations needed to guarantee the clarity of the three distinct elements. This view of orchestration has become increasingly popular during the twentieth century, especially in America. As the climax nears, the composer does add the contrabassoon to the main theme, all the flutes to the middle-ground, and all the trumpets to the background material. Before this moment (m. 240), he was content to have the double basses alone support the brass main theme, and only the first flute joins the sub-sidiary tune, while three of the four trumpets strengthened the back-ground harmony. The crescendo to 31 as well as the one to 32 are greatly aided by a timpani roll and then a bass-drum roll with tim-pani sticks, which make this latter instrument resemble a more artic-ulate timpani. The composer wisely marks both percussion instruments *piano* and then crescendo, because a *fortissimo* roll would obliterate the rest of the orchestra and completely change the emphasis of this passage, which is meant to develop the themes and combine them for the sake of musical tension, not merely to build a climax.

Example XV–31. Schoenberg, *Five Pieces for Orchestra,* Op. 16, No. 5, "The Obligatory Recitative," mm. 423–56

A most sophisticated and complex contrapuntal excerpt, yet clear
and superbly managed in its orchestration. Schoenberg facilitated
the reading of his complex scores by using the following sign to
designate the main idea (or ideas) at every moment of the piece: H⌐
meaning *Haupstimme* (principal voice) and ⌐ when that voice ceases
to be the main gesture; in later scores, he used the sign N⌐ meaning
Nebenstimme (subsidiary voice). He also provided dynamics indicating that the principal gestures were to be played louder than the
subordinate ones. Notice at mm. 425–32 the gestures marked H⌐ are
designated *piano*, while the subsidiary ideas, if they lie in any kind
of piercing register, are *pianissimo*. Study the doublings very carefully and separate the elements. One will find doublings only at pitch
or one octave apart; there are no examples here of wider spacings.
Further, this orchestration is much closer to the luscious nineteenth-
century sound of the orchestra than to the leaner twentieth-century
sound, especially in the full tutti. Naturally, because of the many
diverse elements presented simultaneously in mm. 425–38, Schoenberg is careful to assign each fragment to an instrument that will be
clearly heard in the complex texture. For instance, the major gesture
in the oboe in mm. 425–26 does not need any doubling to speak

clearly, while the flutes can stand the help of the clarinets in their lower register in m. 427. In m. 429 the oboes and first clarinet greatly help to delineate the *Haupstimme*, which would otherwise be made subservient to the rather prominent combination of English horn, Clarinet II, and violas playing a subordinate, but quite active counter gesture. This is not "choir orchestration," but very careful color mixing in order to get the most thrilling kind of effect. The doublings in this excerpt are an extremely subtle effect here, which should be examined carefully so that it may become an integral part of any orchestrator's technique.

Let us look at mm. 447–51. We find the following principal idea:

Example XV–32

In order to give the impression of a very smooth line, the composer has to "sneak in" instruments that can cover this extremely wide range. He begins with a combination of woodwinds (Flutes I, II, Oboes I, II, Clarinets I, II); in order to highlight the high note reached by a skip of a tenth, he adds the second violins and the piccolo clarinet on that note to offset the rather thin, high oboes. For the final beat of m. 448, he brings in the English horn, bass clarinet, and two bassoons, which are able to extend the ranges of their upper cousins and bridge the register gap. The second violins act as continuity instruments to introduce the violas supported by the first violins, in order to complete the phrase. The entrance of the first violins in m. 448 on a dissonant note adds great tension for a moment, and contributes to the feeling of "resolution" or repose when the C♯ is reached in m. 450. It is important to note, that Schoenberg, as mentioned before in this book, considered all instruments equal and would give a soft, high, lyrical solo to a muted trombone rather than to a cello (mm. 452–56). A soft wind chord such as the one in m. 455, is a sonority that a student should place in his orchestral vocabulary for future use. The extreme ranges add to the tenseness and expansiveness of this effectively orchestrated work.

SOME ADDITIONAL THOUGHTS ON ORCHESTRATION AND SPECIAL DEVICES

Throughout this chapter we have discussed melody, the main voice, or the primary gesture. To recapitulate the thoughts concerning this most important element, we must look at some ways of isolating it from other considerations so that the possibilities of effective scoring for a principal theme are clear in our minds.

Here is the famous English horn solo from the *Roman Carnival Overture* by Hector Berlioz:

Example XV–33. Berlioz, *Roman Carnival Overture*, mm. 21–28

Sounding a fifth lower, it could be played by flute, oboe, clarinet, and even bassoon solo (but that would be a bit high and sound strained). It is certainly playable by all the strings, although it would sound terribly awkward on the double bass. Further, it is playable on the trumpet and horn and even the trombone, although the latter instrument would sound most pinched on the very top notes and not be able to project the quiet elegance that the tune seems to demand. In other words, the registral intensity would completely alter the character of this melody. Besides these instruments, the English horn, alto flute, or soprano, alto, and tenor saxophones could successfully negotiate this line.

Here is where choice and intent become paramount. An orchestrator approves the character of the tune in this particular range compass and then assigns it to a solo instrument befitting the emotional as well as the tonal intent. If this same tune appeared an octave higher, a fifth higher, or two octaves higher, the choice would of necessity be a different one. The same would hold true if it appeared a fifth, an octave, or more below this present register.

The dynamic also has a great deal to do with the choice, for knowing the strengths and weaknesses of every instrument in each register, the orchestrator would certainly have to be influenced by dynamic considerations.

If one wished to strengthen the tune or to give it more power, one could use any of the following measures:

1. Double it at pitch, preferably with instruments that have an affinity for doubling with the assigned instrument:

English horn doubled by oboe, bassoon, muted trumpet, viola, cello;

Flute doubled by violin, clarinet (viola and cello when range permits);

Oboe doubled by English horn, flute, muted trumpet and horn, violin, viola;

Clarinet doubled by flute, violin, viola, cello, horn (trumpet);

Bassoon doubled by oboe, English horn, all strings, soft trombone and tuba.

These are only a few of the most utilized at-pitch doublings. One must realize, however, that at-pitch doublings change the basic tonal quality or characteristic of the resulting sound, and this should be seriously considered before one decides on such a mixture.

2. Another effective way of strengthening a passage is by octave doublings. That means adding octaves above or below by any instrument capable of the range. We may call this "organ" doubling, for it resembles pulling the 4' or 2' stops to extend the range one or two octaves upward, or the 16'–32' stops for similar duty in the opposite direction. We have discussed doubling and tripling instruments at pitch or solo passages to gain power, but this should be reserved for very special effects; however, doubling a tune in a three-octave spread of the two flutes and piccolo, English horn, and two oboes, bass clarinet, B♭ clarinet, and E♭ clarinet, etc., is most desirable.

3. An interesting variation on direct doubling is heterophonic doubling, as we have seen in some of our orchestral examples. In addition to the examples of heterophonic doubling already discussed in this chapter, refer back to the *La Mer* fragment in Chapter 8 (see p. 226), which illustrates this technique so beautifully. Here are two rather obvious examples of how this device might work in the case of the Berlioz tune:

Example XV–34

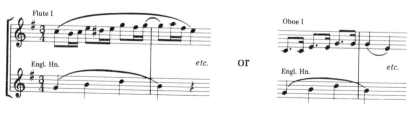

SOME SPECIAL EFFECTS

Scoring sforzandi

Often an accent is not sufficient to emphasize sforzando, and having an entire orchestra as one's instrument, one does not have to be satisfied with any one method of accomplishing this effect. Here are some suggestions:

1. string pizzicato combined with a longer note in the winds;
2. a short sforzando trumpet note combined with long notes in the strings;
3. a short sforzando note in the oboes combined with long notes in the strings;
4. pizzicato note in the violas with the long notes in the violins.

Example XV–35

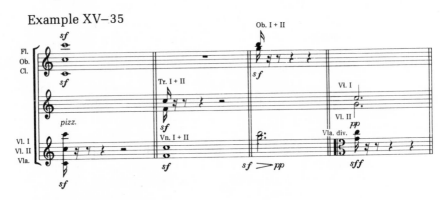

Some More forte subito piano Scorings

This is an effect used often in music today, and the most effective way of scoring it is to have one section play the chord *fortissimo*; then, before that loud sound ends, another choir or combination of instruments enters unperceived at a piano dynamic and simply sustains at that level. When the loud chord cuts off, the *subito* or sudden effect of *piano* will have been accomplished, since the chord is already there at that dynamic. It is essential that the two chords overlap.

Example XV–36

Coloring a Note

This is a similar idea and can be accomplished in a variety of ways. Here are a few:

1. A held C colored:

Example XV–37

2. Each note colored by a different instrument:

Example XV–38

3. A rather recent development: the same instrument or like instruments using alternate fingerings to color a pitch:

Example XV–39

Example XV–38 is the most complex and should be attempted only if the composer can supply exact fingerings for the players, and if he knows that these will work. Consultation with a seasoned professional is urged to accomplish this rather recent, but most intriguing device for coloring a pitch.

A Reminder about Dovetailing or Overlapping

In any kind of passage where there is a color change or a swap between similar instruments, make certain that the seams don't show, unless, as in the example below, one wishes each group of six notes to be accented:

Example XV–40

Pointillistic Scoring

This type of scoring is related a bit to the technique of coloring each note in a melody by using a different instrument, as in Example XV–37. Webern, who is the chief proponent of this kind of scoring, usually does not use one instrument to play a tune but rather assigns each pitch to a different instrument without a "continuity" instrument. Therefore, with some stylistically characteristic octave displacements, our little tune would look (and sound) as follows if it were "pointillistically" scored:

Example XV–41

Notice that each note is assigned a different dynamic, an idiomatic device in this style of composition which adds great interest. The melody is, as a result, quite fragmented, but that is part of the aesthetic that is based on the French school of painting of the same name. Those painters used tiny dots of different unmixed colors to achieve their representational effects. For an authentic page of pointillistic music, study the first movement (mm. 35–39) of the Symphony, Op. 21 by Anton Webern to appreciate the full impact of the technique, which may be used in serial as well as nonserial music.

Klangfarbenmelodie

This German word literally means "tone color melody." Actually, it may refer to a "melody," or an entire piece based on one kind of sound. The most famous example of this procedure is the third of the *Five Pieces for Orchestra* by Arnold Schoenberg, called "Colors" (*Farben*), and subtitled, *Summer Morning by a Lake*. Here Schoenberg simply invents one sonority and repeats it all the way through this short piece, changing it only minimally as far as the harmony or simultaneity is concerned, but coloring it differently every few measures to give the illusion of motion. Very few pieces exist that are entirely *Klangfarbenmelodie*, but the principle, which can be applied to a phrase or a series of simultaneities in any work, is most effective and very important to understand. Here is a reduction of the first eight measures of Schoenberg's *Farben* and then the full score, so that one may study this very sensitive scoring and be able to apply the principles for a most colorful and subtle orchestral effect.

Example XV–42a. Schoenberg, *Five Pieces for Orchestra*, Op. 16, No. 3, *Farben*, mm. 1–8: Reduction

b. Full Score

16

The Orchestral
Transcription

The transcription of a piece of music from one medium to another is very much like the translation of a poem from one language to another. While all those speaking the original language will of course claim that a poem can never be successfully translated and loses its essence in the process, the people who do not understand the original tongue will benefit by being able to fathom something that was beyond their grasp before the transformation was accomplished. There are instances where great poets of one language undertake to translate poems from another, and create magnificent masterpieces. The arguments pro and con have been with us for many years in poetry as well as in music. In our own time, when "purists" maintain that no one should dare tamper with the music of the past or present, history answers with very strong reminders that transcription is perhaps as old as composed music itself.

Let us go back only as far as the Baroque period, and we see overwhelming evidence that even the greatest composers of that time transcribed their own pieces several times over in their lifetimes, besides adapting the works of their contemporaries and predecessors. Some composers of this period wrote works in which they did not even specify the exact instrument that would perform a given line, but simply said, "any C instrument, etc." To cite only a few examples: Bach's version of the violin concertos of Vivaldi; his own adaptations of movements from his instrumental music as sinfonias (for orchestra) for some of the cantatas; or his transcription of his violin concertos to keyboard concertos (the E-major violin concerto became the D-major keyboard concerto); Handel's transcription of the second movement of the D-major violin sonata as a chorus and orchestra piece in his oratorio *Solomon*. These examples don't even begín to describe the frequency of transcription during the Baroque period. The practice grew with each successive decade (Beethoven even made a transcription of his violin concerto for piano and orchestra), until it reached almost epidemic proportions in the nineteenth century, when every great work was transcribed either for piano two hands, piano four hands, two pianos, or violin and piano, etc. It was considered a wonderful way to get intimately familiar with the masterworks in the privacy of their own homes. Liszt transcribed all the symphonies of Beethoven for piano; on the other hand, Brahms, Dvořák, and Grieg transcribed their "ethnic" dances (Hungarian, Slovakian, Norwegian) from piano four hands to orchestra. It is hardly necessary to justify the art of transcription today, since a great many works in our standard orchestral repertoire are transcriptions of original piano works. Besides the above-named dances, Liszt's *Hungarian Rhapsodies*, Bizet's *Jeux d'Enfants* (Children's Games), and almost all the works of Ravel bear witness to this statement. There can be justifiable claims that a work like Mussorgsky's great *Pictures at an Exhibition* is more effective in Ravel's orchestral transcription than in the original piano version, or that Husa's *Music for Prague* sounds better for orchestra than in the band version; conversely, Schoenberg's *Variations* Op. 43 sound better for band than for orchestra. We certainly do not wish to get embroiled in any of these controversies, save to say that the art of transcription is a most valid one and should be carefully mastered. Most important for the mastery of this skill are the following considerations:

1. a thorough and complete knowledge of all the instruments, their capabilities and range characteristics;
2. an intimate knowledge of the form and details, as well as a love for the work to be transcribed;
3. an insight into the orchestral style of the composer whose work is to be transcribed, or if that composer has not written for orchestra, a thorough familiarity with the orchestral practices of the era in which the composer lived;
4. a purpose for wishing to transcribe a particular work:
    a. the best reason to undertake the task is that the work "cries out" for an orchestration;
    b. the original composer wished to orchestrate the work but for some reason was never able to accomplish this;
    c. the all-important pragmatic reason: a conductor asks a composer to orchestrate a work because he wishes to perform it;
    d. certain instruments for which the work was originally scored are not available.

For our immediate purposes, it will be necessary to transcribe the pieces in our workbook for a less glamorous but nonetheless most important reason, and that is to learn the art of transcription.

Besides the conditions listed above, one overriding consideration must guide us, and that is taste. We must respect the work, the composer, and the period in which the piece was conceived, and use our best judgment in every decision we reach about the particular music: the size and composition of the orchestra; the suitability of an instrument to present a certain phrase; and the conviction that our orchestration will clarify the form of the entire composition.

Before we examine the practical aspects of this skill, we should clarify the distinct difference between transcription and arrangement.

Transcription is a transferance of a previously composed work from one musical medium to another.

Arranging involves more of the compositional process, for the previously existing material may be as little as a melody or even a partial melody for which the arranger must supply a harmony, counterpoint, and sometimes even rhythm before thinking about the orchestration.

In this chapter we shall address ourselves primarily to the problem of transcriptions for orchestra from another medium. If an arrangement is called for, the same procedures for orchestration that apply to transcription should then be adopted once the tune has been harmonized and arranged fully in a piano or short score.

Three main areas will be studied: transcribing from

1. keyboard or small chamber combinations to orchestra;
2. band or wind ensemble to orchestra;
3. orchestra to smaller combinations of instruments.

TRANSCRIPTIONS OF MUSIC FOR KEYBOARD OR SMALL CHAMBER COMBINATIONS TO ORCHESTRA

Transcription from keyboard to orchestra is the most common type of medium change, and seems to work well. We have already mentioned the dances of Brahms and Dvořák, but the most amazing transcriptions are those from keyboard to orchestra made in our own century. Ravel wrote all but three of his brilliant orchestral works for piano first, and then orchestrated them. *Daphnis et Chloé*, *Bolero*, and La Valse are the only pieces written originally for orchestra; all the others are transcriptions, even *Tzigane* for violin and orchestra. Bartók wrote the *Dance Suite* and the *Rumanian Dances* for piano first, and what is most surprising, Stravinsky wrote his early ballets initially for piano. This may have been for the purely practical reason that a rehearsal version was essential; nevertheless, it tells us that transcriptions from piano to orchestra can produce idiomatic orchestral music if judiciously executed.

Here are some fundamental considerations:

1. Do not try to simulate the piano, but rather change piano idioms to orchestral ones, retaining the spirit of the music.

Example XVI–1. Ravel, *Ma Mère L'Oye*, "Le Jardin féerique," mm. 20–22

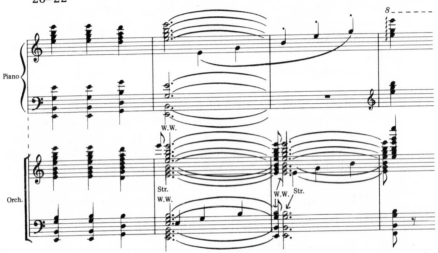

Example XVI–2a. Ravel, *Menuet antique*, mm. 64–66: Orchestral Reduction

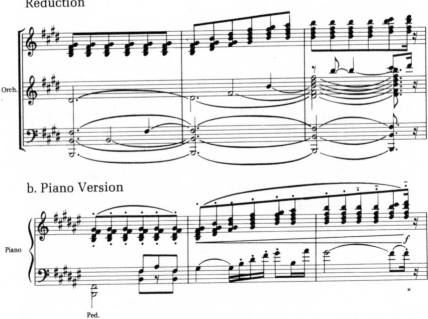

b. Piano Version

2. Remember that the piano is played by one person, while the orchestra is an aggregate of many; therefore, everything must be judged in that light. There are times when a rhythmic simplification, an alteration in notation, or a metric change is necessary for clarity in the orchestra. These may be problems that never interfere with the performance of the pianist.

Example XVI–3a. Bartók, *Mikrokosmos*, No. 5: "Syncopation," mm. 1–3

b. Easier for orchestra in this rhythmically notated version

3. A crescendo, diminuendo, rubato, or even a fermata is made clearer when actually written out in an orchestral score. Ravel, the master of the transcription, does this frequently. Here are some examples by other composers:

Example XVI–4. Beethoven, *Symphony No. 6*, first movement, mm. 305–12

Example XVI–5. Bizet, *Jeux d'enfants*, "La Toupie," mm. 1–5

Example XVI–6. Mahler, *Lieder eines fahrenden Gesellen*, No. 1, "Wenn mein Schatz," mm. 89–96

4. Although it is admittedly impossible to simulate the piano sound, we must interpret important piano notations that can help us render the transcription faithful to the composer's intentions. A prime area of consideration will be the sustaining and *una corda* pedalings in the piano score. *Una corda* literally means "one string" and signifies the use of the soft pedal, which shifts the inside action of the piano so the hammers strike only one or two of the three strings. This effect may be realized for orchestra by muting the instruments in such a passage.

Idiomatic piano writing must acknowledge the physical limitations of the pianist. Chords that can easily be performed by an orchestra need to be arpeggiated for piano because of the limited stretch of the human hand. Layers of linear activity in the music must be studied carefully, because some inner or even outer thematic material may be only outlined in the piano, while in the orchestra these multiple lines can be made to sound and sustain simultaneously without any difficulty. This is also true of implied harmony. The transcriber should be thoroughly familiar with the music, so that all the harmonic and melodic "hints" can be used to enrich the transcription.

When a contrapuntal work is to be orchestrated, the limitless possibilities of an orchestra are even more tantalizing. A pianist, however gifted, is able to apply a very limited coloration to the individual lines of a contrapuntal work, no matter how clever and varied his articulations. The orchestrator has a variety of colors to work with and can easily feature the various lines. When we studied the use of the orchestra in the previous chapter, we cautioned the novice not to become too colorful, lest he confuse the form and upset the musical scheme. This caution must be reiterated even more strongly in regard to transcribing another composer's work. Studying the layers of the music and determining their order of importance is paramount to a successful transcription, whether the piece is homophonic or polyphonic.

Here are some examples that deal orchestrally with the pianistic phenomena mentioned above:

Example XVI–7a. Chopin, *Etude*, Op. 25, No. 6, mm. 39–40

b. Orchestral Version

Example XVI–8. Mussorgsky-Ravel, *Pictures at an Exhibition,* "The Great Gate of Kiev," final 22 measures

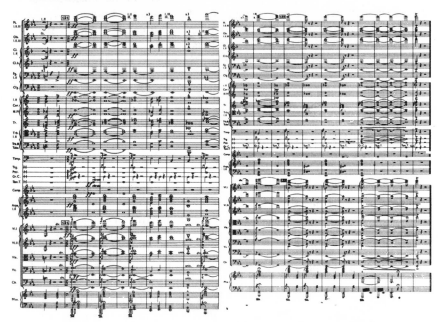

Once again, the very best way of learning how to do these transcriptions in the most professional manner is to study some successful models from the great piano-orchestra transcription literature. Most of these examples are simple and straightforward, but those are attributes toward which we should strive, especially in the beginning.

Example XVI–9a. Brahms, *Hungarian Dance No. 1,* mm. 1–48: Piano 4-Hands Version

b. Orchestral Version

Brahms has created a most interesting and effective transposition of the original piano four-hand version. He heightens the dynamics of the orchestra from *mezzo-forte* to *forte* in the opening string passage, and in m. 5, which is soft in the piano, the winds are marked *forte*. This change adds zest to the orchestral version. Notice the beautiful scoring of the strings with the steady pizzicato bass and the independent cello part giving the "Hungarian" rhythm, while the violins, with first bassoon doubling the violas, play the tune. Also note that the entire harmony is not sounded until the first off-beat in m. 3, so as not to thicken the downbeat suddenly. The wood-wind arpeggio is most imaginatively scored: while the piccolo and first flute are playing it, the two clarinets "flutter" in the opposite direction with the implied harmony notes. At first, the composer entrusts the staccato pitches only to the second flutes, but the first bassoon then doubles them in the second measure (m. 6). Mean-while, a bit of color is added to the sustained note of the violins, by the horns supplying the harmony, and by the addition of the timpani and triangle. In mm. 5–6, the violas join the cellos to articulate the offbeat rhythm. We have quoted this piece at length to show how long Brahms retained the same color combination before changing it. When he finally does, at m. 25, notice how the triplets of the *secondo* part are realized in the violas, and how curious it is that the dynamics are not the same as in the piano version. Here this change is more obvious, for Brahms orchestrates the *mezzo-forte* by dou-bling the violins with horns and oboes.

Example XVI–10a. Dvořák, *Slavonic Dance No. 8*, mm. 1–48: Piano 4-Hands Version

b. Orchestral Version, mm. 1–46

We offer a bit of this exciting transcription for its thrilling tutti opening and the immediate contrast when the tune is played softly. In the first few measures, compare the second violin and oboe parts for the interchange of doublings; notice too the emphasis on the melodic figure, which the composer achieves by the largest amount of doubling (piccolo, flute, first oboe, second clarinet, and first violin). The grace notes of the second violin and the chord of the cello, both of which include open strings, give a special ring to the opening chord. Otherwise, it is a traditionally well-orchestrated tutti with a bit of "dance color" supplied by the cymbal and bass drum. Beginning at m. 9, the orchestration is quite different, with a strong, but soft color for the melody, a light accompaniment, and sustained "harmonic counterpoint" in the strings. Although there is no indication of this "harmonic counterpoint" in the piano part, the pianist would use a slight amount of sostenuto pedal here to reinforce the harmonic notes, which are important enough to be emphasized and sustained in order to complete the harmony without making it heavy.

The repetition of the first strain at m. 17 is a bit more open in the distribution of the chords, particularly in the horns and middle string parts. Without changing the basic color, Dvořák reworked the

tutti admirably, to give it a slightly different hue. The new answer
to this strain (m. 25) is most expertly worked out and should be
closely compared to the piano version. The delay of the oboe
entrance clarifies the tune much better, and makes the last four measures sound truly polyphonic. At m. 33, we have a model of exactly
how one accomplishes a diminuendo from *fortissimo* to *piano*. First
examinine the piccolo part, which has been written an octave lower
than before to enable the player to accomplish the diminuendo to
piano; all other instruments are also in controllable ranges. The
dropout of the strings, which have been playing continuously since
the beginning of the piece, is a great relief here and also serves as a
bridge color to the next section, in which the strings only perform a
supporting role.

Below is another work originally written for piano four hands. It is
a very simple but most sensitive transcription for orchestra with
many valuable devices for us to master. The opening octaves are
excellently distributed and the diminuendo clearly orchestrated,
instead of being left to the players or conductor. A playful kind of
orchestration is used to strengthen the E pedal by "rhythmatizing"
it in the third horn. This gives stability to those measures where the
flutes do not play on the third beat, and provides a light offbeat
accent to the others. Notice that Bizet spells the D♯ in m. 7 enharmonically in the orchestral version, perhaps to clarify the dimin-
ished-seventh-chord effect. Just as he orchestrated a diminuendo in
the beginning, he did the same for the crescendo, mm. 13–18. A
most fascinating addition in the orchestral version may be found at
m. 3, with the "whispering" tritone in the cellos and the roll in the
timpani. The dynamic of the chord was changed from *pp* to *ppp*, but
motion was added to enliven the sustained chord. The triplet run
which follows is an excellent example of dovetailing for absolute
smoothness from the bottom to the top. The repetition of the little
piece should be carefully studied for the slight, but significant
changes Bizet makes in the orchestration to give the repeat a different flavor. It is a fuller version with the sixteenth notes and the melody doubled at pitch. All this was preceded by a chromatic scale in

Example XVI–11a. Bizet, *Jeux d'enfants*, "La Toupie": Piano 4-
Hands Version

b. Orchestral Version

the clarinets and bassoons, which possibly anticipates the new scoring. The fourth horn sustains the pedal, while the trumpets maintain the rhythm previously provided by the third horn, and the pizzicato doubling of the flutes lends great charm. Ten measures before the end, the "whispering" tritone is repeated, but the triplet run this time dovetails through the woodwinds for a real color change. The ending is scored quite traditionally, but the spacing and octave doublings of the final chords should be studied because they are exemplary.

Example XVI–12a. Ravel, *Ma Mère l'Oye*, "Petit Poucet": Piano 4-Hands Version

b. Orchestral Version

It is hard to believe that this suite was first written for piano four hands, because it sounds so completely natural in the orchestra. However, as has been mentioned before, most of Ravel's orchestral music was originally written for keyboard. For that reason, we shall study two of his works: first, this very sensitive short work, and then excerpts from *Alborada del gracioso,* which of course is much more complex.

Petit Poucet (Little Tom Thumb) is a simple adaptation of the piano original, executed with impeccable taste and clarity. The soft background is given to the muted violins in sharp contrast to the oboe's tune. One should notice that the accompaniment, as well as the melody, is essentially an eighth-note movement; therefore, the highly contrasting colors throughout the piece are very necessary to separate the two elements for the listener. Many details are noteworthy: The background dovetails or overlaps at [1], while the melody is taken from the oboe by the darker-hued English horn without overlap and a fresh articulation. The slurring pattern of the violas and cellos remains regular throughout the rather imaginative phrasing of the solo instrument. The sustained G, softly accented by the double basses' pizzicato, is held by the clarinet into the next measure, an effect comparable to that produced by the damper pedal on the piano. In the orchestra version, Ravel is especially careful to notate even the slightest details of articulation as well as decay and cessation of a pitch. It is interesting to see how the composer changes both fore- and background color with each new entrance and how the background sometimes overlaps, while other times there is a new articulation to the phrasing. This makes for a very sustained effect such as that notated in the *secondo* piano part by an unbroken slur. Five measures before [3], we begin another orchestrated crescendo. The harmonic texture is very thin, but because of the intense register of the instruments' and the at-pitch doublings, the colors give the effect of fullness. As they descend and drop out, Ravel is easily able to orchestrate the diminuendo into the short recapitulation of the English horn theme a fifth lower than the first statement. At [5] there are four measures that go well beyond mere transcription. Over a D pedal and with the melody played by the first bassoon accompanied by the muted violas, Ravel has created an atmosphere by sophisticated subtle orchestral effects. The piano part could not possibly duplicate this unless the inside of the piano were used (which was unheard of in Ravel's time). The simple grace note (G♯–A) is replaced by a glissando of harmonics from F♯ chromatically to the A (a characteristic device used by Ravel in many of his transcriptions). An ornament such as a grace note is often varied and extended to give a more coloristic effect. The *sul tasto*, glissando, and tremolo in the first and second violins and cellos add great mystery and a momentary unreality to the rather straightforward atmosphere that has existed thus far in the piece, and will also bring the piece to a close. Study the piccolo part imitated by the second and third solo violin trills, which are quite different from the simple gesture in the piano version. The seemingly unaffected bassoon soloist, with his viola accompaniment, makes the return to a more normative orchestration quite feasible and successful. It is important to note that Ravel does not remind the listener of this strange interlude again, except that nine measures from the end, the cellos play a harmonic, and the resulting chord is similarly colored. The return from [6] to the end is orchestrated in very much the same way as the beginning, but differently colored. The combination of solo cello and piccolo is wonderful, and the contrast with the flute going into its lower regions is very striking. A clever stroke is the return of the exact opening colors for the last five measures, aided by the beautiful viola chord in harmonics.

The student is advised to study other piano-orchestra transcriptions to strengthen his technique from the knowledge gained by such analysis. Here are some transcriptions recommended:

Satie-Debussy, *Gymnopédies*

Stravinsky, *Petrushka*

Ravel, *Le Tombeau de Couperin, Valses nobles at sentimentales, Rapsodie espagnole, Pictures at an Exhibition, Alborada del gracioso*

Dallapiccola, *Variations for orchestra*, a transcription of his *The Musical Notebook of Annalibera*

Copland, *Piano Variations–Orchestra Variations*

Schuman, *America Variations by Charles Ives* (from the organ version)

Respighi-Rossini, *La Boutique fantastique*

Mussorgsky, *Pictures at an Exhibition:* Compare the transcriptions by Ravel and Stokowski.

Now we shall briefly discuss two works transcribed from chamber ensembles to orchestra.

Example XVI–13a. "Pergolesi," *Trio Sonata in G major*, first movement, mm. 1–15

b. Stravinsky, *Pulcinella*, Sinfonia, mm. 1–15

Stravinsky, one of the greatest masters of our century, had the extraordinary ability to take preexisting materials—that is, works written by other composers—and adapt them in his own works. Yet they all sound like Stravinsky. Whether the original works were by Bach, Tchaikovsky, or others, he was always able to manipulate the music so that in the end it had the Stravinsky touch. Stravinsky would invariably fall in love with a composer's entire *oeuvre* and study his compositional and orchestral technique thoroughly. Only after great in-depth exploration did he set about to transcribe a work based on the compositions of another master from another period.

Despite his short life span of only twenty-six years, Giovanni Battista Pergolesi (1710–36) produced a sizable body of work. Stravinsky chose as the Sinfonia for his *Pulcinella* ballet (which he later made into a suite), the first movement of the *G-major Trio Sonata* presumed to be by Pergolesi.

The version of the *G-major Trio Sonata* available to Stravinsky had been edited by Hugo Riemann. Since that time, musicologists have discovered that this work was not by Pergolesi, but rather by one of his contemporaries. Nevertheless, we are able to discuss its transcription and Stravinsky's metamorphosis of it, disregarding its spurious authorship as well as Riemann's incorrect supposition. Although dealing with a secondary source, Stravinsky nonetheless captured the spirit of the period in which the piece was originally conceived and scored it in a manner that can help us do similar transcriptions if we study his methods carefully. Let us therefore try to find Stravinsky's *modus operandi*.

Having great respect for the late Baroque, Stravinsky decided to score it for a combination of instruments which could logically have been employed in that time as well. Further, a duet with continuo could have been the source material for a *concerto grosso*, since the Italian Baroque masters often wrote *concerti grossi* for two violins and continuo as the *concertino* group pitted against a string orchestra (*ripieno*); at times the *concertino* group was made up of wind instruments as well. This is probably the way Stravinsky reached his choice of the instrumentation for this particular work.

As to the adaptation itself, it is rather straightforward. Stravinsky does change the notation for the sake of keeping 4/4 most of the way through. Therefore, he bars the entire piece in a manner that presents fewer ensemble problems than the trio version from the very outset. Further, Stravinsky reinterprets some of the ornaments, such as the one at the end of m. 5 in the trio version, where the mordent becomes grace notes in the transcription. He sets off the two phrases by lightening the texture of the second phrase, dropping out the winds and horns plus the double bass. It must be pointed out that the many dynamic marks in the trio version were placed there by the editor (Hugo Riemann), not by the composer; therefore, it is perfectly permissible for Stravinsky to begin the first phrase *forte* and the second *mezzo forte*, and to change the color so that when the oboe and bassoon play the solos at m. 7, their entrance is very fresh. The harmony and the little counterpoint of the bassoon are Stravinsky's realizations of the figured bass. Riemann chose to do it one way, while Stravinsky does it in a much simpler, more stylish manner, never changing the original harmony or interfering with the melody. His main concern is color change, which he accomplishes as smoothly and gracefully as possible, never breaking up a phrase needlessly, and preserving the shape of the piece. The melodies come through with extraordinary clarity.

We now examine some of the techniques Schoenberg used in his masterful transcription of the Brahms *G-minor Piano Quartet.* On the whole, Schoenberg does not change any of the harmony of the Brahms work, and except for a much greater use of the trumpets and xylophone in the last movement, he tries to give us a Brahms-like orchestral sound. One could argue about the inclusion of the E♭ clarinet, as well as the extraordinary trumpet parts, but the piece is written for the modern orchestra, and we will analyze it to learn how he deals with color distribution or substitution, and also with transcribing the very idiomatic piano part. It is obvious here, as it was in the Pergolesi-Stravinsky example, that Schoenberg loved Brahms and was intimately familiar with his compositional as well as his orchestral style. This cannot be overemphasized as a precondition for transcribing a work.

Let us study five excerpts from the score:

Example XVI–14a. Brahms, *Piano Quartet in G minor,* first movement, mm. 1–10

b. Orchestral Version by Schoenberg

The original Brahms quintet opens with piano octaves, which Schoenberg transcribes beautifully for three clarinets. In m. 4, the logical bassoon-horn combination with the two upper clarinets ends the phrase to prepare for the new entrance. As in the original, a string instrument enters. Schoenberg, instead of doubling at pitch as Brahms did, uses octaves to provide a richer sound, for he does not have two distinct colors (piano and cello); doubling at pitch, the violins and cellos would swallow each other up. The entrance of the viola in the quartet is taken by the horn to point up the upcoming violin entrance. The switch between choirs is not only colorful, but emphasizes the pseudo-fragmented presentation of the theme in the Brahms version: two measures, one measure, two measures and a beat. Mm. 8–10 are the richest continuous orchestration thus far and reflect the original version admirably. At m. 11 a bridge passage begins and with it, an entirely new color.*

There are some important details we can glean from examining mm. 50–59.

1. The cello solo is kept intact from the original.
2. Except for the arpeggiation, the harmony in sustained chords is

* From this point on, the reader is referred to the scores of the work being discussed.

also retained. This technique reflects the use of the sostenuto pedal when the piano performs the passage.

3. There is no actual doubling of the middle parts until m. 53, when the oboes double the second violins and violas, signifying that the cello solo is coming to an end.

4. The violin solo is also kept intact, with sustained as well as arpeggiated harmony.

5. Notice the handling of the arpeggiated triplets. In m. 54–57 they are played as solid chords, then for one measure they are arpeggiated in order to lead smoothly to m. 59, where, as in the original, both the violin and cello play triplets in that manner.

We have chosen one big tutti spot—mm. 75–77—to show how Schoenberg scores the alternation between the piano and strings in the original. He only adds *secco* chords at the beginning of each measure; otherwise, he simply orchestrates what Brahms wrote. Notice, however, the un-Brahmsian trumpet part, which gives an extra sting to the winds. The leanness of the texture (essentially two-part) makes the color and the big chords very successful.

Now, two excerpts from the exciting last movement, where one could argue that the xylophone and the big battery are a bit excessive, but since we are dealing with "Hungarian" or "Gypsy" rhythms and tunes (the movement is called *Rondo alla Zingarese*), one may contend that Schoenberg was trying for the cimbalon sound with the xylophone.

Compare, in mm. 874–92, the figuration of the piano part with the very clever, idiomatic orchestration, first in the strings (mm. 874–76), then in the winds (mm. 877–79). It is interesting that Schoenberg here introduces a completely new rhythm in the timpani, which lends great excitement to the crescendo. In m. 880, the orchestrator is doing a bit more than simply transcribing the score; he adds a nice counterpoint made up of the pitches found in the measure, but having its own rhythm. This "countertheme" continues to enrich the texture to m. 891, first in the second horn and the bassoons, then in the violas—a beautifully orchestrated section.

The cadenza in m. 1106A is a very complicated spot that warrants careful study. Schoenberg thoughtfully bars the "free" piano notation in sextuplets for the Eb clarinet, while solo strings and low flutes provide the "residue" of pitches that would result if the pianist were to sustain the entire run with the pedal. It would be very dissonant; therefore, clusterlike chords result, but by the time the low strings finish the run at m. 1106J, one is left with a thrilling and most unusual impression.

It is urged that the student become more familiar with this fascinating score and study it carefully, always comparing the original with the transcription.

TRANSCRIBING FROM BAND TO ORCHESTRA

The transcriber is confronted here with two large organizations, one of definite and one of indefinite size. We all know that the complement of an orchestra is whatever the composer specifies. Except for the exact number of strings, one can be confident that if one writes for two flutes, exactly two flutes will play the part. Not so in the average band. If one writes three clarinet parts, there may be as many as fifteen clarinet players on each part. During the last thirty years, we have seen the development of the wind ensemble, which differs from the band in that there is only one player on a part, unless otherwise specified by the composer. In music for band, the composer is justified in writing the word *solo* in the first clarinettist's part, for there may be any number of clarinets performing the same part. This does present problems in transcription, and this potentially massive sound should be kept in mind when attempting a transcription from band to orchestra.

We must remind the student once again that the two media have their own peculiar sounds, and no orchestra can be made to sound exactly like a band nor vice versa in any transcription. The argument whether a certain piece sounds better in its band or orchestral version is purely rhetorical, for it depends on the taste of the composer, the performers, or the audiences. It is a moot question to argue whether *Elsa's Procession* by Wagner should still be performed in its band version, for the question should be: If there are no orchestras around, is it not better for the players and the audience to have experienced some of these great works of the past in band transcriptions than never to have heard them at all? On the other hand, if we do transcribe from one medium to another, let us be sure it is accomplished in the best of taste and without loss to the musical content of a work or the basic concerns of the composer as to the quality of each sound. Quality in this context means a sensitive realization of the dynamics, implied colors, and emotional "feel" of a sound or a section.

In examining the following three transcriptions, which were all made by their composers from band to orchestra, let us dwell on the following considerations:

1. How much of the band orchestration was kept in the transcription, and how did the composer's attitude change toward some or any portion of the work?

2. Were there significant substitutions in the solo voices from one medium to the other? Why? Is there any perceivable logic to this change?

3. How were the band instruments that are absent from the standard orchestra handled in the orchestration? What role did the strings inherit?

4. As in piano-to-orchestra transcriptions, were any changes in notation necessary?

Although we have concentrated on the orchestra in this book, you should be able to apply all the observations and techniques in reverse, when called upon to transcribe an orchestral work for band or wind ensemble.

Both the band and the orchestral version of Darius Milhaud's *Suite française* were written to be played by high-school groups. Therefore, Milhaud took great care to minimize all technical difficulties and control the range of the individual instruments.

Example XVI–15. Milhaud, *Suite française*, second movement
Band Version (mm. 25–35)

(continued on next page)

Orchestral Version (mm. 25–36)

1. It is fair to say that although both versions have a great deal of Gallic flavor, the band version is definitely heavier, sometimes even massive, while the orchestral transcription has a chamber-music quality.

Example XVI–16. Milhaud, *Suite française*, fifth movement, opening measures

Band Version (mm. 1–11)

Orchestral Version (mm. 1–10)

2. The band version sustains the same or similar colors for a long passage, while in the orchestral transcription, there is constant alternation between choirs, thereby providing much more coloristic variety.

Example XVI–17. Milhaud, *Suite française*, fifth movement.

Band Version (mm. 50–57)

Orchestral Version (mm. 51–60)

3. Aware that many high school wind players are more seasoned than their string-playing equivalents, the composer doubles the lower octave, letting the flutes carry the upper one by themselves. Here, as in many other places, he leaves out the brass in the orchestra and saves it for the significant entrance at m. 57. A similar lack of high partials is the case where Milhaud wants to save the flute for the entrance at m. 50, but fears the violins could not play that high. It certainly gives this passage a flavor different from the band version.

4.* Let us now look for some more small details which could help us if we were asked to do such a transcription:

a. Third movement, mm. 62–67: The muted trumpet, aided by the first violins, makes a beautiful substitution for the alto clarinet–alto saxophone solo.

b. Fourth movement, mm. 25–42: The muted cornet is transformed into an oboe-viola combination, and when the "open" cornet takes over, a muted trumpet is added to the oboe-viola mix in the orchestral version.

c. Fifth movement, mm. 15–30: It is strange that in the orchestral version the piccolo is not used where it is so effective in the band, as it is here.

d. Third movement, mm. 26–38: At times, there is some lovely rethinking for the transcription. For example, flute, oboe, and clarinet become flute, clarinet, and first violins; then piccolo and muted cornet become flute, oboe, and violins.

Now we come to the most complex of the three pieces, Arnold Schoenberg's *Theme and Variations,* Op. 43A and B, because Schoenberg's orchestral version is more a recomposition of the band version than either of the other works. He did not simply substitute strings for the nonorchestral instruments, but radically changed colors to make the two versions sound completely different. To give a few brief examples:

---

*From this point on, the reader is referred to the score of the work under discussion.

Example XVI–18a. Schoenberg, *Theme and Variations*, Op. 43A
(Band), mm. 1–5

b. Op. 43B (Orchestra), mm. 1–5

The very opening replaces a typically thick band color of clarinets
and oboes in unison with the clear solo voice of a trumpet; even
more important is the radical change in dynamics—*forte* for band,

piano for orchestra. This naturally has immediate consequences in the first variation: the oboe substitutes for the trumpet, which then becomes the principal voice, although it was not marked thus in the original version.

Example XVI–19a. Schoenberg, *Theme and Variations,* Op. 43A (Band), Variation I, first 4 measures

b. Op. 43B (Orchestra), Variation I, first 4 measures

The muted upper strings and pizzicato cellos and basses have a much "softer" color than the clarinets, euphonium, cornets, horns, and saxes. An attitude of greater delicacy in the orchestra pervades the entire transcription, and forces one to admit that the band version is much more "gutsy." There is no doubt that this change of emphasis was deliberate on Schoenberg's part. Knowing what a fine orchestrator he was, we are certain that he could have simulated and mirrored the band quite readily in the orchestral transcription. Therefore, this is an excellent work in which to observe at least two different ways of expressing the same musical idea. Let us study one other variation in greater depth.

Example XVI–20a. Schoenberg, *Theme and Variations,* Op. 43A (Band), Variation IV

b. Op. 43B (Orchestra), Variation IV

Although the flute solo was transferred intact, it is interesting to examine the "toned down" accompaniment in the orchestra.* The clarinet, muted trumpets, and baritones were replaced by solo strings muted or tutti playing *col legno battuto* (mm. 106–13). Then, with the trumpets resuming their original role, solo strings continue their extremely soft accompaniment instead of the much more piercing muted cornets and baritones. At the end of the flute solo (m. 122), the clarinet color is replaced by an oboe–English horn combination and the alto clarinet–alto saxophone mix assigned to a muted trombone. Remember that a section in a band may consist of a multiple of instruments playing a solo part; this would necessitate heavier accompaniment scoring for that, if for no other reason. It is noteworthy to examine the "fluttering" figures which Schoenberg invents in mm. 122–23 of the orchestral version. These have no equivalent in the much more straightforward band setting. Then we observe a drastic change of color in the orchestra when the flugelhorn's theme is played by the low flute and the high bassoon and the baritone-euphonium part is given to the very soft clarinets (mm. 124–25). Strangely enough, this is followed by two measures of exact transcription and a return to the color of mm. 124–25. In m. 129, we feel the lightness that Schoenberg wishes to convey in the orchestra, for the trumpet is kept muted and the oboe melody not doubled. Then (mm. 132–39) we have a wonderful exchange of high and low tessitura when the flutes and clarinets, doubled in the lower octave by the second violin, play the first loud phrase, followed by the violins in the upper register, while the winds double at the lower octave. This is certainly a much more sophisticated and less piercing solution than we find in the original score. Both versions end the variation in a similar manner, except for the violas, which provide a much softer sound than the original flugelhorn. The muted lower strings bring about the beautifully peaceful close.

* Variation VI (the fugue) will certainly verify the statement that the band version is more "gutsy." The orchestral version begins with the violas stating the subject; in the band there is a thrilling brass combination of open horns and baritone. Instead of bringing in another heavy brass combination, Schoenberg leaves the second statement to the first trumpet; however, that means several trumpets will play it, and that can hardly be compared to the second violin color. Nevertheless, let us remember these are two separate works, and the balance of the two strings is fine in the orchestra, while the brasses are well balanced in the band; as we said, the emotional impact is different. Meanwhile, the brass chords are taken by a rather

* The reader is now referred to the scores of the work under discussion.

effective double-reed combination. The pseudo-stretto entrance in mm. 176–77 is truly softened in the orchestra. While in the original the heavy bass color of trombones, baritone saxes, bass clarinets, and bassoons hold forth, in the transcription only the cellos mark the entrance, with the winds coming in with a rather undistinguished color, when compared to the winds in the band (mm. 177–80: high clarinets and alto sax, plus flugelhorn). The next few measures are fairly similar in strength, though the violin pizzicatos in m. 181 are no substitute for the power of the trumpets. At m. 182, Schoenberg drops out the brass except for the horns for a couple of measures, and has the strings take over the high wind parts; this provides a great freshness for the tutti reentrance of the winds in m. 186 and the buildup of the brass from m. 184 to m. 189. The high horns in the orchestra, as substitutes for the entire brass body of flugelhorns, horns, baritones, euphoniums, lower saxes, and clarinets, are quite thrilling, although a good deal lighter.

Study the rest of this marvelous piece on your own. You can learn a great deal about orchestral and band colorations, substitutions, and sensitive alterations, all of which will increase your techniques in dealing with the orchestral as well as the band medium.

TRANSCRIBING TO VARIOUS INSTRUMENTAL COMBINATIONS

We come perhaps to the most important section for many of us who are called upon to transcribe orchestral works for performance by groups, especially school ensembles, which do not always have the full complement of orchestral instruments demanded by a particular score. There is no reason why a great many orchestral, chamber, or piano works should not be adapted to meet the special circumstances in which we may find ourselves. It is very important to expose young people to good music which they can enjoy performing. To transcribe any work, especially a standard orchestral work, to meet the requirements of an often bizarre ensemble may tax our orchestrational skill to the limits. We must not only be aware of the heterogeneous nature of the available instruments, but we need to be conscious of the limited skills that each player brings to the group. These conditions, should, however, only spark our imagination rather than constrain us. For no matter how far-fetched the ensemble, we must be able to include each person present in our transcription.

How does one go about such a task?

1. Reduce the orchestral work to a piano score. If it is a very complex work, a piano four-hand or two-piano score will be even more helpful.

2. Carefully designate the sections as tutti, half tutti, soli, or solo.

3. Label the solo instruments and determine whether you have an adequate player in the group. If a substitution is called for, you may want to choose an instrument that closely approximates the original one, or a combination of two instruments that give a similar result. On the other hand, if this is not possible because of the limited choices you have available, select an instrument that possesses the range as well as the dynamic possibilities suitable to the solo.

There is no reason for rejecting a work for transcription to any medium because, for example, it contains an English-horn solo which simply would not sound right on any other instrument. We must come to grips with the fact that our transcription will of necessity sound differently from the original, but if we follow the steps outlined above, if we respect and love the piece we are adapting, and most of all, if we know the piece well both formally and orchestrally, we will be able to get satisfactory results with our transcription.

If there is a good pianist available in the group, he certainly should be used. However, do not commit the error that so many of us remember from our primary-school experiences, where the pianist played the reduction of the entire piece from beginning to end. Use the piano as just another orchestral instrument: to lend body to tutti sections, to provide arpeggiated accompaniments when called for, to render the harp parts, and to take occasional single line solos, or couple solos, doubling them in the higher registers.

Usually there is a percussion player present who should be used, but only where the music absolutely calls for it. Remember, percussion can obliterate an orchestra; it can do no less for a small group if it is not judiciously handled.

Two important "housekeeping" items for the score. Most amateur performers have problems with extreme ranges. There is an appendix at the end of this book where you will find the approximate, comfortable instrumental ranges for nonprofessionals. We hope that this will be helpful, for if you go much beyond those, your transcription, no matter how brilliantly executed, will not work. Most of the upper portions of the registers on most instruments will cause difficulties, but there are some on which the very lowest notes are problematical as well. This is the case for the flute, oboe, bassoon, horn, trumpet, tuba, and their auxiliaries.

Many orchestration books supply a list of substitution instruments, but that is really too limiting for our purposes. We would prefer that you experiment with the many possibilities and use the knowledge gained from analysis and listening, to decide which is the best substitute. Consider the range, the quality of the sound, and the given register, and what is most important, the skill of the player for which the part is intended.

Let us now invent a typical situation with which we may be confronted in a school or community, and solve it, transcribing a portion of three diverse pieces for our ensemble. After studying these examples, which of course present only one possibility among a great number of solutions, you should be able to cope with similar cases, as well as solve the transcription exercises in the workbook. We shall transcribe a chamber music work and an overture originally written for full orchestra. In each case the original is given.

One further caution: if one has a choice of a work to transcribe, it may be advisable to choose relatively unknown works on two counts: 1) the participants won't feel obliged to compare the transcription with the original, to the former's detriment; 2) performers should be exposed to the vast literature of the past and present which, for one reason or another, has not been widely disseminated.

Here is our fictitious ensemble and the relative technical proficiency of each player or section:

2 Flutes, both rather good *

3 Clarinets in Bb, first very good, others fair

1 Alto Saxophone, quite good

2 Trumpets in Bb, fair

1 Euphonium, very good

1 Timpani (3 drums), not too quick

1 Percussion player; counting is not his greatest strength

5 First Violins; 3 excellent to fifth position, 2 good to third position

4 Second Violins; all rather mediocre, not beyond first position

3 Cellos, the first is excellent, the other 2 mediocre

1 Double bass, not too proficient

This is probably a fairly typical cast of characters, and the gaps are quite usual—no double reeds, no horns, and no violas. There may be a trombone or two, and even a tuba, but all these instruments could be easily accommodated, and in setting quite stringent limitations for our present purpose, the ensemble above will serve.

---

* Please refer to Appendix A1 for instrument ranges (nonprofessional).

Example XVI–21a. Schumann, *Piano Quintet*, second movement, mm. 1–16

b. Orchestral Version

Example XVI–22a. von Suppé, *Poet and Peasant Overture*, 4-hand
Version, mm. 1–37

b. Orchestral Version

17

The Orchestra as Accompanist

The orchestra as an accompanying instrument considerably predates its existence as an independent body. There is more and more evidence that the Medieval and Renaissance vocal music, which we perform *a cappella* today, was in fact accompanied or doubled by a variety of instruments forming an ad hoc orchestral group. Since vocal music was by far the most important body of composed works in Western music until about 1600, instruments were relegated to the role of accompanist. With the ascendancy of opera, the shift of musical patronage from the Church to royalty, and the technical improvement of instruments, the orchestra gradually achieved greater autonomy. At the same time, its older role as the chief accompanying body for both sacred and secular vocal and choral works persisted. Throughout the seventeenth century, with the growth and development of the *concerto grosso* as well as the solo concerto, the orchestral task of accompaniment was greatly expanded, enhanced, and refined.

THE CONCERTO

Concertos have been written for all instruments, especially in the twentieth century. Previously, the piano was by far the favorite instrument for the solo concerto because it mixes relatively well with all instruments but blends with none. Therefore, it is quite easy to feature the piano with an orchestra, since it will stand out in any combination of instruments. All the other orchestral instruments must be treated with greater care and consideration, for they all have the tendency to blend into the orchestra rather naturally. Many orchestration books have stressed the idea that orchestral accompaniments should be assigned chiefly to the strings because of their "unobtrusive" character. This is a simplistic formula, and if one studies the concerto literature, it is easy to see that the facts don't substantiate this concept. There are much better guidelines we can extrapolate from the study of successful concerto orchestration of the past and present:

1. the use of dialogue;
2. separating solo and tutti by rhythmic independence;
3. assigning foreground and background roles to both solo and tutti;
4. distinct color differentiation to feature soloist;
5. consideration of the most transparent types of accompanying textures;
6. spacing and registral placement of solo vis-à-vis the orchestra.

These are six of the basic considerations that should be kept in mind in order to write an effective orchestral accompaniment to an instrumental solo work. Here are some examples from the solo concerto literature illustrating these guidelines:

Dialogue

The principle of dialogue stemming directly from the *concerto grosso* is still valid today, for it introduces the solo instrument by itself, implanting its timbre firmly in the listener's mind. In the simple Beethoven example that follows, we have the principal tune introduced by the solo violin and then immediately repeated in a radically different orchestral color. So conscious was Beethoven of the importance of contrast that even though the strings are contained in the "answering" color, they play pizzicato to add greater variety and to avoid duplication of the solo sound. (Another famous example of such a beginning is Prokofiev's *Violin Concerto in G minor*.)

Example XVII–1. Beethoven, *Romance for Violin and Orchestra,* Op. 40, mm. 1–8

Here is an example of the same principle in a piano concerto. The dialogue enhances the role of the piano as soloist, clarifies the melodic material, and aids in a clearer exposition of the form. There are literally hundreds of examples of this simple dialogue device, one of the most effective tools of the accompanying technique.

Example XVII–2. Schumann, *Piano Concerto,* second movement, mm. 1–4

See also, first movement, mm. 185–93.

Rhythmic Independence of Solo and Tutti

This is a more delicate problem, but perhaps the most crucial one to solve for accompanying purposes.

Tchaikovsky sets himself a difficult task by choosing the string orchestra to accompany the solo violin. For one thing, the range of the solo instrument is not much different from that of the first violins. Therefore, the composer has given the first violins a melodic counterpoint and the rest of the section harmonic figuration, which is quite simple and neither duplicates nor imitates the rhythmic patterns in the solo part.

Example XVII–3. Tchaikovsky, *Violin Concerto*, first movement, mm. 28–37

A similar situation is found in the last movement of the Mendelssohn *Violin Concerto*. In this excerpt we have a radical rhythmic difference between the smooth line of the soloist and the rather "coquettish" figure of the string-orchestra accompaniment.

Example XVII–4. Mendelssohn, *Violin Concerto*, third movement, mm. 107–17

Assigning Foreground and Background Material

It is interesting to note that in most successful concertos roles are frequently exchanged—the foreground material assigned to the soloist and the background to the orchestra, or vice versa.

In one of the most striking of concerto openings, the main theme is assigned to a combination of violins and cellos, while the piano plays chords reinforced by soft, sustained harmonies in the winds:

Example XVII–5. Tchaikovsky, *Piano Concerto No. 1*, first movement, mm. 1–16

The soloist can provide a successful accompaniment to foreground activities of the orchestra. For these purposes, it is important to use the most idiomatic figuration for the solo instrument in order to assure the best results. In the piano, the Alberti bass, or broken chord figuration, is a natural for this role. Here is an example of another solo instrument fulfilling the accompanying task excellently:

Example XVII–6. Saint-Saëns, *Cello Concerto*, mm. 447–61

See also Mendelssohn, *Violin Concerto*, first movement, mm. 335–43.

Brahms, *Violin Concerto*, first movement, mm. 110–31.

Distinct Color Contrasts to Feature Soloist

To introduce the soloist, many composers utilize a distinctly contrasting color combination. For instance, both Dvořák and Tchaikovsky, in the slow movement introductions to their cello and violin concertos respectively, begin with the woodwind choir before the string soloist enters. The solo color is therefore very fresh, even after the first movement has been heard.

Example XVII–7. Dvořák, *Cello Concerto*, second movement, mm. 1–10

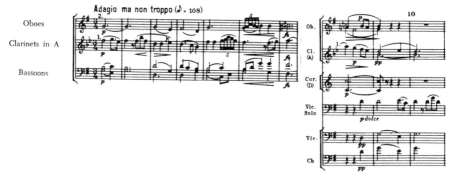

Example XVII–8. Tchaikovsky, *Violin Concerto*, second movement, mm. 1–24

Two examples from Mozart concertos can teach us some other valuable lessons about color contrasts. Example XVII–9, from the *Second Horn Concerto*, shows that the heterophonic doubling of the solo instrument does not diminish the soloist's role in the least, for there is such a vast color contrast between the horn and the first violins. The rest of the strings have more subsidiary harmonic roles. Notice that Mozart never uses the orchestral horns while the solo horn is playing. These are employed only in the introduction and during interludes, so as not to interfere with the solo sound.

Example XVII–9. Mozart, *Horn Concerto No. 2*, first movement, mm. 6–63

The next Mozart excerpt, taken from the final movement of his *G-major Flute Concerto*, illustrates a number of important considerations when a wind instrument is soloist:

1. A sparse accompaniment is provided for the solo runs at Ⓐ in order to give the performer freedom.

2. Notice the color contrast at Ⓑ where the oboes, then the solo flute and first violins play the tune. This is followed once again by solo scales, which are lightly orchestrated to give maximum freedom to the soloist.

3. The soloist is introduced by tutti at Ⓒ, but as soon as the flute enters, the orchestra is reduced drastically, for the flute is playing at the softest part of its range. The sustained D in both the horns as well as the cellos and basses emphasizes the solid return to the tonic G.

4. Mozart uses no orchestral flutes in this work, so that the solo flute will not encounter any color competition.

Example XVII–10. Mozart, *Flute Concerto No. 1*, third movement, mm. 54–94

Texture Considerations

Not only must the varying timbres be considered as valid accompanying devices, but the density and transparency of the texture adds immeasurably to the effectiveness of the solo-material presentation. Here are two wonderful examples in which the solo is separated from the accompaniment in a most advantageous way. In both, the soloist is introduced to the audience in a manner that highlights his best characteristics because of the sparse and transparent texture in which the entrance is couched.

Sibelius creates an atmosphere of expectation into which the soloist enters with a great, fresh sound. Because the accompanying texture is so ethereal, the beautiful, robust melody soars freely and is instantly perceived by the listener, since the background does not intrude at all.

Example XVII–11. Sibelius, *Violin Concerto*, first movement, mm. 1–41

Similarly, in this piano concerto by Béla Bartók, a mood is created by the weaving strings, quietly pulsating timpani, and sustained clarinet chord, which permits the piano free rein in performing its lyrical tune. The rather illusive nature of the background rhythm also strengthens the intricate rhythmic patterns of the main melody by contrast.

Example XVII–12. Bartók, *Piano Concerto No. 3*, first movement, mm. 1–18

Spacing and Registral Considerations

Instruments other than the piano have a strong tendency to blend when used in certain registers and with acoustically sympathetic orchestral combinations. Here are a few successful and ingenious solutions to this problem from the concerto literature:

In the example below from Beethoven's *Violin Concerto*, the soloist replaces the flute in the woodwind combination, and in its most ethereal register easily dominates the situation. The timpani is very important because it plays the motive that separates the two phrases of the melody, while the harmony is provided in a most natural fashion by the other woodwinds.

Example XVII–13. Beethoven, *Violin Concerto*, first movement, mm. 99–109

In the famous "triangle" episode from his *Piano Concerto in E♭*, Liszt writes a characteristic heterophonic flute part to accompany the piano, emphasizing the most important pitches and doubling others. The triangle is also an integral part of the accompaniment, with the pizzicato strings providing the harmonic background.

Example XVII–14. Liszt, *Piano Concerto in E♭*, second movement, mm. 99–104

Once again we quote a fascinating passage from Beethoven's *Violin Concerto*, in which the bassoon in its middle register is pitted against the solo violin playing ornamental passages. The great contrast in the rhythmic activity of the two instruments contributes immensely to the clarity of the passage, as does the simplicity of the harmony in the orchestral strings.

Example XVII–15. Beethoven, *Violin Concerto*, third movement, mm. 135–42

All these guidelines and considerations don't preclude the possibility of a simple accompanying figure in the orchestra which provides harmony to a melody. In this very useful and popular solution to the accompaniment problem, one important fact must be borne in mind: try to keep the accompanying forces registrally distant from the soloist whenever possible. It is true that rhythmic contrast lessens the importance of this consideration. Nevertheless, for utmost effectiveness, especially when dealing with woodwind solo instruments, it is an important idea to remember.

ACCOMPANYING THE VOCAL SOLOIST OR CHORUS

Before embarking on this most important subject, let us review the ranges of the four voice types:

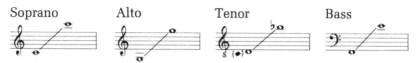

These are the extreme solo voice ranges. Some sopranos can go above the high C easily, and, using "chest voice," may reach a fourth below middle C. Altos can be divided into two categories: mezzo-sopranos, with a range of: 𝄞 and contraltos, with a range of: 𝄞 The tenors cannot, or should not, be placed in different categories, although the quality of the voice easily separates a heavy

Wagnerian tenor from a light, lyric tenor singing Mozart. The bass voice can be classified in at least two ways: the baritone, with a range of: 𝄢 and a "basso profundo," with a range of: 𝄢 We know there are Russian basses who are able to reach even a fourth below this lowest note.

One point of caution: remember that forcing the voice to sing over a thick orchestral accompaniment for long periods of time not only overtaxes and fatigues the singer, but often causes the vocalist to "push" his instrument abnormally, detracting from the beauty of the natural quality. Just like any orchestral instrument, the timbre and power of the register vary with each voice class; unlike the orchestral instrument, these variations differ with almost every individual. Usually the lower fifth of the range carries least well and must be lightly accompanied; the next octave is relaxed and quite forceful; the upper fifth of the range is the most powerful one. However, with many basses and contraltos, the lower part of the range carries much better than the upper portion, which can sound constricted and forced. Conversely, the upper registers of the sopranos and tenors are quite penetrating, while the lower register speaks only very softly.

Remember that the voice is an instrument that produces pitches purely "by ear," without the aid of strings, keys, or valves. It is true that some few singers have absolute pitch, and many others "feel" the placement of tones with astounding accuracy (much as the way horn players do); but most vocalists depend for their pitch orientation on the accompaniment. With this in mind, it is essential to lead a singer to his first pitch, and from then on aid him in every conceivable way with the orchestral accompaniment, so that he will be able to maintain pitch accuracy throughout the work with relative ease. This does not mean that the voice part should be doubled at pitch all the time, but rather the singer should have important points of pitch reference as frequently as possible. The admonition is especially relevant today, when we deal with an expanded harmonic vocabulary, and it is even more crucial when writing for a chorus, which is usually made up of singers less professionally trained than soloists.

The Recitative

The recitative is the simplest vocal piece to accompany, since it usually consists of a few chords necessary to establish and then support the harmony. The most commonly used recitative types are the *secco* recitative and the accompanied recitative. Here are some examples of each:

The *secco* recitative is mostly found in the works of Bach and Handel, etc., and is simply a vocal line accompanied by a figured bass (improvised chords).

Example XVII–16. Haydn, *Creation*, No. 9

See also Bach, *Cantata No. 56* (*Kreuzstab*), "Mein Wandel auf der Welt," mm. 1–10.

The accompanied recitative also consists of chords, for the most part, but more of the orchestra is used, and often orchestral interruptions heighten the drama.

Example XVII–17. Mendelssohn, *Elijah*, No. 13: "Call Him Louder," mm. 1–11

Example XVII–18. Walton, *Belshazzar's Feast*, Recit.: "And in that same hour," mm. 1–8

See also Mozart, *Le Nozze di Figaro*, Act III, scene 4, mm. 14–40

The Aria or Orchestral Song

While the vocalist sings the words, the orchestral accompaniment often provides the interpretation and sets the atmosphere. This is especially true in opera. However, in many of the most successful Italian operas, composers have opted for very simple orchestral accompanying figures in order to permit the singer to emote fully without orchestral interference. Here is an excerpt from Verdi's *La Traviata* which exemplifies this treatment. It is quite simple, containing a clarinet *obbligato* and sustained chords to strengthen the harmony.

Example XVII–19. Verdi, *La Traviata*, Act I, scene 3, "Ah fors' è lui", mm. 29–47

See also Verdi, *La Traviata*, Act III, "Parigi, o cara," mm. 1–35.

The next example is Micaela's aria from the third act of *Carmen*. Notice the wonderful contrast between the high voice and the rather mellow colors used against it. Bizet is very careful to keep the instruments and the voice quite separate rhythmically. Only when the singer reaches her dramatic climax on the word *peur*, does he take the first violins up to double her at a higher octave. The singer is free to make her sad plea with great pathos.

Example XVII–20. Bizet, *Carmen*, Act III, "Je dis que rien ne m'épouvante," mm. 6–24

The next example is not operatic, but is from the orchestral song literature: a short passage from the first song of the *Lieder eines fahrenden Gesellen* by Mahler. Here the orchestra paints the picture of a meadow with flowers and birds chirping all about. The voice is never obscured in this most colorful setting. It is helped in pitch, yet not doubled. One should study the entire song cycle for some of the most beautiful orchestral accompaniments imaginable.

Example XVII–21. Mahler, *Lieder eines fahrenden Gesellen*, No. 1, "Wenn mein Schatz," mm. 44–63

One should not neglect the study of many other orchestral songs, such as (to name only a few):

Berlioz, *Nuits d'été*
Mahler, *Kindertotenlieder* and *Das Lied von der Erde*
Ravel, *Shéhérazade*
Barber, *Knoxville: Summer of 1915*
Messiaen, *Poèmes pour Mi*
Britten, *Serenade* and *Nocturne*
Schoenberg, the solo opera *Erwartung*

We have discussed the solo aria, recitative, and solo orchestral song. It is important that we examine at least one famous ensemble number from the opera stage. The quartet below, a canon from the first act of Beethoven's *Fidelio,* is a brilliant example of wonderful vocal writing, simply and delicately accompanied by the orchestra. Notice that Beethoven doubles the voice parts at all times, either directly or heterophonically, and keeps the texture around the singers extremely light. Study each doubling, for often a bass part is doubled several octaves higher, and conversely, the soprano by a bass instrument. The orchestral figuration adds considerably to the contented spirit that describes at least three of the singers' moods.

Example XVII–22. Beethoven, *Fidelio*, Act I, No. 3

The exciting combination of chorus and orchestra has been a favorite since the time of Monteverdi. As we have already said, one of the most important things to remember is that choral singers are not always professionals and need more pitch support than solo singers. In the Baroque and Classical periods, the chorus, when not doubled, could discern the pitches easily from the clear harmony provided by the orchestra. As the harmonic language grew more complex, composers tried to find a variety of ways to provide good pitch orientation for the choruses:

The following Bach example shows the strong harmony which gives unquestioned support to the contrapuntal choral texture.

Example XVII–23. Bach, *Cantata No. 21*, "Ich hatte viel Bekümmerniss," mm. 1–12

In "The Heavens Are Telling," from *The Creation*, Haydn doubles the entire chorus, and it is interesting to notice that in the second phrase the tenor, alto, and one note of the soprano are doubled on top by the flute. This is a common device, sounding like an harmonic-contrapuntal line, which lends great support to the chorus.

Example XVII–24. Haydn, *The Creation*, No. 13: "The Heavens Are Telling," mm. 1–12

Carmina burana has been a favorite for thirty years now, and even though a large orchestra is employed, Orff always ensures that the chorus sounds through the maze easily. He does so in two ways: 1) by scoring the chorus in its most advantageous range to compete with the "doubling" orchestra; and 2) by setting up an accompaniment figure that does not obscure the chorus while still giving vital pitch and rhythmic assistance. The example certainly bears out these two successful techniques used throughout the work.

Example XVII–25. Orff, *Carmina burana,* "O Fortuna," mm. 1–14

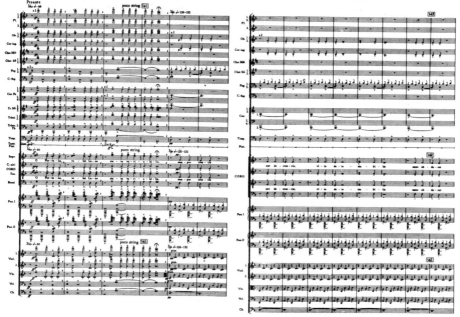

It is vital that the student become familiar with the great choral-orchestral literature, not only by listening to the works, but also by studying the scores to learn the successful techniques for accompanying solo and orchestral passages. Here is a short list of recommended works:

Bach, *B-minor Mass* and *St. Matthew Passion*
Handel, *Messiah* and *Israel in Egypt*
Haydn, *Creation, Seasons,* and *Masses*
Mozart, *Requiem* and *C-minor Mass*
Beethoven, *Missa solemnis* and *Mass in C*
Berlioz, *Requiem*
Mendelssohn, *Elijah* and *Hymn of Praise*
Brahms, *German Requiem* and *Alto Rhapsody*
Verdi, *Requiem*
Mahler, *Symphony No. 2*

Kodály, *Psalmus hungaricus*
Debussy, *The Martyrdom of St. Sebastian*
Poulenc, *Gloria*
Honegger, *King David*
Vaughan Williams, *Flos Campos* and *Hodie*
Britten, *War Requiem*
Walton, *Te Deum* and *Belshazzar's Feast*
Stravinsky, *Symphony of Psalms, Canticum Sacrum, Threni,* and
    Oedipus Rex
Schoenberg, *Gurrelieder*
Bartók, *Cantata profana*
Tippett, *Child of Our Times*
Hindemith, *When Lilacs Last in the Dooryard Bloomed*
Prokofiev, *Alexander Nevsky*
Sessions, *When Lilacs Last in the Dooryard Bloomed*
Berio, *Sinfonia*

This is only a small sample of the works readily available on recordings. There are, of course, many more, especially chorus and orchestra combinations from such operas as *Fidelio, Der Freischütz, Carmen, Otello, Turandot,* and in particular, *Boris Goudonov.*

18

The Preparation of Score and Parts

We know that world leaders are able to change laws and thereby affect our destiny by a flick of the pen. In orchestration, some incorrect flicks of the pen resulting in unclear and error-riddled scores and parts can spell disaster for a performance. It is most appropriate, therefore, that we take this final chapter to discuss and to review the correct procedures for laying out a score and extracting parts in the most professional manner.

Here are the considerations which must govern that process:

1. The score must be clear, easy to read, and as unproblematical as possible. The last phrase means that all new, different, or original notation must be carefully explained, so that when a conductor reads the score it will be self-evident.

2. The score must be organized logically, with every instrument appropriately labeled: the vertical alignment of the music must be accurate so that all notes and beats coincide. The spacing on the page, indicating the separation of choirs, must be immediately discernable, for a conductor has to read all the lines simultaneously.

3. In addition to rehearsal numbers, the score must contain every detail for every instrument, including special instructions concerning bowing, tonguing, or articulations.

THE ORCHESTRAL SCORE SETUP

The instruments of a large symphony orchestra appear on a full score page in an unvarying order:

Piccolo
Flutes I and II
Oboes I and II
English Horn
Clarinet (in D or Eb), indicated at the beginning of the score
Clarinet I and II (in Bb or A), indicated at the beginning of the
    score
Bass Clarinet
Bassoons I and II
Contrabassoon
Horns I, II, III, IV—Keys of the horns must be given at the begin-
    ning of the score.
Trumpets I, II, III—Keys of the trumpets must be given at the
    beginning of the score.
Trombones I, II, III
Tuba
Timpani—The number of drums should be given at the beginning
    of the score.
Percussion—All instruments must be listed at the beginning of the
    score.
Harp
Piano (Celesta)
Strings

If there are additional instruments, these should be fitted into their family, such as Wagner's tubas or euphonium between the trombones and the tuba, or saxophones between the bass clarinet and the bassoons. (N.B.: In some American scores the saxophones are printed below the bassoons or even below the brass, just above the timpani.)

It is imperative to leave space between the choirs on the score page. Leave an empty line between the winds and the brass, between the brass and the percussion, between the percussion and the harp, between the (harp) piano and the strings.

If there is an independent piccolo part in the composition it appears above the flute parts. If the second or third flutes double on piccolo, the piccolo part will appear on the line normally read by that player. The alto flute part is always placed below the regular flute parts, and most often is doubled by the third flute.

Example XVIII–1

TITLE

Alternative way of notating time signatures

This principle of alternation equally applies to a second or third oboist doubling on English horn, a clarinetist doubling on bass clarinet, or a bassoonist doubling on contrabassoon. To indicate that the player is to change instruments, the instruction "change to _____," or in Italian, "muta in _____," should be given well ahead of time and should be written above the player's staff. Further, if a change of key signature or clef is required because of a transposition change in the new instrument, this also appears at the point of instruction.

From time to time, the horns are grouped I–III and II–IV on two staffs, when there is an excess of unisons for the high and low horns; most often, Horns I and II share one staff, III and IV the other.

Trumpets and trombones are written on two staffs respectively. In both cases, Instrument I is separated from Instruments II and III, which share the second staff of their sections.

The score layout on page 523 is for the entire orchestra. Notice that all staffs are connected with a single barline at the beginning of the line; heavy brackets set off the choirs; and an additional brace clarifies instruments of a family. Measure lines should be drawn only through the individual complete choirs. It is absolutely wrong to rule a measure line through an entire score, for it obscures the choirs and is a deterrent to rapid reading by the conductor.

Key signatures should appear in their traditional position right after the clef signs, followed by the time signature. These time signatures may be repeated on every instrumental line or enlarged to one time signature for each choir. It is strongly urged that tempo markings be placed at the top of the score and repeated in the space separating each choir. Dynamics are usually placed below the staff, unless two instruments share a staff and two different sets of dynamics are required.

Up to this point, we have dealt only with the initial page of a score. However, the subsequent pages should follow the same model, except that one may use abbreviations for the instrument names. Unless there is a change from one transposing instrument to another, such as Clarinet in B♭ switching to Clarinet in A in the middle of a work, it is not necessary to repeat the transposition on every page. Some composers try to use all kinds of short cuts, like leaving out clefs or key signatures after the initial page; this custom should be strongly discouraged, even if it is used extensively in jazz charts. On the other hand, the cutout score originated by Stravinsky, and very popular through the '60s and early '70s, is quite valid. In this kind of score, the staffs begin where the particular instrument starts to play, and stop as soon as that instrument ceases to play. Notice in the following example that each instrument is always placed in the correct choir and is labeled every time it enters.

Example XVIII–2. Stravinsky, *Movements for Piano and Orchestra,* mm. 13–39: Cutout Score

THE REDUCED SCORE

After the initial page, subsequent pages may contain more than one system because only a few instruments are playing at a time. Pages like this are called *reduced scores*. Make certain that two heavy slash marks ✦ appear between the systems so that it will be easy for the eye to separate them immediately. Also, it is imperative that all the instruments must be clearly marked in all systems appearing on a page, and that the order of choirs remains the same as on the initial page of the score.

Example XVIII–3. Mahler, *Symphony No. 1*, first movement
a. Fullscore page, mm. 269–75 b. Reduced-score page, mm. 276–89

THE CONDENSED SCORE

When writing educational or commercial music, the composer is often asked to supply a *condensed score*, in which a full score is reduced to only three or four staffs, but all the essential pitches (melodic), rhythms and harmonics contained in the full score are provided. This reduction should all be in C with no transpositions. It may or may not be playable on the piano. If it is to be a *piano reduction*, it should be written on two staffs, omitting all nonessential octave doublings so that it can be played with ten fingers. A regular three- or four-line condensed score most often uses a line for each choir and is prepared for conductors who are not able to read a full score fluently. Here is an example of a condensed score and a piano version of the same passage.

Example XVIII–4a. Brahms, *Symphony No. 1*, first movement, mm. 82–87: Full Score

b. Condensed Score

c. Piano Score

PREPARING INDIVIDUAL PARTS

The clearer the parts, the easier it is to perform a work. This statement is especially valid today, for orchestral music has become more and more difficult. It is essential that all notation, other than the standard, universally accepted symbols, be carefully explained in a "Guide to the Notation" at the beginning of the individual part. If the work contains no unusual notation, this is not necessary.

Here are some important suggestions to follow in extracting parts from a score:

1. Use a good size (9½" x 12½") paper with no more than twelve staffs on each page, and provide each player with his own part. Strings, of course, should have one part per stand.

2. Use ink rather than pencil. The diazo process, in which the score and parts are prepared on transparencies, is highly recommended over other duplicating processes for professional clarity.

3. Make the noteheads at least as large as those printed in a published part for easy visibility. The same holds true for the flags on

eighth or sixteenth notes, the rests, and the thickness of beams denoting rhythmic divisions.

4. Be sure to include rehearsal numbers or letters in both score and parts. Chaos may result if a rehearsal number or a change of meter is omitted because it occurs while an instrument is resting. Make certain that every player has detailed information about what is happening every moment in the performance, whether he is playing or not. Let us suppose a player has sixteen measures' rest, and the score has rehearsal numbers placed every ten measures. Here is the way his part should read:

Example XVIII–5

The same rule would apply if changes of meter occurred within that rest period. Let us suppose that measure 65 is in 3/4, and the rest of the measures are 4/4. This is how the part should read with the added detail:

Example XVIII–6

5. It is imperative that a woodwind or brass player has enough time at the end of a page to make the turn. In string orchestral parts, the person on the inside of the stand turns the page, while the partner on the outside continues to play so that a rest is not essential. The general problem of page turning must be dealt with when you begin to lay out a part on a page. Wind or brass players have been known to leave out an entire passage because there were no rests to free their hands. And even in string parts, you must consider the weakening effect on an important string passage when half the section drops out to turn a page.

6. Cues are often necessary to facilitate re-entry after a long period of rest. Both the instrument playing that particular cue and the place where the cue begins should be clearly indicated. The notes in the cued parts should be smaller than those in the rest of the part. Also, the cue should be transposed to fit the part into which it is written (for example, a violin cue in a clarinet in B♭ part should be transposed into B♭).

Example XVIII–7

7. Quite frequently, parts for oboes, bassoons, violas, or even horns are cross-cued in other parts so that important lines assigned to these instruments will not be lost. Particularly in music for school orchestra, cross-cuing is often advisable. Since violas are scarce in many of our high school orchestras, it may be necessary to supply a third violin and a second cello part which divide up the viola part. These should be used only if no violas are available. However, important oboe lines and English horn parts are often cross-cued in the clarinet, violin, or muted trumpet parts, depending on where they lie in the register. Bassoons are cross-cued in the clarinet or cello parts, and sometimes a tenor saxophone part is supplied if no bassoon is available. As mentioned in the chapter on transcriptions, there is no real substitute for the original instrument. However the best possible solution has to be found to prevent the loss of important lines, even if the cross-cued instrument's sound is a bit removed from the composer's original intention. Be certain that all cross-cuing is indicated in the full score so that the conductor may assign each substitution.

8. Some shortcuts that are permissible when copying out parts:

a. One should use 8va, 15ma, or 8^{basso} designations as much as possible to avoid more than four ledger lines above or below the staff.

b. When a passage is repeated exactly, repeat marks may be used. It is helpful to number the repeated measures for easier execution:

Example XVIII–8

c. The abbreviations *sim., sempre stacc., sempre legato,* etc. are also permissible to avoid repeating details like staccatos, slurs, etc.

Example XVIII–9

9. When two instruments are written on the same staff in the score, they should have separate parts for each player.

Example XVIII–10a. Score

b. Parts

Last but not least, we must mention proofreading. As a general rule, proofreading your own score and parts is a difficult chore. Therefore, it is urged that a two-step process be followed to insure a minimum of errors.

1. Proofread both score and parts thoroughly yourself.

2. Let someone else proof them so as to make certain you have not overlooked even the smallest detail. This can make the difference between a flawless first reading (and first impression) and a tedious rehearsal, which is discouraging to both composer and performers.

For a more detailed study of manuscript preparation, the student is referred to the following books:

Boehm, L. *Modern Music Notation.* New York: G. Schirmer, 1961.

Donato, A. *Preparing Music Manuscript.* Englewood Cliffs, New Jersey: Prentice-Hall, 1963.

Read, G. *Music Notation.* Boston: Allyn and Bacon, 1964.

Read, G. *Modern Rhythmic Notation.* Bloomington: Indiana University Press, 1978.

Risatti, Howard. *New Music Vocabulary.* Urbana: University of Illinois Press, 1975.

Stone, K. *Music Notation in the Twentieth Century.* New York: W. W. Norton, 1980.

Warfield, G. *How to Write Music Manuscript.* New York: Longman, 1977.

Appendix A

1. QUICK REFERENCE TO RANGES OF MOST FREQUENTLY USED ORCHESTRAL INSTRUMENTS

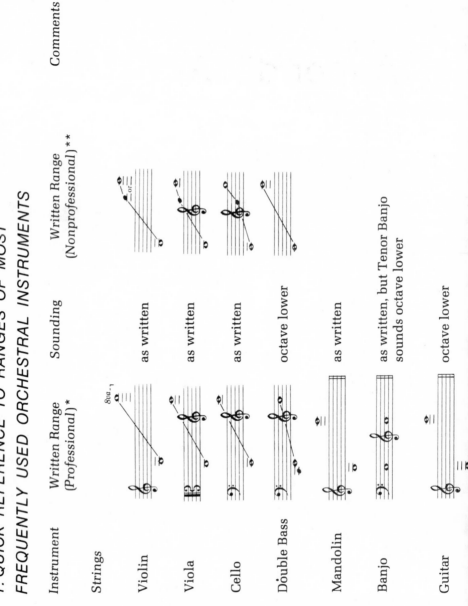

Instrument	Written Range (Professional) *	Sounding	Written Range (Nonprofessional) **	Comments
Strings				
Violin		as written		
Viola		as written		
Cello		as written		
Double Bass		octave lower		
Mandolin		as written		
Banjo		as written, but Tenor Banjo sounds octave lower		
Guitar		octave lower		

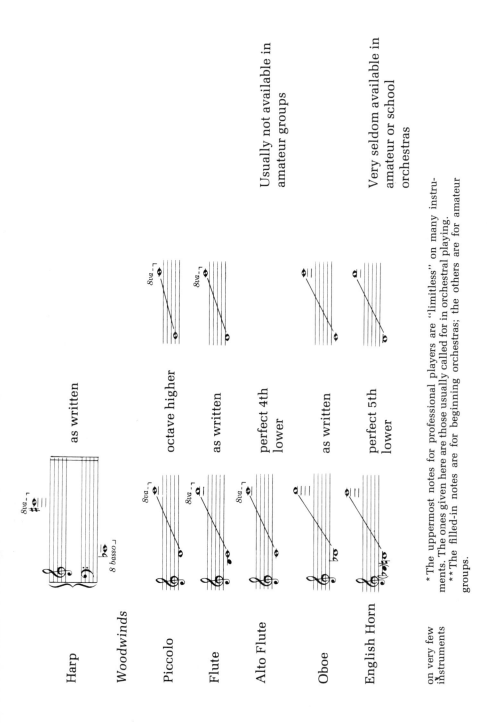

Harp — as written

Woodwinds

Piccolo — octave higher

Flute — as written

Alto Flute — perfect 4th lower

Oboe — as written

English Horn — perfect 5th lower

on very few instruments

Usually not available in amateur groups

Very seldom available in amateur or school orchestras

*The uppermost notes for professional players are "limitless" on many instruments. The ones given here are those usually called for in orchestral playing.
**The filled-in notes are for beginning orchestras; the others are for amateur groups.

Instrument	Written Range (Professional)	Sounding	Written Range (Nonprofessional)	Comments
All Clarinets except Bass		Bb: major 2nd lower A: minor 3rd lower D: major 2nd higher Eb: minor 3rd higher		Usually no D or Eb clarinets in nonprofessional orchestras
Bass Clarinet		major 9th lower; if written in bass clef, major 2nd lower		Usually unavailable in amateur or school groups
Bassoon		as written		Watch lowest and highest notes for amateurs
Contrabassoon		octave lower		Usually not available in nonprofessional groups
All saxophones		Bb Soprano: major 2nd lower Eb Alto: major 6th lower Bb Tenor: major 9th lower Eb Baritone: octave and major 6th lower Bb Bass: 2 octaves lower		If available in amateur groups, the saxophones should not be scored very low or very high
Brass				
Horn		perfect 5th lower		

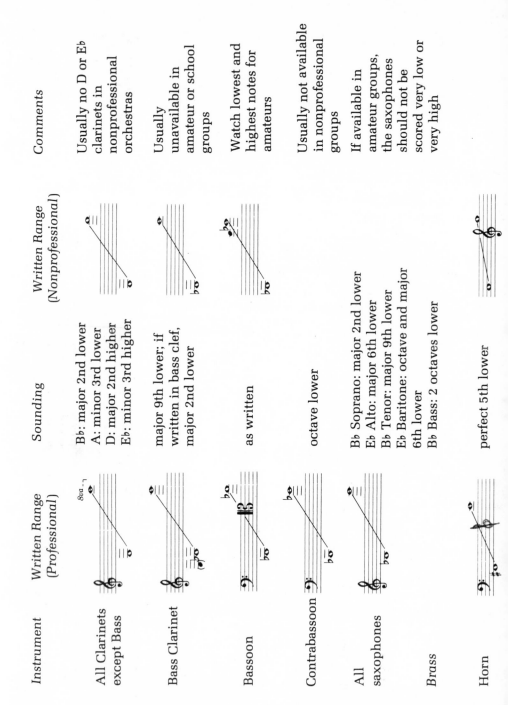

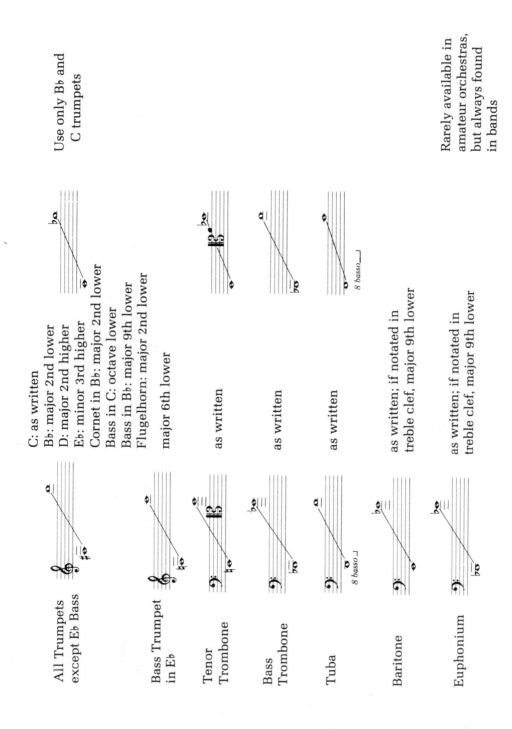

All Trumpets except Eb Bass

C: as written
Bb: major 2nd lower
D: major 2nd higher
Eb: minor 3rd higher
Cornet in Bb: major 2nd lower
Bass in C: octave lower
Bass in Bb: major 9th lower
Flugelhorn: major 2nd lower

Use only Bb and C trumpets

Bass Trumpet in Eb

major 6th lower

Tenor Trombone

as written

Bass Trombone

as written

Tuba

as written

Baritone

as written; if notated in treble clef, major 9th lower

Rarely available in amateur orchestras, but always found in bands

Euphonium

as written; if notated in treble clef, major 9th lower

Instrument	Written Range (Professional)	Sounding
Percussion		
Timpani		as written
Xylophone		octave higher
Marimba		as written
Glockenspiel		2 octaves higher
Vibraphone		as written
Chimes		as written
Keyboard		
Piano		as written
Celesta		octave higher
Harpsichord		as written
Harmonium		as written
Organ		as written

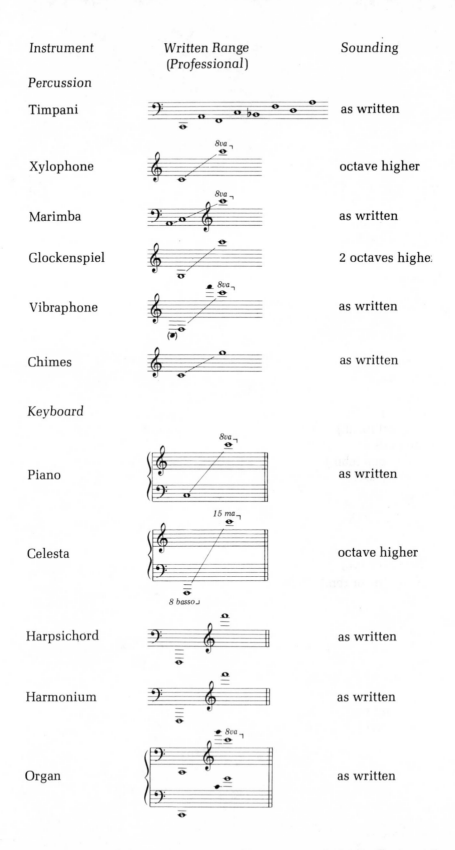

2. NAMES OF INSTRUMENTS IN FOUR LANGUAGES AND THEIR ENGLISH ABBREVIATIONS

English	Italian	French	German
Strings:	Archi:	Cordes:	Streichinstrumente:
Violin (vl.)	Violino	Violon	Violine
Viola (vla.)	Viola	Alto	Bratsche
Violoncello (vlc.)	Violoncello	Violoncelle	Violoncell
Double Bass (d.b.)	Contrabasso	Contre Basse	Kontrabass
Woodwinds:	Legni (or Fiati):	Bois:	Holzbläser:
Piccolo (picc.)	Flauto Piccolo (or Ottavino)	Petite Flûte	Kleine Flöte
Flute (fl.)	Flauto	Flûte	Flöte
Oboe (ob.)	Oboe	Hautbois	Oboe (or Hoboe)
English Horn (Eng. hn.)	Corno Inglese	Cor Anglais	Englisch Horn
Clarinet (cl.)	Clarinetto	Clarinette	Klarinette
Bass Clarinet (b. cl.)	Clarinetto Basso	Clarinette Basse	Bassklarinette
Bassoon (bn.)	Fagotto	Basson	Fagott
Contra Bassoon (cbn.)	Contrafagotto	Contre-basson	Kontrafagott
Saxophone (sax.)	Sassofono	Saxophone	Saxophon
Brass(es):	Ottoni:	Cuivres:	Blechinstrumente:
Horn (hn.)	Corno	Cor	Horn
Trumpet (tr. or tpt.)	Tromba	Trompette	Trompete
Trombone (trb. or tbn.)	Trombone	Trombone	Posaune
Tuba (t.)	Tuba	Tuba	Tuba (or Basstuba)

IDIOPHONES OF DEFINITE PITCH

Percussion	Percussione	Batterie	Schlagzeug
Marimba (mar.)	Marimba	Marimba	Marimbaphon
Xylophone (xyl.)	Xilofono or Silofono	Xylophone	Xylophon

English	Italian	French	German
METAL INSTRUMENTS OF DEFINITE PITCH			
Orchestral Bells (Glsp.)	Campanelli	Jeu de Timbres or Carillon	Glockenspiel
Vibraphone (vib.)	Vibrafono	Vibraphone	Vibraphon
Tubular Chimes (chim.)	Campana Tubolare or Campane Tubolari	Tubes des Cloches	Röhrenglocken or Rohrenglockenspiel
Celesta (cel.)	Celesta or Celeste	Célesta	Celesta
Gong (gong)	Gong	Gong	Gong
Crotales (crot.)	Crotali	Crotales or Cymbales Antiques	Zimbeln
Anvil (anv.)	Incudine	Enclume	Amboss
Musical Saw (saw)	Sega Cantante	Scie Musicale	Spielsäge
Flexatone (flex.)	Flessatono	Flexatone	Flexaton
MEMBRANOPHONES OF DEFINITE PITCH			
Timpani (timp.)	Timpano and Timpani	Timbale and Timbales	Pauke and Pauken
Roto-Tom (r. tom)	Roto-Tom-Tom	Roto-Tom	Tom-Tom-Spiel
MEMBRANOPHONES OF INDEFINITE PITCH			
Snare Drum (s. dr.)	Tamburo Piccolo	Caisse Claire or Tambour	Kleine Trommel
(with snares on)	(Colle Corde)	(avec timbres)	(mit Schnarrsaite)
(with snares off)	(senza le corde)	(sans timbres)	(ohne Schnarrsaite)
Tenor Drum (t. dr.)	Tamburo Militare	Tambour Militaire	Militärtrommel
(with snares on)			

Tenor Drum (t. dr.) (with snares off)	Cassa Rullante	Caisse Roulante	Wirbeltrommel or Tenortrommel
Tom-Tom (tom. t)	Tom-Tom	Tom-Tom	Tom-Tom
Bongos (Bong.)	Bongos or Bonghi	Bongos	Bongos
Timbales (timb.)	Timpanetti or Timbales latino-americani	Timbales Cubaines or Creoles	Kuba-Pauken
Conga Drum (conga)	Tumba	Conga	Conga-Trommel or Tumba
Bass Drum (b. dr.)	Gran Cassa, Cassa, or Tamburo Grande	Grosse Caisse	Grosse Trommel
(upright)	(verticale)	(verticale)	(aufrecht)
(on side)	(orizzontale)	(à plat)	(liegend)
Tambourine (tamb.)	Tamburo basco or Tamburino	Tambour de Basque	Tamburin

WOODEN INSTRUMENTS OF INDEFINITE PITCH

Woodblock (w. bl.)	Blocco de Legno Cinese	Bloc de Bois	Holzblock
Temple Block (t. bl.)	Blocco de Legno Coreano	Temple-Bloc	Tempelblock
Claves (claves)	Claves	Claves	Claves or Holzstab
Castanets (cast.)	Castagnette or Nacchere	Castagnettes	Kastagnetten
Maracas (marac.)	Maracas	Maracas	Maracas

METAL INSTRUMENTS OF INDEFINITE PITCH

Finger Cymbals (fing. cymb.)	Cimbalini	Cymbales Digitales	Fingerzimbeln
Crash Cymbals (cymb.)	Piatti or Cinelli	Cymbales	Becken-Paar
Suspended Cymbal (susp. cymb.)	Piatto Sospeso	Cymbale Suspendue	Hängendes Becken
Sizzle cymbal (sizz. cymb.)	Piatto Chiodat	Cymbale sur Tiges	Nietenbecken

English	Italian	French	German
METAL INSTRUMENTS OF DEFINITE PITCH (cont.)			
Triangle (trgl.)	Triangolo	Triangle	Triangel
Cowbells (cowb.)	Campanelli da Mucca	Cloche de Vache	Kuhglocken
Tam-Tam (tam-t.)	Tamtam	Tam-Tam	Tamtam
Sleighbells	Sonagliera or Sonagli	Grelots	Rollschellen
Automobile Brake Drums (b. dr.)	Auto-Brake-Drums	Auto-Brake-Drums	Auto-Brake-Drums
OTHER SOUND SOURCES OF INDEFINITE PITCH			
Whip or Slap Stick (slapst.)	Frusta	Fouet	Peitsche
Ratchet (ratch.)	Raganella	Crécelle	Ratsche
Sandpaper Blocks (sandp. bl.)	Carta Vetrata	Papier de Verre	Sandpapier or Sandblöcke
Wooden Wind Chimes (w. chimes)	Bacchette di Legno Sospese	Baguettes de Bois Suspendues	Holz-Windglocken
Bamboo Wind Chimes	Tubi di Bambù	Bambou Suspendu	Bambusrohre
Metal Wind Chimes	Bacchette di Metallo Sospese	Baguettes Metalliques Suspendues	Metall-Windglocken
Glass Wind Chimes	Bacchette di Vetro Sospese	Baguettes de Verre Suspendues	Glas-Windlgocken
MALLETS, STICKS, AND BEATERS			
Snare Drum Sticks	Bacchette da Tamburo	Baguettes de Tambour	Trommelstöcke
Rubber Mallets	Bacchette con L'éstremitá di Gomma	Baguettes en Caoutchouc	Gummischlegel

Plastic Mallets	Bacchette di Plastica	Baguettes en Plastique	Kunststoff-Schlegel
Yarn Mallets	Bacchette Ricoperte di Filo o di Lana	Baguettes Recouverte de Fil	Garnschlegel
Timpani Mallets	Bacchette per Timpani	Baguettes de Timbales	Paukenschlegel
Wooden Timpani Mallets	Bacchette per Timpani di Legno	Baguettes de Timbales de Bois	Hölzernen Paukenschlegel
Brass Mallets	Bacchette D'Ottone	Baguettes de Laiton	Messingschlegel
Wooden Mallets	Bacchette di Legno	Baguettes de Bois	Holzschlegel
Rawhide (Chimes) Hammer	Battaglio, Martello, or Battente	Marteau	Glockenhammer
Triangle Beater	Battente da Triangolo	Baguette de Triangle	Triangelschlegel or Triangelstab
Bass Drum Beater	Bacchetta da Grancassa	Mailloche	Schlegel für Grosse Trommel
Two-Headed Bass Drum Beater	Mazzuolo a Doppia Testa	Mailloche à Double Tête	Zweiköpfiger Schlegel
Wire Brushes	Spazzola	Brosses	Besen or Stahlbesen
Bow	Arco or Archetto	Archet	Bogen
Hand	Mano	Main	Hand
Fist	Pugno	Poing	Faust
Finger	Dito	Doigt	Finger
Finger nail	Unghia	Ongle de la Main	Fingernagel
Coin	Moneta	Pièce de Monnaie	Geldstück
Hard	Duro	Dur	Hart
Medium	Medio	Moyen	Mittel
Soft	Soffice or Morbido	Doux or Mou	Weich

3. SOME FREQUENTLY USED ORCHESTRAL TERMS IN FOUR LANGUAGES

English	Italian	French	German
Muted	Con Sordino / Con sordini	Sourdine(s)	mit Dämpfer (or Gedämpft, in horns)
Take Off Mutes	Via Sordini	Enlevez les Sourdines	Dämpfer(n) Weg
Without Mute	Senza Sordino	Sans Sourdine	Ohne Dämpfer
Divided	Divisi (div.)	Divisé(e)s (div.)	Geteilt (get.)
Divided in 3 Parts	div. a 3	div. à 3	Dreifach
Divided in 4 Parts	div. a 4	div. à 4	Vierfach
In Unison	Unisono (unis.)	Unis	Zusammen
Solo	Solo	Seul	Allein
All	Tutti	Tous	Alle
1. (first only), 2.	1°, 2°	1er, 2e	1ste (or einfach), 2te
a 2	a 2	à 2	zu 2
At (near) the Bridge	Sul Ponticello	Sur le Chevalet	am Steg
Over the Fingerboard	Sul Tasto (or Sulla Tastiera)	Sur la Touche	am Griffbrett
With the Wood of the Bow	Col Legno	Avec le Bois	Col Legno (or mit Holz)
At the Point of the Bow	Punta d'Arco	(de la) Pointe	Spitze
At the Frog	al Tallone	du Talon	am Frosch
Bells in the Air	Campane in Aria	Pavillons en l'Air	Schalltrichter auf

Half (a string group)	la metà	la moitié	die Hälfte
Stopped (horns)	Chiuso (Chiusi)	Bouché(s)	Gestopft
Brassy		Cuivré	Schmetternd
Open	Aperto (Aperti)	Ouvert(s)	Offen
With Soft Stick	Bacchetta di Spugna	Baguette d'Éponge (Baguette molle)	mit Schwammschlägel
With Hard Sticks	Bacchette di Legno	Baguettes en Bois	mit Holzschlägeln
Change C to E	Sol Muta in Mi	Changez Do en Mi	C nach E Umstimmen
Change to Piccolo	Muta in Piccolo	Changez en Piccolo	Piccolo Nehmen
Near the Sounding Board (harp)		Près de la Table	
Desk or Stand	Leggio	Pupitre	Pult
In the Ordinary Way (after *sul pont.*, *sul tasto*, etc.)	Modo Ordinario	Mode Orndinaire	Gewöhnlich
String	Corda	Corde	Saite

Appendix B

BIBLIOGRAPHY: BOOKS ON ORCHESTRATION, INSTRUMENTS,
THE ORCHESTRA, INDIVIDUAL INSTRUMENTAL TECHNIQUE

1. Books on Orchestration

Bennett, R. R. *Instrumentally Speaking.* Melville, New York: Belwin-Mills, 1975.

Berlioz, H. Enl. and rev. by R. Strauss. *Treatise on Instrumentation.* Transl. by Theodore Front. New York: E. F. Kalmus, 1948.

Blatter, A. *Instrumentation/Orchestration.* New York: Longman, 1980.

Casella, A. *La tecnica dell'orchestra contemporanae.* Milan: Ricordi, 1959.

Clappé, A. *The Principles of Wind-Band Transcription.* New York: Carl Fischer, 1921.

Erpf, H. *Lehrbuch der Instrumentation* Mainz: B. Schott's Söhne, 1959.

Forsyth, C. *Orchestration.* London: MacMillan, 1942.

Gevaert, F. A. *Nouveau traité d'instrumentation.* Paris: Lemaine, 1885.

———. *Cours méthodique d'orchestration.* Paris: Lemaine, 1890.

Isaac, M. *Practical Orchestration* [for Schools]. New York: Robbins Music, 1963.

Jacob, G. *The Elements of Orchestration.* Westport: Greenwood Press, 1976.

Jacob, G. *Orchestral Technique;* London: Oxford University Press, 1931.

Kennan, K. W. *The Technique of Orchestration.* 2nd ed. Englewood Cliffs: Prentice-Hall, 1970.

Kling, H. *The Art of Instrumentation.* New York: Carl Fischer, 1905.

Koechlin, C. L. E. *Traité de l'orchestration.* 4 Vol. Paris: Max Eschig, 1954–1959.

Kunitz, H. *Die Instrumentation.* 13 Vol. Leipzig: Breitkopf und Härtel, 1956–1961.

Lang, P. *Scoring for Band.* New York: Mills, 1950.

Leibowitz, R., and J. Maguire. *Thinking for Orchestra.* New York: Schirmer Books, 1960.

McKay, G. F. *Creative Orchestration.* Boston: Allyn and Bacon, 1963.

Piston, W. *Orchestration.* New York: W. W. Norton, 1955.

Prout, E. *Instrumentation and Orchestration.* 2 Vol. Boston: Ditson, 1877.

Read, G. *Thesaurus of Orchestral Devices.* New York: Pitman, 1953.

Rimski-Korsakov, N. *Principles of Orchestration.* Transl. by Edward Agate. New York: Dover, 1953.

Rogers, Bernard. *The Art of Orchestration.* New York: Appleton-Century-Croft, 1951.

Wagner, J. F. *Orchestration.* New York: McGraw-Hill, 1959.

Wagner, J. F. *Band-Scoring.* New York: McGraw-Hill, 1960.

Wellesz, E. *Die Neue Instrumentation.* Berlin: Max Hesse Handbücher, 1928.

Widor, C. M. *The Technique of the Modern Orchestra.* London: J. Williams, 1906.

Wright, D. *Scoring for Brass Band.* Colne, Lancastershire: J. Duckworth, 1935.

2. The History of the Orchestra and Orchestral Instruments

Baines, A. *Musical Instruments Through the Ages.* Baltimore: Penguin Books, 1961.

———. *Woodwind Instruments and Their History.* London: Faber, 1967.

Barnes, W. H. *The Contemporary American Organ.* New York: J. Fischer, 1952.

Bate, P. *The Flute.* New York: W. W. Norton, 1979.

———. *The Oboe.* New York: W. W. Norton, 1975.

———. *The Trumpet and Trombone.* New York: W. W. Norton, 1978.

Becker, H. *History of Instrumentation.* Cologne: Arno Verlag, 1964.

Bekker, P. *The Story of the Orchestra.* New York: W. W. Norton, 1936.

Bellow, A. *The Illustrated History of the Guitar.* New York: Colombo, 1970.

Bevan, C. *The Tuba Family.* New York: Charles Scriber's Sons, 1978.

Blades, J. *Percussion Instruments and Their History.* London: Faber, 1975.

Brymer, J. *The Clarinet.* New York: Schirmer Books, 1976.

Carse, A. *History of Orchestration.* New York: Dover Publications, 1964.

———. *Musical Wind Instruments.* New York: Da Capo Press, 1966.

Coerne, L. A. *The Evolution of Modern Orchestration.* New York: Macmillan, 1908.

Geiringer, K. *Musical Instruments.* New York: Oxford University Press, 1945.

Goosens, L., and E. Roxburgh. *The Oboe.* New York: Schirmer Books, 1977.

Gregory, R. *The Horn.* New York: Praeger, 1969.

———. *The Trombone.* New York: Praeger, 1973.

Kentner, L. *Piano.* New York: Schirmer Books, 1976.

Korn, R. *Orchestral Accents.* New York: Farrar, Strauss, and Cudahy, 1956.

Kroll, O. *The Clarinet.* Trans. Hilda Morris. New York: Toplinger, 1968.

Langwill, L. G. *The Bassoon and the Contrabassoon.* New York: W. W. Norton, 1975.

Leipps E. *The Violin.* Trans. H. W. Parry. Toronto: Toronto University Press, 1969.

Marcuse, S. *A Survey of Musical Instruments.* New York: W. W. Norton, 1975.

Menuhin, Y., Wm. Primrose, and D. Stevens. *Violin and Viola.* New York: Schirmer Books, 1976.

Morley-Pegge, R. *The French Horn.* New York: W. W. Norton, 1973.

Nelson, S. M. *The Violin and Viola.* New York: W. W. Norton, 1972.

Niland, A. *Introduction to the Organ.* London: Faber and Faber, 1968.

Randall, G. *The Clarinet.* New York: W. W. Norton, 1971.

Reusch, R. *The Harp.* New York: Praeger, 1969.

Sharpe, A. P. *A Complete Guide to the Instruments of the Banjo Family.* London: Clifford Essex Music Company, 1966.

Tumbull, H. *The Guitar from the Renaissance to the Present Day.* New York: C. Scribner's Sons, 1974.

Wheeler, T. *The Guitar Book.* New York: Harper and Row, 1974.

3. Individual Instrumental Technique

a. STRINGS

Bachman, A. *An Encyclopedia of the Violin.* Trans. F. H. Martens. New York: Da Capo Press, 1976.

Galamian, I. *Principles of Violin Playing and Teaching.* Englewood Cliffs, New Jersey: Prentice-Hall, 1962.

Green, E. A. H. *Orchestral Bowings and Routines.* Ann Arbor, Michigan: Ann Arbor Publications, 1957.

Potter, L. *The Art of Cello Playing.* Evanston, Illinois: Summy Birchard, 1964.

Turetzky, B. *The Contemporary Contrabass.* Berkeley: University of California Pres, 1974.

b. WOODWINDS

Bartolozzi, B. *New Sounds for Woodwinds.* London: Oxford University Press, 1967.

Biggers, C. A. *The Contrabassoon: A Guide to Performance.* Bryn Mawr, Pennsylvania: Elkan Vogel, 1977.

Cooper, L. H., and H. Toplancky. *Essentials of Bassoon Technique.* Union, New Jersey: Toplansky, 1968.

Dick, R. *The Other Flute.* New York: Oxford University Press, 1975.

Dorn, K. *Saxophone Techniques (Multiphonics), Vol I.* Islington, Massachusetts: Dorn Publications, 1975.

Howell, T. S. *The Avant-Garde Flute.* Berkeley: University of California Press, 1974.

Pellerite, J. *A Modern Guide to Fingering for the Flute.* Bloomington, Indiana: Zalo Publishers, 1972.

Putnik, E. *The Art of Flute Playing*. Evanston, Illinois: Summy Birchard, 1970.

Rascher, S. M. *Top-Tones for the Saxophone*. Boston: Carl Fischer, 1941.

Rehfeld, Ph. *New Directions for the Clarinet*. Berkeley: University of California Press, 1978.

Spenser, W. G. *The Art of Bassoon Playing*. Evanston, Illinois: Summy Birchard, 1958.

Sprenkle, R., and D. Ledet. *The Art of Oboe Playing*. Evanston, Illinois: Summy Birchard, 1961.

Stein, K. *The Art of Clarinet Playing*. Evanston, Illinois: Summy Birchard, 1958.

Teal, L. *The Art of Saxophone Playing*. Evanston, Illinois: Summy Birchard, 1963.

Tose, G. *Aristic Clarinet Technique and Study*. Hollywood: Highland Music, 1962.

Weisberg, A. *The Art of Woodwind Playing*. New York: Schirmer Books, 1975.

c. BRASS

Farkas, P. *The Art of French Horn Playing*. Evanston, Illinois: Summy Brichard, 1956.

Franz, O. *Complete Method for the Horn*. New York: Carl Fischer, 1906.

Kleinhammer, E. *The Art of Trombone Playing*. Evanston, Illinois: Summy Birchard, 1963.

Schuller, G. *Horn Technique*. London: Oxford University Press, 1962.

d. PERCUSSION AND OTHERS

Blades, J. *Orchestral Percussion Technique*. New York: Oxford University Press, 1973.

Peinkofer, K., and F. Tannigel. *Handbook of Percussion Instruments*. Trans. K. and E. Stone. Mainz: B. Schott's Söhne, 1976.

Reed, H. D. and J. T. Leach. *Scoring for Percussion*. Englewood Cliffs, New Jersey: Prentice-Hall, 1969.

Salzedo, C. *Modern Study for the Harp*. New York: G. Schirmer, 1948.

Smith-Brindle, R. *Contemporary Percussion*. New York: Oxford University Press, 1970.

Stahl, Wm. C. *Stahl's New Mandolin Method*. Milwaukee: J. Flanner, 1900.

Index